Table of Contents

BAUDELAIRE

A COLLECTION OF CRITICAL ESSAYS

Edited by

Henri Peyre

A SPECTRUM BOOK

Prentice-Hall, Inc., *Englewood Cliffs, N.J.*

Current printing (last digit):

13   12   11   10   9   8   7   6   5

LIBRARY OF CONGRESS CATALOG CARD NO.: 62-18082

Printed in the United States of America

07249-C

TWENTIETH CENTURY VIEWS

The aim of this series is to present the best in
contemporary critical opinion on major authors,
providing a twentieth century perspective on
their changing status in an era of profound
revaluation.

Maynard Mack, *Series Editor*
Yale University

Introduction

by Henri Peyre

In 1917, the gloomiest year of World War I, the death of Degas, soon after that of Renoir and of Debussy, marked the end of an era. This same year, the works of Baudelaire fell into the public domain. They were at once reprinted in dozens of editions, elegant or cheap, included in anthologies for the schools, proposed as texts for academic exercises. Suddenly, half a century after his miserable death in Paris, the poet of *Les Fleurs du mal* outstripped the romantics and the symbolists in popularity. Outside France, especially in the English speaking world, he was the favorite among the French poets, with Verlaine or Villon as his closest competitor.

Criticism had not helped very much to spread the fame of Baudelaire. It had proved notoriously inept at assessing his value while the poet was struggling amid debts and anguish, eager for recognition by his peers or by the public, whom he tried to reach through lectures. Théophile Gautier, in his famous preface to the first volume of Baudelaire's collected works, in 1868, first attempted a faithful portrayal of his dead friend, in which he analyzed the notion of decadence with which *Les Fleurs du mal* was long to be associated, rather unfelicitously. Earlier, in November 1865, in a sensitive article in an obscure periodical, *L'Art*, Verlaine had defined the originality and modernity of Baudelaire as a novice in poetry uncannily perceived it. The same year, in *L'Artiste*, a fervent tribute was paid Baudelaire, linked with Gautier and Banville, by an obscure young poet then exiled in the south of France, Mallarmé: the three whom he acknowledged as his masters were grouped in a "literary symphony," as he entitled it. Rimbaud, as a lad of seventeen, was impressed by Baudelaire's gift of "voyance" in the poems and even more by his prose work, *Les Paradis artificiels*. Another great poet, Jules Laforgue, dead at twenty-seven, left a few posthumous notes on Baudelaire, first published in 1891, evincing an insight into his genius unparalleled then, and for years to come, in professional critics. Just before World War I, Albert Thibaudet restored Mallarmé to his right-

1

ful estate in an important volume (1913), but he devoted, subsequently, only a secondary essay to Baudelaire, in a volume entitled *Intérieurs* (1924). André Gide's preface to *Les Fleurs du mal* (1917), translated in *Pretexts* (Meridian Books, 1959) is but a perfunctory piece. The best pages on Baudelaire, between Laforgue and Valéry, were those of young Jacques Rivière, collected in *Études* (1911), and they were a poetical tribute to the poet by a fervent apostle of modernity in literature rather than a critical interpretation.

The only valid critical work on Baudelaire's poetry, on his aesthetics, on his self-revelation in letters and private journals, on his position in modern letters, and on his immense influence has all been accomplished since 1920 or so. The bibliography of several hundreds or thousands of articles and volumes has been compiled by one of the shrewdest detectives of literary inquiry and most diligent devotee of the poet, Walter T. Bandy, of the University of Wisconsin. The essays which have been retained in this selection, sifted from that overabundant mass of comments, long and short, are deemed the most useful to the present day reader of Baudelaire, eager to understand and to enjoy the poet; they constitute a varied and harmonious sheaf of critical views. Had space allowed and, in some cases, had not the difficulty of securing rights of reproduction stood in our way, more essays might have been added. Those by Benedetto Croce, by Walter Benjamin in German, by T. S. Eliot, Aldous Huxley, Martin Turnell in England were not judged to be so enlightening or so relevant as those which have been retained here. The two or three pages at the beginning of Marcel Raymond's classic, *De Baudelaire au surréalisme* (1933) were too short to hold their own here beside substantial essays in which the reader should be able to follow the critic's elaborate reasoning or to share his sympathy with the poet. A penetrating and original chapter, "Profondeur de Baudelaire," in *Poésie et profondeur* (1955) by the gifted young critic, Jean-Pierre Richard, would have had to be mutilated in order to be included here. It was deemed wiser to refer attentive readers to it.

Paul Valéry's "The Position of Baudelaire," originally delivered and published as a lecture in Monaco in 1924, was later collected in *Variété II*. It remains the most concise characterization of Baudelaire's position between the French romantics, Edgar Allan Poe, and the subsequent poetry of several lands. A more systematic attempt to analyze, not historically but psychologically and aesthetically, both the romantic and the classical aspects of Baudelaire is made in the second essay, by the editor of this volume.

Baudelaire, while eschewing the lack of reserve and the complacent display of feeling which has marred much of romantic literature, strove all his life after that literary sincerity which might enable him to "lay his heart bare," while resorting to diverse masks and occasionally to the antics of a tragic comedian. Any critical estimate of his originality inevitably must refer his poetry to his life—not to the chance events of his biography, but to the lack of will power abjectly displayed in his heart-rending letters (on which J. P. Sartre has built up a distorting view on the poet), and to the firm will power which he reserved for his creation. The two great aspects of Baudelaire's life as manifested in his works are his religious sensibility and his loves, experienced, imagined, and sublimated. The essay by François Mauriac, never before rendered into English, is a youthful piece, written with intense fervor and probably overstressing Baudelaire's Christian leanings. The future novelist, then only known as a poet of some promise, composed it during his soldier's years of World War I and published it in 1920 as *Petits Essais de psychologie religieuse. De Quelques Coeurs inquiets.* Charles du Bos, the most spiritual interpreter of literature among the Frenchmen who wrote after World War I, wrote his long and sinuous, extraordinarily penetrating *Meditation on the Life of Baudelaire* in 1921; he published it in *Approximations* the following year. Never was the case for interpreting Baudelaire as a would-be or an authentic Christian made more honestly and more convincingly. Charles du Bos spent the last years of his life teaching at Notre Dame University; he died in 1939. His last works and his long and very rich *Journal,* of which the last volume appeared in 1962, show him anxious to interpret his favorite authors, without ever betraying them, in the light of his own ardent Catholic faith.

The next essay in this volume is borrowed from *L'École des Muses* (1951), by Étienne Gilson, who prefaced du Bos' posthumous *Choix de textes* (1961). This eminent Catholic philosopher and historian of medieval philosophy, starting from Dante's devotion to Beatrice and Petrarch's adoration of Laura, probes with acute insight into Baudelaire's similar idealization of Mme. Sabatier and of another mysterious woman, Marie, to whom he wrote an extraordinary letter. In it, replying to the woman's avowal that she would not be his and loved another man, the poet declared that he would love her all the more, for he would respect her and he would not be in danger of possessing the person whom he loved. The woman, being inaccessible, was exalted into a pure spiritual figure: she was worshipped in the language of mysticism. Baudelaire needed a muse. Mme. Sabatier, however, to whom he transferred that worship and from whom he asked nothing but that she be a muse—"the sister of his soul," as Shelley addressed Emilia Viviani and other women whom he idealized—then made the fatal mistake of offering herself to him. "The common herd are lovers; poets are idolaters," Baudelaire later remarked to her sister, who mocked his idolatry. To that quest for a muse by a poet often mistaken as decadent and immoral, we are indebted for the purest love poetry in the French language.

T. S. Eliot, in an article published in 1928 in *For Lancelot Andrewes,* praised the essay on Baudelaire by Charles du Bos as "the finest study of Baudelaire that has ever been made." He defined the poet as "essentially a Christian, born out of his due time." In a later essay (1930), he tempered this dogmatic assertion and refrained from driving too far his earlier misleading parallel between Baudelaire and Dante. But he set English readers on their guard against the notion of Baudelaire's satanism, which was, he said, in its deeper moments, "an attempt to get into Christianity by the back door." John Middleton Murry, along with T. S. Eliot the finest critic of the years 1910-1930 in Britain, protested in his remarkably balanced and sensitive essay on Baudelaire, published in 1922 in *Countries of the Mind,* against the view that Baudelaire was a decadent poet. He stressed, on the contrary, his heroism, his masculine strength, his classical deliberateness. Wisely, he directed English Baudelaire criticism away from idle debates on the poet's philosophical and religious position to scrutiny and enjoyment of his form, and particularly of his imagery. "Try to be precise, and you are bound to be metaphorical," remarked the same critic elsewhere. His essay is one of the most perceptive on Baudelaire's exacerbation of the poetical image.

The themes of Baudelaire's poetry, his attitude to the higher philosophical issues ("Philosophy is everything," wrote Baudelaire to his publisher, Poulet-Malassis), his aesthetics, the complexities of his psychology, are treated in the last four essays, while the form and the music of his poems are also discussed. Marcel Proust's pages, never before translated into English, were written hastily, from his sick bed at the end of his life, as a letter to the critic Rivière, then director of the *Nouvelle Revue Française.* In his rambling and discursive fashion, passing from Baudelaire to Hugo, Musset, Vigny, Leconte de Lisle and other poets he loved and quoted from memory, Proust lucidly expressed his admiration for some of the Baudelairian themes (Lesbianism, dramatic evocation of the poor and the aged in Paris) and for his imagery.

Georges Poulet's essay is the most abstract, the most arduous, and probably the most enlightening written on Baudelaire's obsession with original sin and with evil: on his incessant wrestling with time in order to retrieve the past and to "take upon himself the mystery of things, as if he were God's spy," to adapt the cryptic and illuminating lines of *King Lear.* Erich Auerbach, with characteristic modesty, starts his pregnant, closely woven chapter as a commentary on one of the *Fleurs du mal* entitled "Spleen." From a penetrating scrutiny of the metaphors, of the rhythm, of the syntactical unity of the poem, the critic proceeds to uncover the antithesis between the symbolism and the realism of that tragically stark poem, the contradiction between the exalted tone and the undignified nature of the subject treated. He envisions Baudelaire's verse as "of gruesome hopelessness," firmly dissenting from the Christian interpretations offered by Du Bos or Mauriac.

Lastly, the pages culled from Jean Prévost's posthumous book, the best single work in French on Baudelaire's art, illuminate his creative process. With critical decision, even with some dogmatism, yet with sharp insight, banishing all rhetoric and all superfluity from his prose, the critic, who wrote these comments shortly before his death in World War II while fighting with the maquis, fathoms some of the secrets of the Baudelairian genius.

Those secrets are twofold. Some poets are immortal who are not thinkers and do not have to be: Theocritus, Catullus, Herrick, La Fontaine, Pushkin, Verlaine. However, remarks the British critic C. M. Bowra in his volume, *The Creative Experiment* (London, 1949, p. 25), "There are others in whom the intellectual, analytical, ordering faculty is so strong that it has to have a place in their poetry." Aeschylus, Sophocles, Donne, Vigny, Leopardi, and Baudelaire rank among these. In each, Bowra continues, "a powerful mind has absorbed the gifts of the senses and the emotions, understood them, and judged them before putting them into verse. The result is that in such work the intellectual element has a strictly poetical task."

Baudelaire is a poet who thought profoundly, felt intensely, imagined daringly. But he could also express poetically, conjuring up emotions and experiences similar to those he had undergone or imagined, thanks to his mastery of language and to his rare evocative power. If it matters greatly that a poet should feel, and think with what he has felt, it is just as essential for him to be able to communicate what he has felt and thought. Baudelaire, at his least felicitous, wielded a cumbersome panoply of images at times macabre, at times bordering on the baroque, often provokingly ugly and jarring. But a poet must only be assessed at his greatest. Even Homer and Shakespeare occasionally slumbered. Some of Baudelaire's sumptuous images, as Proust remarks in his essay, are among the most haunting and the most harmonious in the French language:

> Ils passeront sur toi comme un lourd attelage
> De chevaux et de boeufs aux sabots sans pitié.

> [They will tramp across you, like a heavy team
> Of horses and oxen with pitiless hoofs.]

Thus the more imperious one of the two "Damned women" warns the younger one of the brutal selfishness of men's loves.

In "Un Voyage à Cythère" the poet gazes at a ludicrous body hanged and pecked by vultures and crows. A physical nausea rises up in his mouth,

> Le long fleuve de fiel des douleurs anciennes.

> [That long bilious stream of ancient woe.]

These, and many other images, succeed in achieving the goal assigned by Baudelaire to poetry in his article on "Philosophic Art": to effect "a suggestive magic, containing at one and the same time the object and the subject, the world exterior to the artist and the artist himself."

The Position of Baudelaire

by Paul Valéry

Baudelaire is at the height of his glory.

The little volume, *Les Fleurs du mal,* which contains less than three hundred pages, outweighs, in the esteem of the literary, the most illustrious and bulkiest works. It has been translated into most European languages: this is a fact on which I shall dwell a moment, for it is, I believe, without precedent in the history of French letters.

French poets are generally little known and appreciated abroad. We are more readily accorded leadership in prose; but poetic mastery is but reluctantly conceded to us. The order and rigor which have reigned over our language since the seventeenth century, our particular accentuation, our strict prosody, our taste for simplification and direct clarity, our fear of overstatement and absurdity, a sort of modesty in our expression and the abstract tendency of our thought have resulted in a poetry which differs considerably from that of other nations and which generally makes it inaccessible to them. La Fontaine seems insipid to foreigners. Racine is a closed book. His harmonies are too subtle, his design too pure, his language too elegant, too full of delicate light and shade, not to seem lifeless to those who have not an intimate knowledge of our tongue. Victor Hugo himself is scarcely known outside of France except by his novels.

But with Baudelaire, French poetry at length passes beyond our frontiers. It is read throughout the world; it takes its place as the characteristic poetry of modernity; it encourages imitation, it enriches countless minds. Men like Swinburne, Gabriele d'Annunzio, and Stefan George bear magnificent witness to the Baudelairean influence in foreign countries.

Thus I can say that, though there may be French poets greater and

"The Position of Baudelaire." From *Variété II* by Paul Valéry. Translated by William Aspenwall Bradley and published as *Variety: Second Series.* Copyright 1938 by Harcourt, Brace & World, Inc. Reprinted by permission.

more powerfully endowed than Baudelaire, there is none more *important*.

Whence comes this extraordinary importance? How has a man so peculiar, so far removed from the average as Baudelaire, been able to engender so widespread a movement?

This great posthumous favor, this spiritual richness, this supreme glory, must depend not only on his own value as a poet but also upon exceptional circumstances. Critical intelligence associated with poetic proficiency is such a circumstance. Baudelaire owes to this rare alliance a capital discovery. He was born sensual and exacting; he had a sensibility whose exigencies led him to make the most delicate formal experiments; but these gifts would doubtless have made him merely a rival to Gautier or an excellent Parisian artist, had his mental curiosity not led him to the discovery of a new intellectual world in the works of Edgar Allan Poe. A demon of lucidity, a genius of analysis and an inventor of the newest, most seductive combinations of logic and imagination, of mysticism and calculation, a psychologist of the exceptional, a literary engineer who studied and utilized all the resources of art—thus Poe appeared to him, and filled him with admiration. So many original views and extraordinary promises enthralled him; his talent was transformed by them, his destiny magnificently changed.

I shall return shortly to the effects of this magic contact of two minds. But now I must consider a second remarkable circumstance of the molding of Baudelaire.

He arrived at man's estate when romanticism was at its height; a dazzling generation was in possession of the Empire of Letters. Lamartine, Hugo, Musset, Vigny were masters of the day.

Place yourself in the situation of a young man who came to the writing age in 1840. He has been brought up on the authors whom his instinct imperiously orders him to wipe out. His literary existence provoked and nourished by them, thrilled by their fame, determined by their works, is, however, necessarily dependent upon negation, upon the overthrow and replacement of those men who seemed to him to fill all fame's niches and to deny him: one, the world of forms; another, that of sentiments; a third, the picturesque; a fourth, profundity.

The point was to distinguish himself at any cost from a group of great poets whom some stroke of chance had exceptionally assembled in full vigor in the same period.

Baudelaire's problem then might, and probably should, be thus stated: "To be a great poet but to be neither Lamartine nor Hugo nor Musset." I do not say that these words were consciously uttered, but the thought must have existed in Baudelaire. It was even essentially

Baudelaire. It was his *raison d'État*. In the domains of creation, which are also the domains of pride, the need to distinguish oneself cannot be separated from existence itself. Baudelaire wrote in the outline of his preface for the *Fleurs du mal:* "Illustrious poets have long divided the richest provinces of the poetical domain among themselves. . . . Consequently, I shall do something else. . . ."

In short, he is led, constrained, by the state of his soul and its environment, more and more clearly to oppose the system, or the absence of system, called romanticism.

I shall not define this term. To attempt to do so it would be necessary to have lost all sense of strictness. My present task is merely to reconstitute the most probable reactions and intuitions of our poet "at the state of birth," when confronted with the literature of his age. From it, Baudelaire received a certain impression which we may reconstitute without much trouble. Indeed, thanks to the sequence of time and to later literary developments—thanks even to Baudelaire, to his work and its success—we possess a sure and simple means of introducing a little precision into our necessarily vague idea, sometimes accepted, sometimes wholly arbitrary, of romanticism. *This method consists in the observation of what followed romanticism,* of what altered, corrected and contradicted it, and finally took its place. It suffices to consider the movements and the works which were produced after and against it and which were inevitably, automatically, *exact responses* to what it was. Romanticism thus regarded was, then, what naturalism countered and what Parnassus assembled its forces against; it was what determined Baudelaire's particular attitude. It was what roused almost simultaneously against itself the will to perfection—the mysticism of "art for art's sake"—the demand for observation and an impersonal recording of things; the *desire,* in a word, *for a more solid substance and for a subtler, purer form.* Nothing throws more light on the Romantics than the ensemble of the programs and tendencies of their successors.

Can it be that the vices of romanticism are only the excesses inseparable from self-confidence? . . . The adolescence of new things is always somewhat pretentious. Wisdom, calculation, and, in a word, perfection appear only when strength comes to be economized.

However this may be, the period of scruples began with Baudelaire's youth. Gautier had already protested and reacted against the slackness in formal conditions and the indigence or imprecision of the language. Soon, each in his own way, Sainte-Beuve, Flaubert and Leconte de Lisle were to take arms against impassioned facility, stylistic inconsistency, and the excesses of silliness and eccentricity. . . . Parnassians and realists consented to lose in apparent intensity, in abundance, in oratorical dynamism, what they gained in depth, in truth, in technical and intellectual quality.

To sum up, I will say that the replacing of romanticism by these diverse "schools" may be regarded as the substitution of reflective for spontaneous action.

The romantic output, *in general,* ill supports a slow and unsympathetic reading by a difficult and refined reader.

Baudelaire was such a reader. Baudelaire had the greatest interest—a vital interest—in picking out, in calling attention to, in exaggerating all the weaknesses and lapses of romanticism observed at close quarters in the work and personalities of its greatest men. *Romanticism is at its apogee,* he might say; *consequently it is mortal;* and he was able to consider the gods and demigods of the day, much as the suspicious eyes of Talleyrand and Metternich, about 1807, regarded the world's master. . . .

Thus Baudelaire regarded Victor Hugo, and it is not impossible to conjecture what he thought of him. Hugo reigned; he had acquired over Lamartine the advantage of infinitely more powerful and more precise *working materials.* The vast range of his diction, the diversity of his rhythms, the superabundance of his images, crushed all rival poetry. But his work sometimes made concessions to the vulgar, lost itself in prophetic eloquence and infinite apostrophes. He flirted with the crowd, he indulged in dialogues with God. The simplicity of his philosophy, the disproportion and incoherence of the developments, the frequent contrasts between the marvels of detail and the fragility of the subject, the inconsistency of the whole—everything, in a word, which could shock and thus instruct and orientate a pitiless young observer toward his future personal art—all these things Baudelaire was to note in himself and separate from the admiration forced upon him by the magic gifts of Hugo, the impurities, the imprudences, the vulnerable points in his work—that is to say, the possibilities of life and the opportunities for fame which so great an artist left to be gleaned.

With some malice and a little more ingenuity than is called for, it would be only too tempting to compare Victor Hugo's poetry with Baudelaire's, with the object of showing how exactly *complementary* the latter is to the former. I shall say no more. It is evident that Baudelaire sought to do what Victor Hugo had not done; that he refrained from all the effects in which Victor Hugo was invincible; that he returned to a prosody less free and scrupulously removed from prose; that he pursued and almost always captured the production of *unbroken charm,* the inappreciable and quasi-transcendent quality of certain poems—but a quality seldom encountered, and rarely in its pure state, in the immense work of Victor Hugo.

Moreover, Baudelaire did not know, or barely knew, the last Victor Hugo, the creator of extreme errors and supreme beauties. *La Légende des Siècles* appeared two years after *Les Fleurs du mal.* As for Hugo's later works, these were published only long after Baudelaire's death. I attribute to them a technical importance infinitely superior to that of all Hugo's other poems. This is not the place, and I have not the time, to develop this opinion. I shall only sketch a possible digression. What strikes me in Victor Hugo is his incomparable vital energy. Vital energy is longevity and capacity for work *combined*—longevity *multiplied by* the capacity for work. During more than sixty years, this extraordinary man was at his desk every day from five o'clock till noon! He unremittingly sought to bring about new combinations of language, to will them, to solicit them and to have the satisfaction of hearing them respond. He wrote one or two hundred thousand lines of poetry and acquired by that uninterrupted exercise a curious manner of thinking which superficial critics have judged as best they could. But, in the course of this long career, Hugo never wearied of realizing and fortifying himself in his art; and he unquestionably sinned more and more against selection, he lost more and more the feeling for proportions, he clogged his verses with indeterminate words, vague and vertiginous, and he studded them so abundantly and facilely with "the abyss," "the infinite," "the absolute," that these monstrous terms lost even the appearance of profundity which usage had given them. Yet, what stupendous poems he wrote in the last period of his life—poems incomparable in extent, in external organization, in resonance, in plenitude! In the *Corde d'airain,* in *Dieu,* in the *Fin de Satan,* in the piece on the death of Gautier, the seventy-year-old artist—who had seen all his rivals die, had seen a whole generation of poets born of himself and would even have profited by the inappreciable lessons that the pupil would have given the master had the master lived—attained the highest point of poetic power and of the noble science of versification.

Hugo never ceased to learn by practice; Baudelaire, the span of whose life scarcely exceeded the *half* of Hugo's, developed in quite another manner. One would say he had to compensate for the probable brevity and foreshadowed insufficiency of the short space of time he had to live, by the employment of that critical intelligence of which I spoke above. A score of years were vouchsafed him to attain the peak of his own perfection, to discover his personal field and to define a specific form and attitude which would carry and preserve his name. Time was lacking to realize his literary ambitions by numerous experiments and an extensive output of works. He had to choose the shortest road, to limit himself in his gropings, to be sparing of repetitions and divergences. He had therefore to seek by means of analysis what he was, what he could do, and what he wished to do; and to unite, in himself, with the spontaneous virtues of a poet, the sagacity, the skepticism, the attention and reasoning faculty of a critic.

This is why Baudelaire, although originally a romantic, and even a romantic by taste, sometimes appears as a *classic*. There are infinite ways of defining the classic, or of thinking to define him. For today we shall adopt this one: *a classic is a writer who carries a critic within him and who associates him intimately with his work.* There was a Boileau in Racine.

After all, what was there to *choose* in romanticism and how was there to be discerned in it a good and an evil, a false and a true, weaknesses and virtues, unless one were to treat the authors of the first half of the nineteenth century as the men under Louis XIV treated the authors of the sixteenth? *Every classicism assumes a preceding romanticism.* All the advantages that are attributed to "classic" art, all the objections that are made to it, are related to this axiom. *The essence of classicism is to come after.* Order assumes a certain disorder to be overcome. *Composition,* which is artifice, follows some primitive chaos of natural intuitions and developments. *Purity* is the result of infinite operations on the language, and the pursuit of *form* is nothing but the meditated reorganization of the means of expression. Classic consequently implies voluntary, concerted acts which modify "natural" production in conformance with a *clear* and *rational* conception of man and art. But, as the sciences have taught us, we can make a rational work and construct in orderly fashion only by means of a group of *conventions.* Classic art is recognized by the existence, the clearness, the absolutism of these conventions. Whether it is a matter of the three unities, of the prosodic precepts, or of verbal restrictions, these apparently arbitrary rules constitute its force and its weakness. Little understood today and now difficult to defend and almost impossible to observe, they none the less arise from an ancient, subtle, and deep understanding of the conditions of *unmixed* intellectual enjoyment.

Baudelaire, in the midst of romanticism, reminds us of a classic, but he merely reminds and nothing more. He died young, and he moreover lived under the execrable impression given to men of his time by the miserable survival of the old classicism of the Empire. It was in no sense a question of breathing life into what was distinctly dead but, perhaps, of reaching by other means the soul which no longer inhabited the corpse.

The romantics had neglected practically everything demanding concentrated thought. They sought the effects of shock, enthusiasm, and contrast. Neither measure nor rigor nor depth tormented them excessively. They were averse to abstract thinking and to reasoning—and not only in their works, but also in the preparation of their works, which is infinitely more serious. The French seemed to have forgotten their analytical talents. It is fitting to note here that the romantics revolted against the eighteenth century much more than against the seventeenth and readily brought charges of superficiality against men infinitely more learned than they ever were themselves—more curious of facts and ideas, more anxious for precision and for thought on a grand scale.

At a time when science was about to undergo extraordinary developments, romanticism manifested an antiscientific state of mind. Passion and inspiration are persuaded that they are self-sufficient.

But, under quite another sky, in the midst of a population wholly occupied with its material development, still indifferent to the past, organizing its future and giving the most complete liberty to experiments of every kind, there appeared about this time a man who was to consider the things of the mind with a clearness, a sagacity, a lucidity which had never been encountered to such a degree in a head endowed with poetic invention. And among these things was literary production. Until Poe, never had the problem of literature been examined in its premises, reduced to a psychological problem, and approached by means of an analysis in which the logic and the mechanics of effects were deliberately employed. For the first time, the relations between the work and the reader were elucidated and given as the positive foundations of art. This analysis—and this circumstance assures us of its value—applies and is verified as clearly in every domain of literary production. The same observations, the same distinctions, the same quantitative remarks, the same directive ideas adapt themselves equally to works destined to act powerfully and brutally on the emotions—to conquer a public in love with strong emotions or strange adventures—and the most refined types of literature and the delicate organization of the poet's creations.

To say that this analysis holds good for the short story as well as for the poem, that it is as applicable to the construction of the imaginary and fantastic as it is in the reconstitution and literary representation of the probable, is to say that its generality is truly remarkable. A characteristic of what is really general is its fecundity. To arrive at a point from which one dominates a whole field of activity is necessarily to perceive a quantity of possibilities—unexplored domains, roads to be traced, lands to be exploited, cities to be built, relations to be established, methods to be extended. Thus it is not astonishing that Poe, possessing so effective and sure a method, should be the inventor of several different varieties, should have offered the first and most striking example of the scientific tale, of the modern cosmogonic poem, of the novel of criminal investigation, of the introduction into literature of morbid psychological states, and that all his work should manifest on every page an intelligence which is to be observed to the same degree in no other literary career. This great man would today be completely forgotten had not Baudelaire introduced him into European literature. Let us not fail to observe here that Poe's universal glory is weak or contested only in his native country and England. This Anglo-Saxon poet is strangely neglected by his own race.

Another remark: *Baudelaire and Edgar Allan Poe exchanged values.* Each gave to the other what he had, received from the other what he had not. The latter communicated to the former a whole system of new and profound thought. He enlightened him, he enriched him, he determined his opinions on a quantity of subjects: philosophy of composition, theory of the artificial, comprehension and condemnation of the modern, importance of the exceptional and of a certain strangeness, an aristocratic attitude, mysticism, a taste for elegance and precision, even politics. . . . Baudelaire was impregnated, inspired, deepened by them.

But, in exchange for what he had taken, Baudelaire gave Poe's thought an infinite extension. He proffered it to the future. It was Baudelaire's act, translation, prefaces, that opened this expansion which, in Mallarmé's great line, changes the poet in himself, and assured it to the shade of the unhappy Poe.

I shall not examine all that literature owes to the influence of this marvellous inventor. Whether we take Jules Verne and his disciples, Gaboriau and his like, or whether, in far more elevated styles, we consider the productions of Villiers de l'Isle-Adam or of Dostoevsky, it is easy to see that the *Adventures of J. Gordon Pym,* the *Mystery of the Rue Morgue, Ligeia,* the *Tell-Tale Heart,* have been for them models abundantly imitated, thoroughly studied, and never surpassed.

I only wonder what Baudelaire's poetry, and more generally French poetry, may owe to the discovery of the works of Poe. Some poems in *Fleurs du mal* derive their sentiment and their material from Poe's poems. Some contain lines which are exact transpositions; but I shall neglect these particular borrowings whose importance is, in a sense, merely local. I shall retain but the essential, which is the very idea that Poe had formed of poetry. His conception, which he set forth in various articles, was the principal factor in the modification of Baudelaire's ideas and art. The fermentation of this theory of composition in Baudelaire's mind, the lessons which he deduced from it, the developments it received from his intellectual posterity—and particularly its great intrinsic value—necessitate our stopping a moment to examine it.

I shall not conceal the fact that the basis of Poe's thoughts is associated with a certain personal metaphysical system. But this system, if it directs and dominates and suggests the theories in question, by no means penetrates them. It engenders them and explains their generation; it does not constitute them.

Poe's ideas on poetry are expressed in several essays, the most important of which (but that which least concerns the technique of English verse) is entitled *The Poetic Principle*. Baudelaire was so deeply struck by this essay, he received so intense an impression from it, that he considered its contents—and not only the contents but the form itself—*as his own property*.

Man cannot help appropriating what seems so exactly made *for him* that, in spite of himself, he regards it as made *by him*. . . . He tends irresistibly to take over what suits his own person so closely; and language itself confuses, under the name of *possession,* the notion of what is adapted to someone and satisfies him entirely, with that of this person's property. . . .

Baudelaire, although enlightened and obsessed by the theory of *The Poetic Principle*—or, rather, because he was enlightened and possessed by it—did not include his translation of this essay in Poe's own works, but introduced the most interesting part, scarcely changed, in the preface to his translation of the *Histoires extraordinaires*. This plagiarism would be open to discussion if the author had not himself, as will be seen, drawn attention to it: in an article on Théophile Gautier he reproduced the whole passage in question, preceding it with these very plain and surprising lines: "It is occasionally permissible, I believe, to quote oneself in order to avoid paraphrasing oneself. I shall consequently repeat. . . ." Then follows the borrowed passage.

What then were Poe's views on Poetry?

I shall briefly sum up his ideas. He analyzes the psychological requirements of a poem. Among these, he puts in the first rank the ones which depend upon the *dimensions* of poetical works. He gives exceptional importance to the consideration of their length. He moreover examines the very conception of these works. He easily establishes that there exists a great number of poems concerned with notions for which prose would have been an adequate vehicle. Neither history, science, nor morality gains by being set forth in the language of the soul. Didactic poetry, historical poetry or ethics, although honored and consecrated by the greatest poets, strangely combine the materials of discursive or empirical knowledge with the creations of the inner being and the emotive forces.

Poe understood that modern poetry should conform to the tendency of an age which drew a sharper and sharper distinction between forms and provinces of activity. He understood that it could claim to realize its own object and produce itself, to some degree, in a *pure state*.

Thus, by analyzing the requirements of poetic delight and defining "absolute poetry" by "exhaustion," Poe showed a way and taught a very strict and fascinating doctrine in which he united a sort of mathematics with a sort of mysticism. . . .

If we now regard *Les Fleurs du mal* as a whole and take the trouble to compare this volume with other poetic works of the same period, we shall not be surprised to find that Baudelaire's work is remarkably consistent with Poe's precepts and consequently remarkably different from the productions of romanticism. *Les Fleurs du mal* contains neither historical nor legendary poems; nothing based upon a narrative. There are no flights into philosophy. Politics here make no appearance. Descriptions are rare and always *pertinent*. But all is charm, music, powerful, abstract sensuality. . . . "Luxe, forme et volupté."

In Baudelaire's best poems there is a combination of flesh and spirit, a mixture of solemnity, warmth and bitterness, of eternity and intimacy, a most rare alliance of will with harmony, which distinguishes them clearly from romantic verse as it distinguishes them clearly from Parnassian verse. Parnassus was not excessively kind to Baudelaire. Leconte de Lisle reproached him with sterility. He forgot that a poet's true fecundity does not consist in the number of his poems but rather in the extent of his effects. They can be judged only in time sequence. We see today that the resonance, after more than sixty years, of Baudelaire's unique and far from copious work, still fills the whole poetic sphere, that it is still influential, impossible to neglect, reinforced by a remarkable number of works which derive from it and which are not imitations but the consequences of it. Consequently, to be just, it would be necessary to join to the slender collection of *Les Fleurs du mal* several first-rate works and a number of the most profound and finest experiments that poetry has ever undertaken. The influence of *Poèmes antiques* and *Poèmes barbares* has been less diverse and less surprising.

It must be recognized, however, that this same influence, had it been exerted on Baudelaire, would perhaps have dissuaded him from writing or from retaining some very slack verses that are to be found in his book. Of the fourteen lines of the sonnet "Recueillement" one of his most charming pieces, there are five or six which, to my never-failing surprise, are undeniably weak. But the first and last verses of this poem are so magical that we do not feel the ineptitude of the central part and are quite ready to hold it for null and void. Only a very great poet can effect a miracle of this kind.

A minute ago I spoke of the production of "charm," and now I have pronounced the word "miracle." Doubtless these are terms which must be used sparingly because of the emphasis of their meaning and the facility with which they may be employed; but I should not know how to replace them except by an analogy so long and perhaps so debatable that I shall perhaps be forgiven for sparing him who would have to make it, as well as those who would have to listen to it. I shall remain vague, confining myself to suggesting what it might be. It should be shown that language contains emotive resources mingled with its practical, directly significant properties. The duty, the work, the function of the poet are to bring out and render active these forces of enchantment, these stimulants of the emotional life and intellectual sensibility, which are mixed together in the customary language with the signs and means of communication of ordinary superficial life. Thus the poet consecrates himself to and consumes himself in the task of defining and constructing a language within the language; and this operation, which is long, difficult, and delicate, which demands a diversity of mental qualities and is never finished, tends to constitute the speech of a being purer, more powerful and profound in his thoughts, more intense in his life, more elegant and felicitous in his speech, than any real person. This extraordinary speech manifests itself and is recognized by the rhythm and harmonies which sustain it, and which should be so intimately and even mysteriously bound to its origin that the sound and the sense can no longer be separated, responding to each other indefinitely in the memory.

Baudelaire's poetry owes its duration and the ascendency it still has to the plenitude and the unusual clearness of its timbre. At times, this voice yields to eloquence, as happened a little too frequently in the case of the poets of the period; but it almost retains and develops an admirably pure melodic line and a perfectly sustained sonority which distinguish it from all prose.

Baudelaire, in this, reacted very happily against the tendency to prosaic style which has been observable in French poetry since the middle of the seventeenth century. It is remarkable that the man to whom we owe this return of poetry to its essence is also one of the first

French writers to be passionately interested in music. I mention this taste, which was shown by the celebrated articles on *Tannhäuser* and *Lohengrin,* because of the later development of the influence of music upon literature. . . . "What was baptized Symbolism is summed up quite simply in the intention common to several families of poets to take back from music what belonged to them. . . ."

To render less imprecise and less incomplete this attempt to explain Baudelaire's importance today, I must now recall what he was as an art critic. He knew Delacroix and Manet. He sought to weigh the respective merits of Ingres and his rival, as he had compared the quite different "realisms" of Courbet and Manet. For the great Daumier he had an admiration which posterity shares. Perhaps he exaggerated the value of Constantin Guys. But, on the whole, his judgments, invariably motivated and accompanied by the finest and most substantial considerations on painting, remain models of their kind, which is so terribly facile, hence so terribly difficult.

But Baudelaire's greatest glory, as I have shown at the outset, is without question to have inspired several great poets. Neither Verlaine, nor Mallarmé, nor Rimbaud would have been what they were had they not read *Les Fleurs du mal* at the decisive age. It would be easy to point in this collection to poems of which the form and the inspiration foreshadow certain pieces by Verlaine, Mallarmé, or Rimbaud. But these are so clear that I shall not enter into details. I shall confine myself to indicating that the sense of the intimate and the powerful, uneasy mixture of mystical emotion and sensual ardor which are developed in Verlaine; the frenzy for evasion, the impatience excited by the universe, the deep consciousness of sensations and their harmonic resonances which render Rimbaud's brief, violent work so energetic and active, are clearly present and recognizable in Baudelaire.

As for Stéphane Mallarmé, whose earliest poems might be taken for the most beautiful and compact of *Les Fleurs du mal,* he pursued in their subtlest consequences the formal, technical experiments of which Poe's analyses and Baudelaire's essays and commentaries had communicated to him the passion and taught him the importance. While Verlaine and Rimbaud continued Baudelaire in the order of sentiment and sensation, Mallarmé carried his work forward in the province of perfection and poetic purity.

Baudelaire, Romantic and Classical

by Henri Peyre

Literary criticism has long and lavishly played with the words "classical" and "romantic." They may well tempt lazy pens, for they lend themselves to restful confusions and may serve alternately as praise or blame. To resort to them, Paul Valéry once submitted, one must have lost all sense of intellectual rigor. But who has ever refrained from using them or other similarly confusing terms like "greatness," "profundity," "sincerity"? Not even Valéry himself, who vainly pursued the "obstinate rigor" which he imagined to have discovered in E. A. Poe and in Leonardo. Stern professors have held learned conventions in which they urged the banishment of those ambiguous terms from the language of criticism; but all to no avail. The only wisdom lies in making clear the significance which each of us attaches to the words "classical" and "romantic," and to avoid juggling inconsiderately with them. It is indeed a denial of rigor to apply an adjective like "romantic" to Shakespeare, or to Virgil, or to Euripides, or to Prometheus, Cain, Eve, or Satan himself. Romantic moods existed long before the word came to denote them. But because the word did not then exist, and because the opposition to other moods which seemed antithetic to romanticism had not yet become established, the romantic spirits who lived before 1760 had no clear awareness of their innate and unformulated romanticism. Whether we like it or not, the word "romantic" has unavoidably become laden with historical connotations.

Baudelaire's aesthetic meditation began, and was long pursued, in close relation to the great romantic movement which had shaken the generation which preceded his, all over Europe. He and his contemporaries, born like him around 1820 (Leconte de Lisle, Flaubert, Fromentin, Renan), had to find and to define themselves both as the successors to the great Romantics born twenty years earlier and as their opponents who would redress or eschew some of their errors. "Romanticism is the most recent, the most modern expression of the beautiful," Baudelaire observed in his *Salon de 1846*. He rose above the technical controversies which had centered on dramatic rules or minor questions of language and of prosody; for, he added, with a clear-sightedness not frequently to be found in a young man of twenty-five, that "Romanticism lies not precisely in the choice of subjects nor in their exact truth, but in the manner of feeling." And in the same critique of an annual exhibition of painting, he defined romanticism (which to him meant Vigny, Hugo, Balzac, Delacroix, Daumier, all born near the dawn of the century), as "intimacy, spirituality, color, aspiration toward the infinite." Romanticism had invaded all literary genres, all arts, and even the daily lives of average men and women in Europe, with what in a broad sense may be termed poetry. Even the upstarts and the ambitious men of affairs of Balzac, even the characters in Hugo's dramas and novels greedy for domination, were athirst for poetry and illumined the material details of life with a halo of passionate energy. Baudelaire doubted whether he could ever equal the creativeness of those imaginative giants.

But he soon realized what perils lurked in that effusiveness of the romantic poets, in the debauchery of color by painters allured by ambitious and, at times, rhetorical subjects. He feared the tendency to exaggerate, the feverish motion which ended in sheer restlessness and waste of talent. Repeatedly, in his intimate papers, he recalled to himself the precept of Emerson: "The hero is he who is immovably centered," and observed that productive concentration of the ego must at all costs replace the seductiveness of dissipating its energies. He acutely perceived all that had been unfinished, artificial, inflated in the art of the romantics. His originality proceeds from that profound duality in him; two souls wrestled in his breast as in that of Saint Paul or of Faust.

Other men may have reached greatness through achieving some cohesiveness and felicitously wedding all their contrary impulses into a synthesis which afforded them some serenity. Goethe is the model of such supreme artists. But such a unity is seldom attained without the forcible silencing of rebellious voices, judged too jarring by the man who, at forty or fifty, is inclined to conform, perhaps to stagnate. Still, even in his advanced years, irruptions from his unconscious and visitations from his "daimon," and a resurgence of loving ardor in the septuagenarian that he was at Marienbad, are what move us most in Goethe. But there are many natures less concerned with the portrait of themselves sketched in their writings; progress, for them, does not consist in a serenely calculated evolution toward more light and more harmony. In such men, as events prompt it, one or another layer of their deeper self is tapped;

at one time, they plumb the most tragic abysses of self; at another, they restfully play at the surface.

In Baudelaire, there cannot be said to have been a marked evolution, in the conventional sense of the word, or an ascending and then declining curve. Even as a critic, he rose no higher in 1859 than he had done in 1846. He never endeavored to reconcile his contradictions or to mutilate, through weariness and resignation or the need for easy intellectual comfort, the rebellious sides of his being. The late C. G. Jung, in his book on *The Unconscious in Psychological Life,* asserted that "disagreement with oneself is the distinctive mark of the civilized man." If so, Baudelaire was supremely civilized and truly schizophrenic, like many other great men. What we may call his romanticism and his classicism were not the manifestations of a calculated alternation or of an orderly succession—as may have been, according to some pigeon-holing scholars, the stoical, epicurean, and positivistic phases of Montaigne's wisdom, and as are the naïvely coquettish wiles of Gide or of Montherlant cultivating their oscillations. The romantic and the classicist in him interpenetrated each other, corrected and reinforced each other. T. S. Eliot may have simplified things when he defined him peremptorily as "inevitably the offspring of romanticism and by his nature the first counter-romantic in poetry."

The doctrines and the superficial agitation of the Romantic *cénacles* impressed Baudelaire but little. He saw beyond that and further; with lucid insight he declared, at the outset of his career, that romanticism was an infernal or a celestial grace to which he and others owed eternal stigmata. It had freed literature from the shackles of the old aesthetics, from social and ethical conformity, exacerbated the rebellion of the individual; it had also enriched literature with many examples from abroad, discovered the profound meaning of symbols, and even approached the deeper mysteries of the "surreal." Lands hitherto uncharted had been explored by the romantic pioneers: the Bible, Dante, Shakespeare, Calderón, Gothic art, the subterranean vibrations of music. The unconscious was proclaimed by philosophers and by poets to be the fountain from which genius draws its originality. Artists would henceforth plunge inward into those depths, as Novalis, Goethe himself, Balzac, Michelet, Hugo, then Baudelaire advocated, even if evil, cruelty, self-destruction, a strange fascination with death lay there. But having delved deeper into his own "selva oscura," man leaped much more boldly upward. He wanted to become an Icarus or an angel; he aspired to a paradise where his vices would be washed clean, and the Satan lurking in him would be rehabilitated and saved. From Romanticism on, literature was to turn into a gospel of self-deification by man, a drive toward a superman.

Baudelaire is a romantic first because of his life, or rather because of the way in which he lived his poetry and allowed himself to be devoured by his own creation. Men of the Renaissance, in Italy and in England especially, had likewise sacrificed their existence to a harsh and unequal struggle with their destiny. It was left to nineteenth century creators, Hölderlin, Kierkegaard, Nerval, Baudelaire, to turn relentlessly against their own selves in order to feed the unforgiving Moloch of their demon. Still, there lingered among those desperately sincere men many an oversumptuous drapery—a screen of gaudy works and of sonorous strains —interposed between them and the reader, and even between themselves and reality. With all its virtues, French romanticism is at times all too prone to rhetoric and to a variegated display of brilliant hues. It strove for sincerity passionately, but perhaps only reached it with those of its writers who were least touched by romanticism: Stendhal, Constant, Nerval, Mérimée. More surely than any of his predecessors in France, Baudelaire reached that "authenticity" of which the moderns make so much; all else was sacrificed to that pursuit. The phrase which he borrowed from his elder brother from overseas, E. A. Poe's "my heart laid bare," well conveys the tense obsession which haunted him to mirror the secrets of his deeper self as faithfully as possible.

The fragments which Baudelaire left and which are grouped under that title, "Mon coeur mis à nu," do not come anywhere near to rivalling, as Baudelaire had for a time rashly hoped, Rousseau's *Confessions.* They are devoid of the aesthetic distance with which even a self-portraying author should view himself, too vibrant with the poet's hatreds, fits of anger and of self-blame. Yet his own drama, half divined through some incensed cursing of God, of women, or of men, or through a few snatches of abject confession closer to Dostoevsky than to Montaigne or Gide, grips us all the more powerfully. There lingers no rhetoric in those bare avowals. "We make out of the quarrel with others, rhetoric, but of the quarrel with ourselves, poetry," noted, in *Per Amica Silentia Lunae* (1918), W. B. Yeats, whose poetry often transfigures experiences he had lived. Of all the French poets of the last century, Verlaine excepted, Baudelaire is the last of those who confided to the reader or—as he put it in a famous letter to the man whom he judged least able to understand him, Ancelle—poured "into an atrocious book all his heart, all his tenderness, all his religion, all his hatred." Mallarmé, Valéry, Claudel himself, St. John Perse will not follow him along that path of intimate confession to a mistress or to a reader.

Baudelaire is profoundly romantic also through the role which he grants, in the work of art, to sensibility and to sensuality.

At all times poetry has naturally sprung from men whose power to feel rose far above that of average creatures. But tides of taste alternately lead to taming and muffling the expression of that sensibility, or to its shameless display. Baudelaire loudly scorned Musset's elegiac and complacent histrionics and sided with Flaubert and the stern Parnassian, Leconte de Lisle, who insisted on the concealment of the self in art. If, however, he wished to purify and sublimate, or perhaps to transpose and disguise his sensibility in his poetry, he never attempted to stifle it altogether. His own sensitiveness, as he well knew, was acute, easily bruised by life, feminine in part, due perhaps to the immense influence of his mother upon the youth of a child who hardly knew his father and to his early saturation in the "mundus muliebris" of which he speaks when he conjures up his childhood memories. Many of his stanzas are pleas to be understood and loved:

> Et pourtant aimez-moi, tendre soeur! Soyez mère
> Même pour un ingrat, même pour un méchant.
> ("Chant d'automne")

> [And yet, love me, tender sister! Be a mother
> Even to an ungrateful, even to a wicked one.]

However, behind that tidal wave of sensibility submerging the whole being, under that vaporous and languid language which many romantics had cast as a deceptive veil over their sensibility, Baudelaire perceived the full originality of the discovery made by the late eighteenth century: that sensuality also must have its place in the work of art. With Laclos, Rétif, Sade, Casanova himself (who is often a man of great delicacy and a piercing psychologist), with Diderot and Rousseau, sensation became one of the primary foundations of modern letters. Baudelaire realized that angelism, an almost Platonic attempt to transcend the body, could not satisfy a reader of poetry who had also reveled in the vivacious prose of the previous century. His own sensations were keen, almost to the point of *morbidezza*. He provoked them, he prolonged them, he blended them in a whirlpool where they underwent what he calls "a mystical metamorphosis." He increased their range through adding to them fear, a sensation before which much poetry had recoiled until Poe, the anguish of the spleen, the vertigo of destruction. A strangely disturbing sonnet, "Destruction," opens the most stark and infernal section of his book, "Flowers of Evil," a title taken up again for the volume as a whole. In one of his most tragic avowals, he noted: "I have cultivated my hysteria with enjoyment and terror." Thereby his poetry became the poetry of each of us, and not just a game which briefly touches us or a meditation which provokes an ephemeral dream or lures us into reflections of a general order.

Lastly, Baudelaire is romantic in two more senses of the adjective: in his passionate advocacy of modernity and through the role which he grants to strangeness as a component of beauty. To him, the word romantic denoted modern art, as it had for Stendhal, whose definition seems to have attracted him. There had been other directions in the French romantic movement: nostalgia for the past, Hellenic or medieval, dreams of an exotic elsewhere, thrust toward a better future and a deified man rivaling God. But with Delacroix, Balzac, and Hugo, romanticism had flown in the face of the timid aesthetes or conservative doctrinaires for whom beauty had to be stylized, idealized, stripped of all that might make it the thing of one country and of one age. Baudelaire's "Tableaux parisiens" may occasionally recall Boileau or Gay and eighteenth century urban realism. But because the poet had understood how poetical we can be in our cravats and our patent leather boots he was able to rediscover the poetry of the past preserved in the streets of the metropolis.

Baudelaire succeeded better than anyone else before him in extracting from the modern what is all the more seductive in it for being short-lived, all the more dearly to be cherished because, as Vigny put it, it will not be seen twice. Walter Pater, toward the end of the century, was, in a striking sentence of his *Appreciations,* to define romanticism as "the addition of strangeness to beauty." Another Englishman, Theodore Watts-Dunton, who stood close to the Pre-Raphaelites and to Baudelaire's admirer, Swinburne, defined romanticism as "the renascence of wonder." All that was dimly anticipated by the French poet. "The Beautiful always is bizarre," he pronounced. To him, astonishment and surprise made up the most valuable element of beauty. Several of Baudelaire's aesthetic dicta, perhaps acquired from Poe, recall the romantics of Great Britain: Coleridge at times; Blake even more, for whom everything exists in human imagination; or Keats, who wanted poetry to surprise by a fine excess and proclaimed beauty to be truth when it was perceived by human imagination. Baudelaire's discovery of "the loneliness of terror," and of the enjoyment of ugliness by temperaments powerful enough to drink that strong potion, can be logically traced back to the romantics.

No less romantic, in its deeper manifestations, was Baudelaire's fondness for "la révolte": a rebelliousness which expanded and exalted the nature of man and was to acquaint him with all vices, all excesses, to make him hover on the verge of many an abyss and to cherish death itself in order to live more courageously, since, as Camus later exclaimed, "True artists are always on the side of life, not of death." "The intoxication of art," Baudelaire clear-sightedly declared, "is better fitted than any other to throw a veil over the terrors of the abyss." The lucid aesthetician who complemented and supported the poet in Baudelaire always protested against any general and insipid conception of beauty which reduced it to an unbodied common denominator. From romanticism, he had learned the value of the concrete and the primacy of passion. "The particular element of each beauty comes from passion, and as we have our particular passions, so have we our beauty," he had already written of the 1846 salon. The subtitle of "Revolt" given to a whole section of his poems was no mere caprice or desire to antagonize the bourgeois who misjudged him. There may have been in it, as Sartre stubbornly contends, some adolescent need for compensation and some pose, a desire to flout the conventions which he was in fact observing. But it was also a metaphysical revolt, as that of Sade had been, as that of Rimbaud, of Henri Michaux, of Camus was later to be: a refusal of the terms meted out to existence, an aspiration to the lost innocence of childhood or to some forsaken Eden. Through indulging a devilish sneer, uttering blasphemies, and pampering with brutish satisfactions the lowest in man, the poet also hoped to arouse the angel in him and to incite the sinful creature to stand up and offer some justification for the world. Baudelaire, with Balzac, Nerval perhaps, Hugo, the Mallarmé of *Igitur* and "Le Coup de Dés," and Rimbaud, must be counted among those many French rebels who, in the century of Dostoevsky's Kirilov and of Nietzsche, dreamt of transcending man by becoming Satanic or angelic supermen.

The paradox is that many successors of Baudelaire have lauded the classic in him and turned to him to defend themselves, through his example, against romantic spells and wiles. T. S. Eliot went so far as to hint that he was close, not to Dante, but rather to "a later and more limited Goethe." There was indeed in Baudelaire a being who needed to fight precisely that in him which nurtured his genius and to maintain the validity of two contradictory and simultaneous positions.

First, he was perspicacious enough as a man of letters to realize how ruinous might have been for him the role of an imitator. There are artists who, fully confident of their creative force, may accumulate materials which they fetch and hew in quarries as yet unexplored. Baudelaire admired, with some envy, those brutal, violent, imaginative creators. He praised Delacroix, Balzac, Hugo himself, and Wagner more glowingly than he did Ingres, Stendhal, Vigny, or Mozart. Lucidly, writing on Delacroix, he defined "that dual feature of great artists which drives them, as critics, to praise and to analyze more voluptuously the qualities which they most need as creators and which are contrary to those qualities which they have in superabundance." He belonged to another family of minds: those who polish materials already hewn and carved, and, by dint of reflection and impregnation of the material by the intellect and by memory, succeed in transmuting what has appeared familiar into something rare and strange. His originality is deliberate, acquired, refined. Valéry rightly presented Baudelaire as one who chose to differ from his romantic predecessors, who had shared among themselves the realm of poetry and only left for him to extract the beauty lurking in evil. In 1845, Baudelaire clearly understood that one no longer could be a romantic as others had been in 1830. It was necessary to become a classic of romanticism.

"I take pity upon poets who are guided by instinct alone; I find them incomplete," Baudelaire remarked in his essay on Richard Wagner; and he added that it was hardly possible for a poet not to contain a critic. Baudelaire's poetry as well as his poetics are characterized by the virtues of lucidity and patient calculation. Therein, he parts company with those romantic temperaments which would rather trust the enthusiasm of inspiration.

He too celebrated enthusiasm, but, he made clear, as "quite independent from the passion which is the intoxication of the heart and from the truth which is the nourishment of reason." His most sardonic barbs were aimed at those sophisms and confusions which had been ushered into France by "the disorderly era of romanticism" and the ridiculous motto of "the poetry of the heart." Such antiromantic reaction was then, around 1850-1870, also that of the Parnassians and of Flaubert, of Matthew Arnold and other British poets weary of the antics of latter-day Byrons and Mussets. But Baudelaire was thus rediscovering the tradition of the French classicists whose concern was above all to see clearly into themselves and, if not to reject darkness, at least to illuminate it. His "alter ego" in the opening poem of the volume, "Bénédiction," alludes to "the vast lightnings of his lucid spirit." That lucidity is what appeals most ardently today to the admirers of Baudelaire, who are often the same as the devotees of Laclos, Stendhal, and the seventeenth century moralists. It is more seldom to be found in a poet than in a novelist. Thanks to it, Baudelaire was able to enrich poetry with the best gifts of the novelist without taming his wild soaring flight. He must have been expressing his own dual nature when he pronounced, apropos of Banville, that "the lyrical soul takes strides as vast as syntheses; the novelist's mind delights in analysis."

Baudelaire is classical through his fondness for analysis, in which he tapped springs of poetry still richer than the fountains of imagination. French romanticism had been tempted to lose itself in exoticism, picturesqueness, nature, in a word, in all the world without. Its great champions seemed to be daunted by the earlier achievements of Pascal, Racine, Bossuet: their exploration of the world within. For that penetration into the recesses of the consciousness is what the Frenchman is most eager to find in his literature. Sooner or later, and also inevitably as he reaches middle age, he becomes indifferent to lyrical poetry, unless it leads him to the inward exploration of that perpetually enigmatic being which man is to man, "tourmenté de s'aimer, tourmenté de se voir," in Vigny's noble line.

Victor Hugo had been aware of it, and after his sumptuous display of sound and sparkling light in his *Orientales,* he had attempted to make lyrical poetry the vehicle of psychological self-knowledge, of revery and of dream, even of philosophical mysticism. Lamartine had tired of pure lyricism after 1830 and turned to a familiar epic with character analysis, *Jocelyn.* A similar enrichment of the content of poetry was then being accomplished in Britain by *In Memoriam, Men and Women,* the poetry of Arnold and Clough, and of Meredith's *Modern Love,* which traces the slow death of love, killed by "that fatal knife,"

> Deep questioning, which probes to endless dole.

If *The Flowers of Evil* bear being read over and over again after a century, it is because they fulfill our need for analysis and for classical values, in the very midst of lyricism.

Baudelaire is also classical through the eminent role which he granted to the virtues of order; and architecture is the quality which he most wished critics to discover in his individual poems and in his volume. Therein also Baudelaire indicated his affinity with those men of the seventeenth century who lauded the beauty of order as primary among the forms of beauty: Bouhours, Malebranche. His poetry never rolls turbidly like a torrent. Jacques Rivière compared it to one of those rivers or canals of the French countryside, which glide along nonchalantly between two rows of poplars, harmonious in their sinuous wanderings. Even in its evocation of madly rebellious or of morbidly destructive moods, it maintains the orderliness of a Racinian tirade, the lucid moderation of a landscape by Claude Lorrain, the serene nobleness of a La

Tour interior illumined by a mystical candle. "I wish to illuminate things with my spirit," declared Baudelaire.

The paradox of Baudelaire's life, often distorted by his biographers, lies in the total transference of his will power from his life, abjectly deprived of planned organization, to his art. From his youth on, in declarations which amounted to more than the paradoxes of a dandy, he announced repeatedly his intention to proscribe chance from the work of art. The peremptory "There is no chance in the work of art," was uttered as early as 1846. Asselineau, who knew him best of all his friends, reveals in his small book on the poet: "Very seriously he believed in prepared miracles, in the possibility of arousing such and such a sensation in the reader, with deliberateness and absolute certainty." The word "will" often recurs in his aesthetic reflections. The example of Delacroix had appeared to him as that of an indomitable will power married to boundless passion or, as he puts it also, of energy stemming from the will. Poe had likewise stressed the role of the will as calculating its effects, imposing sacrifices, encompassing art inside bounds.

Through his fondness for constraints and gleefully confronted difficulties, Baudelaire is classical, in the sense that Goethe before him and Valéry after him were. He praised rhetoric and prosody as "rules demanded by the very organization of the spiritual being." Those rules, he added in his 1859 salon, have always helped originality to emerge. He stubbornly clung to rhythm as conditioning poetical thought. In one of his most curious letters, he begged his correspondent to acknowledge that a patch of blue sky framed by a dormer-window and thus limited produced a more powerful impression of the infinite than the whole sky expanding above our heads. His definition of beauty is famous: "It is the infinite within the finite." Through consenting on the surface to those limits and restraints which, in Goethe's oft-quoted phrase, reveal the true master, Baudelaire dug more deeply his voluntarily restricted, but in truth inexhaustible domain. He plunged low into the mud and evil, then ascended all the higher for that previous descent into infernal depths, and, reaching artistic balance, recovered the very essence of classicism.

Fortunately the victory of that classicism over a latent and prior romanticism always remained precarious with the poet of *The Flowers of Evil*. Fate, which in other ways treated him unkindly, spared him at any rate that desiccation which, after forty, afflicts many artists who have codified their aesthetics and acquired the knack of achieving very exactly what they set out to do. Valéry's poetics was, in the end, to turn Valéry into an official personage, coolly taking very subtle springs and delicate machinery to pieces: too-docile disciples of the master were thus waylaid into blind alleys. They would have been better off to acknowledge that, from the *Album* of his youth, through the alternating strains of resignation and confused and bellicose revolt in the *Jeune Parque* and other poems of *Charmes,* even to the Dionysian masterpiece of his old age, *Mon Faust,* most of his achievement stood in contradiction to his poetics. Mallarmé, perhaps the most profound thinker of all these poets, thought not so much in and with concepts as with playful words, veiled coquettishness, wily enigmas, and libertine suggestions.

Baudelaire is a complete poet and a supremely moving one also because he aspired to classicism but never stayed secure in it and never imprisoned himself in it as in a set attitude. The very same man who praised the deliberate calculation of the poet as craftsman confessed, at other times, that the role of the will in art is not so vast as is believed. He who had railed at the romantic display of sentiment elsewhere gave the warning: "Do not scorn anyone's sensibility; the sensibility of each person is his genius." He pretended at times to survey his work with the haughty glance of his Don Juan in hell, "staring at the wake and not deigning to see anything," but the creator in him was one with his creation and desperately involved in it. Never in his work serene or still; it unceasingly tends upward or it is drawn downward by carnal and satanic impulses. It aims at a formal classicism, the better to set off an inner disorder which ravaged the poet. Never did Baudelaire find God with any finality, or the serene satisfaction of concentration in his work of which he naïvely dreamt, or perfected beauty, or any degree of triumph over his nerves and his emotions, or any control over his fear of the abyss. He never ceased to search. He remained a dual creature. If to be modern means, as Valéry once put it, to unite in oneself the most contradictory features and to live with that monstrous juxtaposition of opposites, Baudelaire represents the most modern interweaving of those eternally hostile and fraternally bound features which we like to call romantic and classical—and of many others besides.

Charles Baudelaire the Catholic

by François Mauriac

Je sais que vous gardez une place au Poète,
Dans les rangs bienheureux des saintes légions,
Et que vous l'invitez à l'éternelle fête
Des Trônes, des Vertus, des Dominations. . . .

[I know that you keep a place for the poet
In the happy ranks of the heavenly hosts,
And that you invite him to the eternal feast
Of Thrones and Virtues and Dominations. . . .]

I

Because Charles Baudelaire died some fifty years ago, journalists throw themselves on the great memory avidly. I dread for it indiscreet friendships more than I do insults. One commentator asserts that the Catholic was but a subtle mystifier, another swears that that debauchee died a virgin. Fine subjects indeed for articles! But let us ask Charles Baudelaire alone to show us "his heart laid bare." We Catholics shall not reject that sorrowful brother without close scrutiny. Down to his dying day, he listened to his poor soul and he confessed it. The flowers of evil are the flowers of sin, of repentance, of remorse and penitence. He suffers, but he knows why.

Soyez béni, mon Dieu, qui donnez la souffrance
Comme un divin remède à nos impuretés,
Et comme la meilleure et la plus pure essence
Qui prépare les forts aux saintes voluptés!

"Charles Baudelaire the Catholic." From *De Quelques Coeurs inquiets, Petits Essais de psychologie religieuse* by the Société Littéraire de France. Translated by Lois A. Haegert. Copyright 1920 by François Mauriac. Reprinted by permission.

[Blessed be Thou, O God, who givest suffering
As a divine remedy to our impurities,
And as the best and the purest essence
Which prepares the strong for holy delights.]

He is humiliated, but "those humiliations have been graces sent by God" (*Mon Coeur mis à nu*); Pascal likewise had written: "To offer oneself to inspirations through humiliations." Baudelaire prays, like a child of the Church:

> The man who says his prayers at night is a captain who places sentinels; he then can sleep. . . . Every morning, make my prayer to God, the reservoir of all strength and of all justice, to my father, to Mariette [the maid he had had as a child] and to Poe as intercessors; pray them to impart to me the strength I need to fulfill all my duties and to grant my mother a life long enough so that she may witness my transformation. . . . Trust God, that is to say, justice itself for the success of my projects; make every night a new prayer, to ask God for life and strength for my mother and myself. . . . Do not punish me in my mother and do not punish my mother because of me. . . . Grant me the strength to do my duty immediately every day and thus to become a hero and a saint. (*Mon Coeur mis à nu*)

Elsewhere Baudelaire wrote: "Beads are a medium, a vehicle; they are prayer put within the reach of all." The sorrow of men of genius, of the beacons, as he calls them, appears to him through the centuries like one indefinite prayer:

> Car c'est vraiment, Seigneur, le meilleur témoignage
> Que nous puissions donner de notre dignité
> Que cet ardent sanglot qui roule d'âge en âge
> Et vient mourir au bord de votre éternité!
>
> [For it is truly, O Lord, the best proof
> We may give of our dignity,
> This ardent sob which rolls from age to age
> And dies on the shore of Your eternity!]

The revelations which we owe to his friend Nadar and to the two women who were loved by Baudelaire seem to leave scant doubt as to what his strange ideal was: he wanted to possess the loved one in chastity. In his eyes, woman always remains "my child . . . , *my Sister* . . ." Eyes radiant with light go in front of him as he says:

Me sauvant de tout piège et de tout péché grave
("Le Flambeau vivant")

[Escaping every snare and every grave sin.]

On December 8, 1848, apropos of Jeanne Duval, he wrote to his
mother: "It is peculiar that you, who have so often and so long spoken
to me of spiritual feelings, of duty, should not have understood *that
singular liaison* in which I have nothing to gain and in which the chief
part is played by expiation and the wish to remunerate." What candid
love in the man who was denounced as a debauchee, who scandalized
the Voltairean middle class and the unbelievers among the journalists!
Unacknowledged as he was, he took a delight in irritating those people.
He mystified them. Today, the descendants of those journalistic critics,
of Pontmartin, Villemain, and their ilk, go on tearing their clothes and
shouting cries of blasphemy. Yet Baudelaire it was who wrote: "To be a
great man and a saint for oneself is the only thing that matters." A mistake no doubt, for we should not remain unconcerned in the eternal salvation of stupid fools. Yet how well we understand Baudelaire! In spite
of his unknown miseries, he does not cease conversing with God.

Jules Lemaître asserts that Baudelaire's thoughts are but a pretentious
and painful stammering and that no less philosophical head can be imagined. Neither a philosopher nor a scientist, I agree. But because he
believes in the dogma of original sin, the poet holds the key to the universal enigma. Lemaître derides this maxim which he quotes: ". . . The
one and supreme voluptuous delight of love lies in the certainty of doing *evil*. Man and woman well know, from their birth, that in evil all
that is voluptuous has its roots." I do not see that there is matter for
laughter here. Those few words illuminate the human heart better, for
me, than all the confusions and postures of theatrical people. Lemaître
assures us that the Catholicism of *Les Fleurs du mal* is scarcely Christian,
impious and sensuous. Facile blasphemies, deliberately exaggerated, will
not avert us from those poems, where a poor soul, torn with remorse, is
hungry and thirsty for perfection and knows the price of sorrow. True,
he is fond of making his title of Catholic sound aloud, as a young lord
does with his noble name. He takes glory in his baptism in a France
"where everyone resembles Voltaire." To me, such pride appears legitimate. I am not scandalized by such spiritual dandyism. Still a danger
lurks there. Today also, the vulgarity of the free-thinking middle class
may well lure some young Catholics to laud God for having made them
such admirable creatures. I fear ostentatiousness for them more than human respect.

But to that Catholic attitude, and that religious dandyism, there corresponds in Baudelaire a heart truly pursued by Grace. A few experiences with opium and hashish, a few excesses with alcohol do not alter the fact that "the frightening grip of God" weighed on that soul. Whenever I read his poems, I have the feeling that they do not bear their true title. With those three words, "Flowers of Evil," at the very threshold of his book, that great poet slanders himself. I remember how, at fifteen, I opened in secret that forbidden collection of poems, but almost nothing in that music disturbed my child's heart. Sin maintained all its ugliness in it; man severed from God was abandoned to his solitude and misery; the heart kept its craving for love, its need to possess someone beyond the blood, beyond the flesh.

Echoes responding to Pascal's lyricism are audible in Baudelaire's poetry. "Man does not know at what rank to place himself," Pascal wrote. "He is clearly lost and fallen from his true estate, and he can not retrieve it. He seeks it everywhere restlessly and unsuccessfully, through impenetrable darkness." Amid that impenetrable darkness where Baudelaire gropes his way as a wanderer of original sin, he is guided by a love unknown to Pascal: Beauty. But he fears it and he hates it, when it asserts itself as carnal and criminal. He merely wishes that it might open in front of him the gate

> D'un infini que j'aime et n'ai jamais connu.
>
> [Of an infinite which I love and never have known.]

His yearning for "the voyage," for "elsewhere," do they not transcend the world? It is beyond the setting suns that the ships of the "Invitation au voyage" carry the poet, and woman does not lead him away from the unattainable horizon:

> . . . Et rien, ni votre amour, ni le boudoir, ni l'âtre
> Ne me vaut le soleil rayonnant sur la mer.
>
> [And nothing, neither your love, nor the boudoir, nor the hearth
> Equals for me the sun radiant over the sea.]

The last of the *Fleurs du mal,* "Le Voyage," in a manner unequalled in its splendor, expresses that need of the human heart to escape from the finite. First it is the earthly departure that is sung in the poet's lines, that desire to

> Bercer notre infini sur le fini des mers,
>
> [Cradle our infiniteness on the finite seas,]

to destroy memory, to obliterate the trace of kisses; but the world is too small, the poet only yearns for the ultimate crossing. He weighs anchor for ever, he trusts death to lead him to God. . . . That celestial Father whom we hope, after a martyrdom without name, Charles Baudelaire at last found.

II

If they do not deserve their title, *Flowers of Evil,* Baudelaire's poems are indeed sickly flowers, as he himself called them in his dedication to Gautier. But Catholicism is balance. Holiness is health itself. There exists a subtle temptation which consists in loving, in the Church, a source of delights, a moving vision of the world and of oneself, the evil pleasure of challenging a prohibition and of disobeying someone; that taste for sinning can be perceived in Baudelaire even by the least attentive of readers. Before he became resigned to the strait gate, the poor poet scratched his hand at too many of its bars. His very purity, which I have praised, is undeniably suspect. It is given to man to discover a worse quest in abstinence, and, if he did not sin through his body, his intellectual debauchery knew no restraint. With the unconscious hypocrisy of a great love, I was too anxious to quote the Christian pages of *My Heart Laid Bare.*

Elsewhere, Baudelaire also confesses, lays his poor soul bare, uncovers for us wounds which, with a patient and mournful self-knowledge, he envenoms. As every young writer will do, he exposes himself complacently in his first piece of writing, that *Fanfarlo* which was turned down by the *Revue de Paris.* The great and pitiful Baudelaire is there to be found, body and soul.

But now? I remember that, one day, from the pulpit of Saint-Étienne du Mont, Father Sertillanges described to us those souls whom Grace crosses in order to reach other souls. The "accursèd poets," in the century of Hugo and of Béranger, with their hands soiled by iniquity, sheltered the flame of ineffable Catholic poetry. They did more: like those uninformed children to whom a hunted priest, during the Terror, entrusted the holy Eucharist, they preserved the sense of the supernatural in order to transmit it to our generation. They bequeathed to us "the living, almost the physical impression of the supernatural." Thus Paul Claudel expresses it when he brings, before God and before us, his testimonial of the unhoped for light which that frantic and blaspheming adolescent, Arthur Rimbaud, brought to him.

Baudelaire's posthumous writings also served as lights on Claudel's way, and we see grace cross the soul of the "accursèd poet" for remote ends. He did not remain untouched by its burning mark. Grace wrought a miracle in him that such a lover of Beauty might not be satisfied with the world of shapes. Among the perfumes, the colors, the sounds, Baudelaire, in order to broaden the universe in which he feels stifled, creates correspondence. He sees nature as a forest of symbols. He prolongs his life in the realm of appearance with the imagined splendor of an "anterior life." But it is in vain; and he forsakes all the appearances to the extent of only tolerating a bare and stripped landscape, a landscape, as he puts it in his prose poems, "made with light, and the mineral and the liquid to reflect them." His poems, like vessels sailing to far-off seas, intoxicate the restlessness of wandering hearts. They suggest a flight toward impossible climates and they constrain us to love death like a supreme departure. They can be summed up in the cry which everyone of us, at some time in his youth, has uttered: "Anywhere out of the world!"—the cry, not of a reconciled Christian, but of a sinner who cannot be resigned to sin. What is refused to Baudelaire, to his ilk, to his brethren, by merciful powers, is the gradual acceptance and the habit of sin; he returns to his nausea, but he is aware that it is but nausea. The most alluring blandishments of the prince of this world do not dim his clear-sightedness. Baudelaire's work illustrates Faust's derisive remark in Goethe's tragedy: "What hast thou to give, poor demon? Thou hast only food which does not satiate."

Never satiated, his thirst always unslaked, aggravated by that trickery of sin, by that deceitful decoy of the senses, why does he not surrender to God the father? Because, on the path of the prodigal son, in the night, the lamps of evil houses burn. It cannot be doubted that the poet used and abused drugs, the criminal delights of which he described for us in his *Artificial Paradises*. But never does he lose the lucidity of one who has not renounced true religion: in more than one passage the *Artificial Paradises* evince a passionate and Pascalian logic. In the entrancing resort to poisons, Baudelaire denounces, as Pascal might have done, the perversion of the taste for the infinite: "Alas! man's vices, full of horror as they may be imagined to be, contain the proof (were it but in their infinite expansion!) of his passion for the infinite: but that passion is often waylaid. . . . Everything leads to reward or to punishment, two forms of eternity. The human spirit brims over with passions . . ." ("The Taste for the Infinite," in *Artificial Paradises*).

Conscious and remorseful lucidity, such is the torment to which grace condemns the poor poet gone astray. Even when he writes on hashish and opium, he knows with absolute certainty that he sits under the watchful gaze of the Trinity and, not to lose heart altogether, he utters a cry of hope toward God in one of his prose poems: "O Lord, my God, you, the servant, you, the Master; you who established law and freedom, you, the sovereign that tolerates; you, the judge that forgives; you who are full of motives and of causes and who perhaps placed in my spirit the taste of horror in order to convert my heart, like the healing at the edge of a blade. . . ."

I know not whether, at the deathbed of Baudelaire, the prayer for the commending of the soul to divine mercy was recited. But his soul deserved, more than any other, that such a testimonial be granted it: "Although it sinned, it denied neither the Father nor the Son nor the Holy Ghost; it believed in them." Some teachers of youth worry: Shall we invite every adolescent to drink, without discernment, from those turbid waters? There are, not only in the commonplace vituperations of preachers, books which are harmful. But the peril is twofold: one consists in inducing young people, for the love of art, to indulge in morbid reading; the other was not eschewed by the priests whose textbooks fostered in me, when I was sixteen, a nefarious sense of irony. To the poison of Balzac and of Flaubert, those pious educators opposed the antidote of the most insipid Sunday School literature. Neither Baudelaire nor Verlaine, needless to say, was granted a single mention in their books, nor any of the poets whom we cherish.

There is no ground for smiling light-heartedly at such pious deceit: I know what storm brews in a young heart when it deems itself exiled, through its faith, from all the paradises whose odor it breathes; when the notions of mediocrity, of childish silliness are married in his thought with religious practice. What! The highest geniuses of the last century and of ours have, according to Nietzsche's phrase, "dropped in collapse at the foot of Christ's cross," and you propose edifying and insipid beverages, as specifically Catholic, to the teenager? I grant that he should be put on his guard against modern writers; that, until he is fortified in his faith, reading them should be forbidden him, in the name of that demanding truth which obliges us to forsake the remotest occasions for sinning; and yet I hold that we should teach young souls the immense role of God in contemporary art, showing them that the lyricism of Baudelaire, of Verlaine, of Rimbaud, Jammes, Claudel, in different degrees, proceeds from the Father, like that of Bossuet and of Pascal.

A young Catholic priest from Denmark confided to me that, on landing in Paris, his first care was to discover the tombs of Baudelaire and of Verlaine, to kneel down there; and, as I expressed my surprise, he was astonished at my very astonishment. What, in Verlaine's work, is abominable, should not, in truth, detract us away from the sobs of *Sagesse*. Verlaine and Baudelaire belong to the Catholics. I am not as disinterested as the Christians who see no reason for rejoicing in the humble prostration of inspired poets. But no family ever took pride in poets in its midst. Baudelaire's errors and transgressions would only exclude him from Catholicism if they were not sins. If he could have committed them without becoming a sinner, then he would not be one of ours. But in Baudelaire every fault becomes a sin; he confesses it as such. By that sign, acknowledge him as my brother. A man whose life was clearer and purer, Taine for example, does not belong to our spiritual family; that wretched Baudelaire does. "The sinner is an inhabitant of Christendom. The sinner may utter the best prayer. No one perhaps is as deeply Christian as Villon. . . . The sinner and the saint are, may we say it firmly, two integral parts of the mechanism of Christianity." Thus avers Péguy, in one of his *Cahiers de la quinzaine,* with his slow and sure logic, his thick, substantial, pregnant logic.

As he neared the end of his life, Baudelaire, deep in the pangs of suffering, found the strength to submit to God. He died a penitent. To be sure, such a death does not exorcize the work of the poet. But in its very blasphemies, that work is the advancement of a heart which, in order to reach God, follows the longest road. Everything delays the poet, because he sees what others do not perceive; solitude, silence, "the incomparable chastity of the azure sky," long avert his gaze from what lies beyond them. The "mute language" of flowers, of skies, of the setting sun cover up the inner voice of God. They may be mistaken and mad in that temporary blindness of theirs. But let us repeat in humility the prayer of Baudelaire's *Poems in Prose:* "O Lord, take pity upon the mad ones! O Creator! can there exist monsters in the eyes of him alone who knows why they exist, how they became thus, and how they might not have thus become monsters?"

Meditation on the Life
of Baudelaire

by Charles du Bos

Soyez béni, mon Dieu, qui donnez la souffrance
Comme un divin modèle à nos impuretés,
Et comme la meilleure et la plus pure essence
Qui prépare les forts aux saintes voluptés!

[Blessed be thou, O God, who givest suffering
As a divine remedy to our impurities,
And as the best and the purest essence
Which prepares the strong for holy delights!]

My only way out of difficulties is by *explosion;* yet what living makes me
suffer is unspeakable.　　　　　(Letter to his mother; Christmas, 1861.)

Les morts, les pauvres morts, ont de grandes douleurs.

[The dead, the wretched dead, have great sorrows.]

I

We here propose nothing more than a meditation on the life from
which the *Fleurs du mal* sprang. Previous critics have considered the
work alone, by itself, in order to evaluate it and to win for it the place
it deserves, and thanks to them, that place has been won for all time.
Today Baudelaire's life no more needs apology than does his work:
everywhere unbared, spread out before our gaze like some gigantic
wound, no centurion's lance can any longer threaten it. Yet on contem-

"Mediation on the Life of Baudelaire." From *Approximations* by Charles du Bos.
Translated by A. Hyatt Mayer. Copyright 1931 by *The Hound and the Horn* and
Lincoln Kirstein. Reprinted by permission of Lincoln Kirstein and Madame Charles
du Bos.

plating it we receive so many lessons, so pure and so urgent, that it becomes our duty to gather them in. We would show that although the *Fleurs du mal* could have grown in a sense only from such a life, yet that it nevertheless remains a miracle that they did so grow from it, and we would show that they grew from the life in spite of it, through a triumph, not of the will, this time, but of the most hidden and inalienable prerogative of the spirit. Baudelaire's case shows more clearly than any other how, in the hidden foundations of moral life and practice, every "because" carries an "in spite of," and every incentive a corresponding inhibition. No man ever more exactly deserved Joubert's maxim: "I have no strength except a certain incorruptibility."

When Baudelaire's letters to his mother were published in 1918, the *Fleurs du mal* appeared for the first time against their proper background. The mass of evidence in Crépet's two collections and the insistent gloom of the letters to Poulet-Malassis and Ancelle had indeed already opened a crack of unbearable bleak and blank light, but this time the whole room is disclosed and each angle of sordidness brought out. These letters might be called *Ma Vie mise à nu* and set up as a diptych against *Mon Coeur mis à nu,* since they further deepen the pit from which that last cry rises.

II

We must realize that Baudelaire's plight is really not unique. Life was just such a problem for many another great artist. Yet in Baudelaire's case we can neither blame the events nor the actors nor any of those jangled instruments that life plays on so harshly, since his supreme tragedy is this, that even if life had set out to give him everything, it had nothing to offer that his disposition could take to. His originality took the dreadful form of a hatred for life that extended far beyond any of its contingencies, the bare spirit's absolute and incompatible hatred.

When such a feeling is found in its pure state, rising above any personal motive in an abrupt and ageless autonomy, it terrifies, like a lonely peak, blacking the valley. With most of us life deals even-handedly and brings us compensations, as Emerson loved to remark

> Et propter vitam vivendi perdere causas.
>
> [And for life's sake, to love the reason for living.]

Even while life steals one by one our reasons for living, our successive centers of gravity, it at the same time, often unnoticed by others, almost always unnoticed or at least unrealized by ourselves, replaces them with those petty satisfactions that solidify a person and enable him to pass from yesterday to tomorrow—those hidden props to so many lives that seem to have nothing left them. Now Baudelaire was congenitally unable to feel these petty satisfactions; his whole being flung them savagely off. I have heard Baudelaire shrewdly called lean; if this means the man and not the artist, then how profoundly true! Baudelaire was indeed lean in the sense that nothing in him functioned as a circulatory system. He never knew any normal vegetative life, any of that well-being diffused throughout the body by a medley of feelings of which no single one rises clearly to consciousness. He knew vegetative life only in the form of dreaming, of such ever brooding meditation as produced the Sibyls of Michelangelo, Dürer's Melancholia, some tomes of de Vigny, and so many of the *Fleurs du mal*. Baudelaire's sole contact with life itself came through his nerves, forever unbared and rasped upon. When we read his letters the same anguish grips us as when we see the trembling and chilly twigs that winter whips with wind.

III

"Greatness does not show itself in pushing to any one extreme, but in straddling opposites and filling all the middle ground." Pascal was here treating of virtues; but whatever the point his mind bore upon it, thereby became the center of a circle embracing all human experience. The extreme must here be taken as height and depth, without, however, restricting these terms to an exclusively moral sense, and their deviation is determined for each man by his character; the middle ground, on the contrary, is furnished us by life itself, and it becomes our task to "fill" it. But how fill what you have not got? Baudelaire has neither Pascal's middle ground, nor the middle ground of life, so that most men's normal state is spiritual death for him. Seen from without, the vegetative life may seem a mere doze, but the man who gives himself up to it feels nothing consciously but the vague fulfilment of repose. Baudelaire knew every form of laziness and idleness, but through them never attained repose. His disposition could not bear the very repose he longed for, whence the all-powerful nostalgia of the *Fleurs du mal* and its wide archangel wings.

Under some form or other, the middle ground of normal life protects men of genius from their genius itself; they regather their strength in a kind of anonymity, which armors their originality, frees it only at its season and takes charge of the interim. This interim, if prolonged, will kill the artist, but often it saved him simply by keeping the man alive.

Now I think no mind was ever made up more exclusively of originality than Baudelaire's, by which I mean more incapable, not only of any expression, but of any way of thinking or feeling that does not bear his personal stamp. He shares this complete lack of anonymity with Constant and Stendhal, the only two recent Frenchmen whose originality seems to me to equal his, but with both of them life by turns attracting or paining them or rousing their curiosity, also stimulated their action, that is, released the intellectual activity that eases originality merely by exercising it. Baudelaire's thought certainly fed on all appearances (few men reflected the spectacle of life so profoundly) but life itself never sufficed to make him act; this is where his originality turned against him and showed itself so murderous, not only by giving him no rest, but by answering no outside appeal. His originality obeyed no commands except those itself laid down.

Now life, whether assimilated or rejected, knows how to impose its middle ground, and torture the man of genius who refuses to admit its plea, as Baudelaire's letters inexorably show. Already at eighteen he wrote thus to his mother:

> I am worse than I was at school. There I did little in class, but at least I did something, and later, when I was dismissed, that shook me, and I still did a little something for you—but now *nothing, nothing at all,* and it is no pleasant indolence, nor poetic, no indeed, but sulky and silly. . . . At school I worked now and then, read, wept, sometimes got angry, but at least I lived. Now not at all. As abject as can be, swarming with faults and no longer with pleasing faults. If only at least this painful sight drove me to change violently, but it doesn't, and of all that spirit of activity that drove me now toward good and now toward evil, I have nothing left, nothing but indolence, sulks and boredom.

Except for the word "silly," by which Baudelaire anticipated what he dreads he might become (although he is one of the very few men who never passed through silliness), the first stage of his malady is already complete. Later we shall track the roundabout ways by which he regains his "spirit of activity," though never rejoining it directly, since he lacked any category of the "given": in one sense he always had to start off from nothing, which multiplied a hundred fold the difficulties of the start, that every self-respecting writer feels. Thus this somber portrait darkens and is increasingly more loaded by the very lifelong growth of Baudelaire's spirit. Each essential element of his exceptional genius brought with it a devastating force, each one sufficient to batter down the whole. If incorruptibility had not been both Baudelaire's inalienable privilege and his essential virtue, we would have neither the *Fleurs*

du mal nor the *Spleen de Paris;* but to maintain this incorruptibility
and through it to rescue his work, he was driven to destroy himself. May
I be forgiven for insisting on this point that is the sole reason for writing these pages?

Baudelaire's fundamental and constant aim, pursued through thick
and thin, was what he liked to call the "perfecting of his spirit." In time
that spirit became an infallible instrument, as incapable of error as most
of ours are of truth. Even in youth Baudelaire had a high faculty for
judgment, which developed until, during the last fifteen years of his life,
it seemed to work independently of his own will, so that the spirit could
not err even though the man might wish it to. I know no more impressive intellectual sight than this unswerving judgment that looks down
from ever higher upon a life irrevocably condemned. At Brussels he was
obsessed and torn by the weight of abandonment by hearing nothing
from the book shop upon which his whole uncertain future depended,
by piercing sickness, by utter inability to work, and by a frightful thirst
for vengeance, and yet he could write thus to Sainte-Beuve in 1865:

> I have re-read the *Salâmmbo* article and the reply. Our good friend is
> certainly right in seriously defending his dream. You were right in laugh-
> ingly making him aware that it is not always wise to be too serious, but
> you seem, in places, to have laughed a little loudly.

No more need be said, and what an earnest and saddened ring! Could
a lapse be more tactfully and delicately pointed out to an elder who is a
friend in spite of everything? French poetry has no greater nor more
scrupulous artist than Baudelaire who thus wrote to Poulet-Malassis, at
the time when the *Fleurs du mal* were in the press: "You yourself once
owned to me that you thought, as I do, that in every kind of creation,
nothing was worth considering but perfection." Baudelaire gave ear to
every objection, which he would scrupulously weigh, and welcome if he
found it the least bit justified, even though it came from men he otherwise despised. From a friend he solicits criticism: "My note on Revolt
is loathsome, and I wonder that you did not call me down for it." He
was tireless in retouching, and never let go of anything, whether the
most sustained poem or some simple note whose perfection lay in absolute exactitude, unless he had first brought it to the highest polish he
thought it could stand. And yet the work of art was never all in all for
him as it was for others, for him technical perfection was not an end in
itself, but a mere evidence of the essential perfection of the spirit. On
this score Baudelaire deserves Paul Bourget's acute remark on Leonardo,

both being alike in "slow preparations, deep reflection, and works of art that are means for study rather than ends in themselves, stages in intellectual exploration and opportunities for the progress of thought."

Although Leonardo, and later Goethe, found their salvation in this "progress of thought," nevertheless they sought it through creative activity. Leonardo called painting, *cosa mentale*, and would have said the same of everything, and yet, as Valéry remarks, "he comes back to reality without effort, models a horse as a handsome and thinking animal in its lithe relaxation, able to gallop or leap or swim, changing gaits upon its rider's slightest hint, and with a wise nimbleness." If Goethe seems at times too willing to nod with Homer, be sure that that master of wisdom, whose life is a matchless treatise on intellectual economy, knew perfectly well what he was about, and what awakenings he was preparing. Spiritual perfection, when left to itself, is anything but an incentive to creation, and unless it is allied, as in Joubert, with a very special constitution, with that seldom found aptitude for spiritual happiness whose experiences are distilled drop by drop in the *Pensées*, it becomes, as with Baudelaire, the most subtle and ingenious instrument of torture. The perfection of Joubert's spirit has the fullness and bloom of a fine fruit; Baudelaire has the sharpness of the double-edged sword whose name he bore, a sharpness never sheathed; let a mist arise, such as those that the very act of creation gives off—dangerous, but also blessed because they give the strength to keep on—and instantly this sword is on it, cuts it off, and remakes the void. In Baudelaire's mind every mist corrupts, not only those rising from the world, but even those that his own genius might be tempted to emit.

If only this "perfecting of his spirit," to which all is subordinate, could find a free field for its exercise. But no, a first comer has already seized the field, the "leaning for dreams." These daydreams, which were finally to give France a poetry not unworthy of English poetry, appear to us only in their apotheosis in the *Fleurs du mal*, but our gratefulness demands that we confront them with their origins. Twenty years of the most tragic experience lay behind Baudelaire when he wrote: "Immediate work, even though bad, is better than daydreaming." "I shall not tell you my fearful struggles with myself, my despairs, my daydreaming." Baudelaire undoubtedly expanded into his vast boundaries through his immense and complex daydreaming, so rich and searching, and it is thence that he brought up those never-ending lines, those strophes that exhaust man's breath, that swell as strong as tides, and whose organ shudderings are pierced by the sharp delights of fifes. But before reaching that result, dreaming had poisoned him with a "hideous lethargy";

his "mind is absolutely lucid" and his "ideas are forever active," yet the
drug takes quick effect, for "the immensity of dreaming soon swallows a
man" and its corrosive strength is intensified by the obsession of the irreparable past, which haunted Baudelaire more destructively and more
awesomely than any other man. On this his word is final: "The thought
of the past strikes mad." The illness grows by mere duration, and yet
during its growth the victim enjoys a matchless bliss:

> O bliss! What we usually call life, even in its happiest unfolding, is
> nothing to this supreme life now revealed to me, which I sip minute by
> minute, second by second. No minutes have ceased longer, and so have
> seconds, for time has foundered and there reigns an everlastingness of
> delight.

And now the awakening:

> But a dreadful knock has struck the door, and I feel as though, in some
> hellish dream, a pickaxe has struck my stomach.
> And there the Specter stands: some constable who comes to rack me in
> the name of the law; an infamous concubine who comes to whine and
> unload the pettiness of her life upon the sorrows of mine; or else it is some
> editor's office boy who demands the completion of a manuscript.
> The heavenly room, the idol, the mistress of dreams, the Sylph, as the
> great René called her, all that magic has flown at the Specter's brutal
> knock.
> Horrible! I remember! I remember! Yes, this den, this prison of unend-
> ing boredom, is indeed mine. This is my stupid, dusty, battered furniture,
> my cold hearth, fouled with spit, my sad window panes where the rains
> have guttered the dust, my manuscripts, scribbled over or unfinished, my
> calendar, pencil marked at sinister dates!
> And instead of the fragrance of another world enrapturing my perfected
> feeling, alas, I smell stale tobacco smoke, mixed with indescribable, nausea-
> ous rottenness, the rancid breath of desolation.
> In this world whose closeness is packed with disgust, only one familiar
> thing smiles at me, my vial of laudanum, my old and frightful friend, lavish
> like every woman I have known, with caresses and betrayals.
> Ah yes, Time is back again, Time is now enthroned, and the hideous
> old man has brought his fiendish train of Memories, Regrets, Spasms,
> Fears, Agonies, Nightmares, Rages, and Panics.
> As each Second ticks out of the clock it speaks thus: I am your life, most
> insupportably, implacably your life.
> In all man's life one Second only is sent with good news, the *good news*
> that sets every man inexplicably to trembling.
> Yes, Time rules and has caught back his brutal dictatorship, and drives

me, like a beast, with his double goad: Pull ox. Sweat, slave. Live, and be damned.[1]

IV

If only the lethargy vanished with the dream that brought it—but it does not, and the lethargic spell stays on, sometimes for months. On awakening he feels sometimes "a resignation worse than fury," but mostly fury itself, and rage (no word recurs so often in his letters); nothing is left of the daydream but its ravages, and it is easy to see why Baudelaire cries: "Ah, how I am disgusted, and have been so for years, with this having to live twenty-four hours every day. When shall I live with pleasure?" Lethargy and anger, such is the chasm from which these two unforgettable stanzas arise:

> Quelquefois dans un beau jardin,
> Où je trainais mon atonie,
> J'ai senti comme une ironie
> Le soleil déchirer mon sein;

> Et le printemps et la verdure
> Ont tant humilié mon coeur
> Que j'ai puni sur une fleur
> L'insolence de la nature.

> [Sometimes in a fair garden,
> Where I dragged my dull apathy,
> I have felt like an irony
> The sun tear my breast;

> And the spring and the verdure
> Humiliated my heart so
> That I punished on a flower
> The insolence of nature.]

There would seem but one way out of such a state; through the will. No one knew this better than Baudelaire, who always judged himself so severely, and who was soon to show the deepest humility in *Mon Coeur mis à nu*. But here we must distinguish. Gautier noticed in him a "dogged will that backed his inspiration" and Baudelaire did indeed

---

[1] *Le Spleen de Paris*: "La Chambre double." This poem throws light on his note in *Mon Coeur*, "While still a small child, two feelings warred in my head: the horror of living and the ecstasy of living. The state of an idle neurotic."

have a will such as few geniuses ever had, which we must oppose to the will by calling it a will to *see,* since it clings unshaken to every turn of inspiration, as incapable of compromise as it is of blindness. But although the will to see superintends all Baudelaire's completed work, it never, either with him or with anyone else, gives the first impulse, which always comes from the will to do. Now the will to see, because of the level on which it works, is not only unable to bring the will to do into play, but sometimes even obstructs it. The will to see just because it does foresee far ahead—because it beholds every detail of work before a stroke has been done to make it—thereby overwhelms some men with disgust, makes them feel that nothing is any use, as men are apt to, whose device is Baudelaire's: "Spleen et idéal." [2]

Although only the will to see can give a work its eternal stamp, it makes the execution torture inch-by-inch. ("How hard it is, not to think a book out, but to write it!") Time and again, Baudelaire shows that work was never a pleasure for him. In his closing years, moved by the wish to make good and by his increasing isolation, he wrote:

> The great and single object of my life is work, the hardest and most boring thing in the world, which only habit can make bearable. I am a great culprit—to have wasted my life, my faculties, my health, to have squandered twenty years in daydreams, which puts me below the herd of boors who work every day.

He wrote again, four months before the end:

> I say to myself with a kind of terror: I must get used to working and make that churlish companion my only joy, for the time is coming when I will have no other.

[2] "For several months I have lain in one of those frightful languors that stop everything; I have not had the courage to touch the proofs that are piled up on my table since the beginning of the month, yet a time always comes when I have to wrench myself, with dreadful pain, from this chasm of indolence." (*Letters to His Mother,* p. 148.) "The page before was written a month, 6 weeks, 2 months, ago, I cannot remember when. I have fallen into a ceaseless nervous terror, with frightful sleep, frightful awakenings, and can do nothing. My copies lay a whole month on the table before I found the courage to put them in envelopes. . . . How hard it is, not to think a book, but to write it without weariness." (*Letters to His Mother,* p. 319.) "I feel an immense discouragement, a feeling of unbearable isolation, an entire distrust of my strength, a total lack of desires, inability to find any amusement whatsoever. The odd success of my book and the quarrels it has stirred up interested me for a while, and then I relapsed. . . . I constantly ask myself, What use is this? What use is that? This is the true spirit of spleen." (*Letters to His Mother,* p. 150, dated December 30, 1857, six months after the *Fleurs du mal* were published.)

We must not be led astray in this respect by the haughty penetration of his "Advice to Young Writers" of 1846, for there Baudelaire's judgment of himself dictates a code from what he wished to be, not from what he was. The admirable axiom: "Inspiration is the sister of daily work" is indeed taken from his experience, but from his negative experience.

Baudelaire appears never to have had much will to *do*. He refers somewhere to the "varying treasure of the will," but his, like the small fortune he inherited, was squandered during the years of leisure through which his genius grew.

Ah, dear mother, have we still time for happiness? I no longer dare believe so: 40 years old, my money in trust, huge debts, and last and worst of all, my will lost, spoiled.

Elsewhere he says:

I have sinned against myself. This disparity between the will and the faculty is more than I can understand.

How was he to make hope from hopelessness, a will from slackness?

It is doubtful if, in a man of such uncompromising superiority, the will to do can find sufficient reasons for acting in purely internal motives. Let me explain: in the last analysis, the will to do is always the most personal of creations. But the man whom vulgar incentives do not touch, who is strong in his incorruptibility and weak in all else, often requires an ideal or real stimulus to come from without and give him the courage to forge his needed will. Whether he subordinates himself to a single love or to a high duty, his effort is inner, but the stimulus comes from outside him. Now Baudelaire never would consent thus to subordinate his intimate self to something greater than it and existing independently; and when 'at last he did consent his game was up, for sickness gripped him. "Too late, perhaps," is the deathknell that strikes across his last cries:

> Loin des sépultures célèbres,
> Vers un cimetière isolé,
> Mon coeur, comme un tambour voilé,
> Va battant des marches funèbres.

> [Far from celebrated graves,
> Toward an isolated cemetery,
> My heart, like a muffled drum,
> Set out to beat funereal marches.]

Baudelaire never begins by working; it takes the excess of his crisis to fling him into work. No one ever listened more to the "fiend of procrastination," and the following quotation seems to be his final statement in this matter:

> Then add to this suffering one which you perhaps will not understand: when a man's nerves are harassed by anxieties and suffering, then the devil, in spite of every resolve, slips into his head every morning in the shape of this thought: Why not rest for one day in forgetfulness? Tonight, at one stroke, I will do all I have to do.—And then night comes, and the mind is overwhelmed by the mass of things overdue; sadness crushes one's strength, and on the morrow the same comedy is played again, in good faith, with the same confidence and the same conscience."

Such is Baudelaire's middle ground of life. Was I wrong in saying that it was really an inner death? Yet he could not escape it, for it was the very stuff of his daily existence. Where is the end? Baudelaire is unable to reestablish his will to do in its sphere, so that nothing is left him but Pascal's "extremes." And we shall see how the very reaction of tossing from one extreme to the other is what allows him, although at the price of his life, to salvage his work.

V

Spirituality is not only Baudelaire's peak but also his bedrock. Every great man uses certain words so personally that his whole being passes into them and charges them with their utmost meaning. Spirit is the word for imperious genius that Baudelaire's stamped above all others. Without ever losing sight of its original meaning of breath (*spiritus*), so that the word seems always airy, he used it in all senses except that of *wit* (*esprit*), a meaning he loathed, as shown in the following line: "Et l'esprit me fait mal." He twice uses the word in its fullest sense, in calling Guys "a spiritual citizen of the world," in speaking of conversation as "That great, that single pleasure of a spiritual being." Even Baudelaire's intelligence was always spiritual, I mean even in its beginning, even before that artistic working over that with other men, and great men too, supervenes to give the illusion of spirituality. This is a most rare phenomenon in France, and, aside from Pascal who is so much above all the rest that he must always be thought of separately, I can think of no others but Joubert and Maurice de Guérin. But if we shift from Baudelaire's intelligence to his sensibility, there spirituality[3] informs every part. We will not yet speak of his sentiments, but he had no sensation, however, heavy, charged, and base by origin, that was not at once mirrored in spirituality. Every passing sensation becomes the "truly spiritual" chamber of the prose poem quoted above, a poem that is essential for insight into Baudelaire's daily drama, since his "horror" of awakening, his "hideous lethargy," and his "anger" arise above all from this fact that when deserted by his spirituality, Baudelaire can feel literally nothing.[4]

Such is the extension, the indefinite expansion, that Baudelaire gives to one meaning of the word *spirit;* but in his case the word has another and more important meaning, its traditional and strictly Christian usage. *Poeta christianissimus* is the subtitle of Rudolf Kassner's essay on Baudelaire. Here is one of Baudelaire's very rare references to his childhood: "Even in childhood I leaned toward mysticism. Conversations with God." That Baudelaire had a religious life at this most susceptible age is still further shown by a letter from his mother to Ancelle, written during the worst of the family quarrels, when the separation occurred and the poet was giving way to his most violent utterance. His mother is answering Ancelle, who has written her about his last interview with her son, and she concludes with these words: "Nevertheless I thought he had a base of religion, without exercise, but still with faith." Doubtless Baudelaire's hatred for his stepfather, and his exasperation at having his money put in trust kept him for years from showing anything to his mother that might console her; and then, his other "passion for all the plastic arts that lasted from childhood" so flourishes from 1842 to 1850 that it hides his base of religion and for the time being seems to "deprive him of faith" in the strict acceptance of the term. But when did loss of faith ever stop a man from being a Christian? Christianity

---

[3] "And also, my dear friend, not too much wit; it jars on my present way of life. . . . Some months ago Christophe gave me a number of the *Journal d'Alençon* in which you let it be known that the translator and admirer of Poe would end like his model. That is wit. . . . I am sure, for my part, that you misunderstand that genius. You have talked with the rowdy gusto of wit about a man you do not know." (*Letter to Poulet-Malassis,* 1853.) "France especially annoys me because every Frenchman is like Voltaire." (*Mon Coeur. . . .*) Baudelaire had an impertinence, even an insolence that dotted an *i* and clinched a nail in a characteristic way; but any impression of wit comes from Baudelaire's objective seriousness and imperturbability in contrast with the unworthiness of the object. Baudelaire himself was of course the first to relish this.

[4] *Letters,* p. 376 (Mercure de France). Both these texts relate to his conversation and confirm Gautier's remark: "Baudelaire's conversation was wholly metaphysical. He talked much of his ideas, very little of his feelings, and never of his actions."

is not so lightly ousted; indeed nothing stamps human organizations more indelibly. In some cases loss of faith even deepens the original furrow since the conviction of sin is not always lost as well, and when that stays without its antidote of belief, and (above all) of Christian exercise, it fastens on the soul to gnaw. Original sin is a fundamental part of Baudelaire, and to the problem of the existence of sin in the world, he had a right to say *ego te intus et in cute novi,* since he constantly felt it in him in the shape of St. Paul's prodigious "law of the members." It has even been said that the idea of original sin flattered Baudelaire's vanity, but that is merely a sample of the wit that Baudelaire despised. His immanent Christianity is so clear, and can be proved by so many texts, that I purposely choose one in which his sincerity has been doubted:

> I was once present where some men were asking what was the greatest pleasure of love. Of course one answered: to receive; and another: to give oneself. This man said: the pleasure of pride; and that man: the gratification of humbleness. All these muckrakers talked like the *Imitation of Christ.* At last one impudent Utopian spoke up and said that the greatest pleasure of love was making little citizens for one's country. I, however, said: the one and supreme gratification of love lies in the certainty of doing *evil,* and both men and women know, from birth, that nowhere but in evil do they find gratification.

When this axiom, which condenses all Baudelaire's most frightful intimate experience, was first printed in Crépet's book, it was called an epigram of glib perversity and a flat paradox. Yet this throughgoing equation between gratification and sin is indeed profoundly Christian. But Baudelaire's immanent Christianity could not do without the aid of the spirit. "De Maistre and Edgar Poe taught me to reason." We can leave out Poe, whose influence was chiefly aesthetic, but the extent of De Maistre's action on him is clear in pages like this one from the *Soirées:* [5]

> Man *gravitates,* if I may say so, toward the regions of light. No beaver, swallow, or bee tries to know more than its predecessors. All beings stay

[5] Voltaire, in "Les Oreilles du comte du Chesterfield," makes a jest of this immortal soul that is lodged for nine months between excrements and urines. Voltaire, like every lazy man, hated mystery. The Church, being unable to suppress love, wished at least to disinfect it, and so established marriage.

"In this placing he might at least have seen some of Fate's malice or satire against love, and in the manner of our begetting a mark of original sin. In truth, we **can** make love only with excretory organs." (*Journaux intimes,* p. 66.)

quietly in their places. All are debased, but do not know it. Only man feels it, and this feeling is proof at once of his greatness and of his wretchedness, of his sublime rights and of his unbelievable debasement. His sad plight does not even allow him the happiness of not knowing himself: he cannot help looking ceaselessly at himself, and cannot do so without blushing; his very greatness humiliates him, since the lights that uplift him as high as angels serve but to reveal his abominable cravings that debase him as low as beasts. He searches the depths of his being for some sound particle, and cannot find it, for evil has tainted everything, and *the whole of man is sickness.* . . .

Being an unthinkable jumble of two different and incompatible powers, an aborted centaur, man feels himself the outcome of some unknown wrong, of some hateful mixture that has tainted him to the core.

And then there are the two last lines of "Un Voyage à Cythère":

Ah! Seigneur, donnez-moi la force et le courage
De contempler mon coeur et mon corps sans dégoût!

[Ah! Lord, give me the strength and the courage
To contemplate my heart and my body without disgust!]

To this strong intellectual framework from De Maistre, whose disciple he loved to proclaim himself, one has but to add the spectacle to Baudelaire's daily life. Baudelaire proves himself Christian by his bonds to sin, bonds tightened by his very failings, and although he is utterly unlike the great Christians in his exercise, for him, as for them, there are two poles, Satan and God. "Every man, at every minute, feels two simultaneous postulates, one towards God, the other towards Satan." The part that Satan plays in Baudelaire's work is very much greater than is usually thought, and it must be our task to bring this influence to light. Those who see mere affectation and puerility in Baudelaire's[6] frequent references to Satan should read the end of his letter to Alphonse Toussenel:

Your letter rouses many dormant ideas in me, and with regard to *original sin* and the *form patterned on the idea,* I had often thought that the destructive and disgusting beasts might perhaps be merely the coming to life, the embodiment and the birth into matter of man's *evil thoughts.*

[6] "And for a man like you to throw mud just casually, as if at some mere editor of the *Siécle,* at De Maistre, the great genius of our time, *a seer.* . . . All the heresies I just spoke of are after all nothing but the outcome of the great modern heresy of the artificial teaching, put in place of the natural teaching, I mean, the suppression of the idea of *original sin.*" (*Letter to Alphonse Toussenel,* 1856. *Lettres,* p. 84 [Mercure de France]).

"The coming to life, the birth into matter of man's evil thoughts,"
the "destructive beasts" and the satanic attributes spring from Baudelaire's anguish, whence their whole validity; Satan's presence around
him, inside him, that is what gives this conception its body, its urgency
and its intimacy.

> Sans cesse à mes côtés s'agite le Démon;
> Il nage autour de moi comme un air impalpable;
> Je l'avale et le sens qui brûle mon poumon
> Et l'emplit d'un désir éternel et coupable. . . .
>
> Il me conduit ainsi, loin du regard de Dieu,
> Haletant et brisé de fatigue, au milieu
> De plaines de l'Ennui, profondes et désertes. . . .
>
> [Unceasingly by my side the Demon frets;
> He swims around me like an impalpable air;
> I swallow it and feel it burning my lung
> And filling it with an eternal and guilty desire. . . .
>
> Thus it leads me, far from the gaze of God,
> Panting and broken with fatigue, into the midst
> Of the plains of Boredom, profound and deserted. . . .]

"Loin du regard de Dieu": there is Baudelaire's torture, for the "two
postulates" are "at every minute simultaneous." This calls to mind
Paul Bourget's penetrating remarks:

> When Catholicism educates a man it reveals the world of spiritual
> realities to him. This revelation is unimportant for many, who already
> from their youth believed in God, though merely mentally, never feeling
> Him as a living person. Such men are satisfied with an abstract faith in
> ideas, that lends itself to any transformation. Needing no vision, but a
> dogma, they change their original belief in God into belief in liberty, or
> in revolution, or in socialism, or in science. Such transformations are to be
> seen daily in oneself and in one's neighbors. Another fate awaits a mystical
> soul, such as Baudelaire's, for this soul, when it believes, is not content
> with a faith in an idea. It *sees* God. He is no mere word, no mere symbol,
> no mere abstraction, but a Being with whom the soul dwells as with a
> father who loves, knows, and understands it. . . . A mystic can have no
> keener anguish than the thought, that his need for belief might be merely
> subjective, that his former faith issued from himself and was all his own
> making.

Baudelaire had indeed a mystical soul, and how deeply! He never wrote anything more sincere than this beginning of "De Profundis Clamavi":

> J'implore ta pitié, Toi, l'unique que j'aime,
> Du fond du gouffre obscur où mon coeur est tombé.

> [I crave your pity, You, the only one whom I love,
> From the depths of the dark abyss into which my heart has fallen.]

He had indeed a right to say "Toi, l'unique que j'aime," since it was only God that he loved, as will become clear later on when we turn to Baudelaire's conception of love. But he loves God as the climate proper to his genius, the air in which his wings can stretch themselves:

> Envole-toi bien loin de ces miasmes morbides;
> Va te purifier dans l'air supérieur. . . .

> [Take your flight very far from those morbid miasmas;
> Go and purify yourself in the higher ether. . . .]

Everything in Baudelaire is a function of his genius, a genius which thirsted above all for a God to pray to, without, I might almost say, believing in Him:

> In this horrible state of mind, helpless and desperate, I was again tempted by suicide (I can tell you now that it has passed) and at all hours of the day this temptation dogged me. That way absolute escape seemed to lie, escape from everything. This *lasted three months,* and at the same time, by a contradiction that only seems strange, I was praying constantly (to whom, to what definite being, I absolutely do not know). . . .
> And God, you will say. I long with all my heart (and with what sincerity only I can know) to believe that someone, invisible and outside me, takes an interest in my fate; but what to do to believe this?

He never wholly escaped from this great sign that Christianity stamps upon a soul, this obsession for prayer in the very face of unbelief. The notion of sin, and deeper still, the need for prayer, seem to be two realities even more fundamentally imbedded than faith itself. This brings to mind Flaubert's saying: "I am at bottom a mystic and I believe in nothing." He and Baudelaire always understood each other like brothers.

VI

But though spirituality is a part of Baudelaire, it does not follow that the spiritual state of grace can be lastingly maintained. A jotting of *Fusées* shows well enough what Baudelaire thought in this respect: "Serena's portrait by Seneca. Stragiros' by St. John Chrysostom. Acedia, the monks' complaint." This acedia, this apathy, always the terrible affliction of those who live according to the spirit, fastened itself more fixedly on Baudelaire than on anyone I can think of. In a sense he always had but one problem, to recapture at any cost and hold that state of spirituality which many, but fleeting, experiences have proved to be the only state which could free the powers of his genius. He is one of those great and unhappy men who feel only at the peak of their being that they live. Baudelaire never lost sight of this spirituality, his source of inspiration, but saw it infinitely aloft, and saw himself shackled to earth by the "law of numbers."

> Mon esprit, tu te meus avec agilité,
> Et, comme un bon nageur qui se pâme dans l'onde,
> Tu sillonnes gaîment l'immensité profonde
> Avec une indicible et mâle volupté.
>
> [My spirit, you move with agility,
> And like a good swimmer exulting in the sea,
> Cheerfully you furrow the deep immensity
> With an ineffable and virile delight.]

But before each of these sovereign flights, the "strong swimmer" went under, and how many times! The closer one knows Baudelaire the more one sees him as a drowning man grasping wildly for a life preserver. From 1852 to the end of 1857 he seems to have sought this life preserver in love, and nothing takes us deeper into a knowledge of Baudelaire than an investigation of what he means by love.

The chief piece of evidence for this is his letter to a model, Madame Marie X, whom he met at the house of a friend. When he declared his love to her, she sent him away, saying that her heart belonged to another. He then wrote this letter:

Madame:
   Can it really be that I must never see you again? This question haunts me, for my heart has already come to feel your absence as a great privation. When I learned that you had stopped posing, and that I was unwitting cause, I felt strangely sad.

I wanted to write you, even though I am not given to writing; one almost always regrets it. But I run no risk, since my mind is made up to give myself to you for good and all.

You know our long talk on Thursday was most strange. It has changed my whole state and makes me write this letter.

Think of a man saying: "I love you," and begging, and a woman answering: "Love you? I? Never! There is but one I love, and woe to anyone who follows, for he would earn my coldness and contempt." And this same man, for the pleasure of looking longer into your eyes, lets you talk of another, talk of nothing but him, warm your blood for him alone, and think only of him. All these avowals have changed you, most strangely, from a merely desirable woman into a woman that I love for her candor, for her passion, for her directness, for her youth, and for her folly.

I have lost greatly by these explanations, since you were so decided that I had to submit at once. But you, madame, have greatly gained, for you have inspired my respect and deep esteem. Live ever thus and treasure the passion that makes you so lovely and so happy.

Come back, I beg, and I will make my longings gentle and modest. I deserved your contempt when I answered that I would be content with crumbs. I lied. Oh, but if you only knew how lovely you were that evening. I dare not be commonplace with compliments, but your eyes, your mouth, your whole living and moving person comes before my closed eyes and I feel it has come to stay.

Come back, I beg you on my knees. I do not say that you will find me free from love. However you cannot keep my longings from haunting your arms, your lovely hands, your eyes where all your life is gathered, your whole adorable body, no, you cannot stop that. But fear not; you are something I worship, and could never defile. I shall always see you as radiant as I did. Your whole person is so good, so beautiful, and so sweet to breathe. For me you are life and motion, not so much because of your quick gestures and the violent side of your nature, as because of your eyes, that cannot but inspire a poet with deathless love. How can I tell you how much I love your eyes and all your beauty? You blend two warring graces, the grace of the child and the grace of the woman. Oh, believe me when I tell you from the bottom of my heart that you are adorable and that I love you deeply. The feeling is virtuous that binds me to you forever. Do what I will, you are henceforth my talisman and my strength. I love you, Marie, there's no denying that, but the love that I feel is the love of the Christian for his God. It would be sacrilege to give an earthly and often shameful name to this bodiless and mystical cult, this suave and chaste attraction that unites my soul to yours, whether you will or no. I was dead and you gave me life. Oh, you little know how much! I own you, for your angel glance struck unknown joys into me, your eyes drew me into the soul's bliss, into all that is perfect and delicate. Henceforth, you are my one dream, my passion and my loveliness; you are the part of myself that a spiritual essence has shaped.

Through you, Marie, I shall be strong and great. Like Petrarch, I will immortalize my Laura. Be my guardian Angel, my Muse and my Madonna, and lead me on the path to Beauty.

Do answer me one word, I beg you, just one. Everyone's life has doubtful and decisive days when a token of friendship, a look, a scribbled something will fling us into silliness or madness. I swear to you that I am in such a state. A word from you would be a blessing to gaze on and learn by heart. Could you but know how I love you. Here, I fling myself at your feet: one word, say one word. . . . No, you will not!

Happy, a thousand times happy, must be the man whom you have chosen out of all, you who are so wise and fair and gifted, all desire, spirit, and heart. What woman could ever take your place! I dare not ask to see you, lest you refuse. I had rather wait.

I shall wait for years, and when you see yourself loved with respect, with complete disinterestedness, then you will recall that you started by treating me badly, and you will own that you did wrong.

Anyway, I am not free to ward off what blows the idol may please to strike at me. You were pleased to show me the door. I am pleased to adore you. The matter is settled.

Baudelaire shows his whole attitude toward love in these pages that are so beautiful and so clear that I have scruples about touching them; and yet I must, to bring out the main feature. The episode of Marie X is all the more significant in that it begins with a simple desire. The refusal of this desire "changes his whole state" and occasions the letter. This changed state is simply love in the only sense in which Baudelaire could ever conceive or feel it. Let us not be misled: here is none of that exasperation of desire, none of that will to possess that obstacles usually redouble. Instead of the "bloody scaffoldings of destruction," as Baudelaire calls the *durus amor,* there is a yearning for contemplation that needs only the presence, and that really possesses only because it possesses nothing. "I was dead, and you gave me life." A man like Baudelaire must feel himself dead in the relative anonymity of desire, as of life. When he says: "The feeling is virtuous that binds me to you forever," one cannot but think of Dante and Petrarch. Love becomes the stair of essential virtue, which consists for Baudelaire in being faithful to his genius. "Through you, Marie, I shall be strong and great. . . . Be my guardian Angel, my Muse and my Madonna, and lead me on the path to Beauty."

We have only this one letter to Marie X. It is printed immediately before the first of his letters to Madame Sabatier, which shows well enough that Baudelaire did not seek in love the favors of any particular goddess, but the permanence of the cult itself. Today we know the whole story of this tragic meeting. From 1852 until the publication of the

Fleurs du mal, Baudelaire, an often silent guest at the Sunday dinners, wrote Madame Sabatier a series of letters and accompanied each by one of his most beautiful poems. He sent these anonymously until the following incident occurred:

> For the first time I write you in my own handwriting. Were I not over-whelmed with business and letters (my hearing comes day after tomorrow) I would take this opportunity to ask you forgiveness for so much folly and nonsense. But then, have you not punished me enough already, especially through your little sister? The little beast! She froze me when she met me one day and burst out laughing in my face and said: "Are you still in love with my sister and do you still write her those grand letters?" I realized two things, that when I had wanted to hide myself, I had hidden very badly, and that the charm of your face masked but little charity. Brats *love,* but poets *worship,* and I fear that your sister is hardly made to understand eternal things.
>
> Allow me, even at the risk of making you laugh also, to renew those protestations that caused that little fool such loud laughter. Imagine a medley of dreaming, sympathy and respect, with endless nonsense full of earnestness, and you will have some idea of that deep sincerity that I can define no better.
>
> I can never forget you. They say there have been poets who have lived their whole lives with their eyes fixed on one dear image. I think indeed (although I am biased) that *faithfulness is one of the marks of genius.*
>
> You are more than a dear image of dreams. You are my *superstition.* When I commit some blunder, I say to myself: "Lord, if she saw that!" When I do something good, I say: "There is something that brings me closer to her—in spirit."
>
> And the last time that I had the happiness (in spite of myself) of meet-ing you (for you cannot imagine how elaborately I flee you) I said to myself: "How odd if that carriage were waiting for her. Perhaps I had better take another street." And then: "Good evening," with that beloved voice whose ring enchants and shatters me. And I went away saying: "Good evening" over and over as I walked, and trying to catch your voice.

This latter is dated August 18, 1857. Less than two weeks later, on August 31st, Baudelaire wrote again, with a sincerity whose frightfulness betrays the effort it must have cost him:

> I have destroyed the mass of nonsense on my table. It was not serious enough for you, dearly beloved. I have reread your two letters and make a fresh answer, for which I need some courage, since my nerves are so fright-fully on edge that I could shriek; and I awoke still disturbed by that unac-countable moral unrest with which I came away. . . . Absolute lack of shame.

For that I love you all the more.

. . . I feel that I have been yours since the first day I saw you. Do what you will with me, I am yours, body and soul.

Woe to you if you do not hide this letter! Do you really know what you are saying? The law imprisons those who fail to pay promissory notes, but the violation of vows of friendship and of love goes unpunished.

I said to you yesterday: "You will forget me, you will betray me. He who amuses you now will soon bore you." And today I add: "Only he will suffer, who, like a fool, takes matters of the soul in earnest." You see, dear heart, what hateful prejudices I have about women. In short, *I have no faith*. Your soul is beautiful, but, after all, feminine.

See how a few days have upset our position. First of all we are obsessed by the dread of hurting a good man who has the happiness still to be in love. And then, we are afraid of our own storm, because we know (I especially) that some knots are hard to loosen.

And then and then, a few days ago you were a goddess, something so convenient, so beautiful and inviolable. And here you are a woman.—And if, to my sorrow, I should ever earn the right to be jealous! The mere thought is horrible, for with a woman like you, whose eyes smile on and allure all the world, it must be torture.

Your second letter bears an English seal whose gravity would please me better were I sure that you understood it. *Never meet or never part.* That certainly means that never to have met were best for us, but now that we have met, we must never part. This might not be without its point on a letter of farewell.

Well, let come what will. I am a fatalist. But this I know, that I have a horror of passion, because I know it and all its slavery—and here the dear image that ruled all my life's adventures is becoming too seductive.

I dare not reread this letter. I might have to tone it down, for I dread hurting you. I fear I have unbared some of the vileness of my nature.

I cannot make you go like this into that foul rue Jean-Jacques-Rousseau. And yet I have much more to tell you. Do write me how and where.

Let me know a few days beforehand if our little plan becomes possible.

Farewell, dearly beloved. I somewhat resent your being so very charming, for when I carry away the scent of your arms and your hair, I also carry away the longing to return, and that is an unbearable obsession.

I must certainly take this myself to the rue Jean-Jacques-Rousseau lest you be going there. It will reach you earlier.

Possession had exactly reversed the places of the man and the woman. In the beginning Madame Sabatier seems to have been merely touched by the quality and the perseverance of Baudelaire's devotion, and probably also by the poems she inspired. We cannot be sure that she loved him when she gave herself, but she certainly did afterwards. The four scraps of her letters, quoted by Jacques Crépet, show once again how singleness and sincerity of passion sharpen a fine woman's intelligence, instead of dulling it. When she writes of Baudelaire: "Listen, dear, may I say what I think? You do not love me," she speaks as a woman and from a woman's point of view she is absolutely right. She is so positive simply because women feel things in wholes; when they love, it is with a single rush that so fuses body, mind and heart, that they can neither admit nor conceive acting otherwise. A divided mind in a woman is almost always the result of perversity, unless it be caused by successive despairs. A woman starts out with singleness, and how deep is her unhappiness when she finds no singleness in a man. For Madame Sabatier to make distinctions, she would have had to falsify the integrity of her love itself.

But a man, on the other hand, is split up almost in proportion to his greatness, and only a heroic effort can reduce him to singleness. For a man like Baudelaire this was the end of the adventure, for with him there was not merely a split, but absolute incompatibility between loving and possessing. This antinomy is a fundamental part of his nature. What could the celebration of the most lofty cult have in common with the gratification of the basest appetite? What bond was there between love, the treasury of strength, the goad of genius, and possession, the unrivalled means of forgetfulness? In keeping these two orders apart, Baudelaire entered a blind alley, and yet he obeys the deep logic in his inner self, and this experience must have shown him once for all that he could not fuse the two. He wrote to Madame Sabatier: "I am an egoist. I am using you." As long as he possessed nothing the image of Madame Sabatier watched over his genius and inspired it; but the instant he profanes the idol, all is over, and Madame Sabatier can do no more for him from the moment when she gives him everything.

Baudelaire had made this likely frustration inevitable, when he sent Madame Sabatier "L'Aube spirituelle" with this English dedication: "After a night of pleasure and desolation, my soul belongs to you." . . . Baudelaire was then lost. Until then he still had a right to hope for salvation from Madame Sabatier's image; from then on, he had to pass through debauchery to recover the image in its purity. As long as he resists, the two elements struggle in him freely, but as soon as yielding becomes a habit, a rhythm of automatic reaction settles in that swings him from love to debauchery and back again. The result is a kind of mechanical functioning of the inner life that is probably the sharpest punishment that debauchery can inflict on a higher man. The minute that Baudelaire lets this rhythm set in, then possession cannot extinguish his love, since Madame Sabatier serves a different purpose.

Must we understand by this that Baudelaire was incapable of love? If so, would we not thereby incriminate Dante, Petrarch, and that whole

notion of love that produced chivalry and culminated in the idea of the
Lady? It would be above all highly unjust not to allow for the deep and
incalculable disturbance that genius brings into the life of the affections.
Because the works of genius are stamped with calm, with mastery and
control, we too readily assume that their beginnings must resemble their
ends. We fall heir to the order of the artist, and then we turn against
the man and take him to task for his disorder, as though it were not
the wretchedness and the sufferings produced by these very disorders
that had struck forth, at favored hours, the *lucidus ordo*.

Thus Baudelaire failed to base any abiding state of grace on love. He
then sought nothing but a moment's oblivion, and had no way to find
it but through all the kins of drunkenness—opium, wine, hashish, and
above all debauchery—because there he expected the deepest oblivion,
and probably because he gambled on the ensuing reaction.

> Si ce n'est par un soir sans lune, deux à deux,
> D'endormir la douleur sur un lit hasardeux.

> [Unless it be, by an evening without moonlight, you and I,
> To lull sorrow to sleep on an unexpected bed.]

Yet even here there are degrees. Beneath the guardian Angel, stands
the Idol; beneath the worship whose fervor is intensified by distance
from its object, stands the contemplation of the presence, Baudelaire's
theme.

> Elle était donc couchée, et se laissait aimer,
> Et du haut du divan elle souriait d'aise
> À mon amour profond et doux comme la mer
> Qui vers elle montait comme vers sa falaise.
>
> . . . . . .
>
> Et son bras et sa jambe, et sa cuisse et ses reins,
> Polis comme de l'huile, onduleux comme un cygne,
> Passaient devant mes yeux clairvoyants et sereins:
> Et son ventre et ses seins, ces grappes de ma vigne,
>
> S'avançaient plus câlins que les anges du mal,
> Pour troubler le repos où mon âme était mise,
> Et pour la déranger du rocher de cristal,
> Où calme et solitaire elle s'était assise.

[She was then lying down and allowed herself to be loved,
And from the top of the couch she smiled with contentment
To her love, profound and kind like the sea
Which toward her rose as toward its cliff.

. . . . . .

And her arm and her leg, and her thigh and her loins,
Polished like oil, undulating like a swan,
Passed before my eyes, clear-sighted and serene,
And her belly and her breasts, those clusters of my vine,

Drew forward more caressingly than the angels of evil,
To disturb the rest in which my soul was laid,
And to unseat it from the crystal rock
On which, calm and solitary, it had sat down.]

Baudelaire's supreme delight was to contemplate a woman's beautiful body, and when her beauty was perfect, he seems to have attained a moment of full calm, a spiritual beatitude. But fleeting, for contemplation cannot continue without tempting. Baudelaire's vice is indeed vice, since it does not spring from a primitive blind thirst, but from the gradual and irritating infiltration of an idea.

In the beginning, you are free to reject this idea, but once accepted, you can no longer control it, and desire seems to become more resistless than in an actual need. Wilde's deep word comes to mind: "Yes, one of the great secrets of life is to cure the soul through the senses, and then the senses through the soul." But whoever has come to that, is doomed to the worst circle of a moral hell.

VII

It is easy to see why Baudelaire thus ends his account of a visit from Meryon, who was already going mad:

After he had left, I asked myself how it could be that I, whose mind and nerves have always had everything needed for going mad, could still be sane. Seriously, I rendered Heaven the thanks of the Pharisee.

Yes, Baudelaire had every right to go mad. But instead

Comme montent au ciel les soleils rajeunis
Après s'être lavés au fond des mers profondes

[As ascend toward the sky the rejuvenated suns
After having washed themselves in the depths of the seas]

the *Fleurs du mal* arise.

Despising everyone and despising myself, I long to redeem myself and to appease my pride in the stillness and loneliness of the night. Souls of those I have loved, souls of those I have sung, strengthen me, uphold me, uplift me out of the falsehood and the rotting mists of the world. O Lord my God, grant me grace to write a few beautiful poems and prove to myself that I am not the lowest of men, that I am no better than those whom I loathe.

Who does not recall the beginning of this prose poem, the account of that day that was to sweep a thousand like days into its net? "Despising everyone and despising myself"—there is the push that at last starts his inspiration. This push once given, each destructive element becomes a cornerstone to bear up the formidable building, a shelter for the strong.

O moine fainéant! quand saurai-je donc faire
Du spectacle vivant de ma triste misère
Le travail de mes mains et l'amour de mes yeux?

[O lazy monk! when shall I ever know how to make,
Out of the living sight of my sad wretchedness,
Handiwork for my hands and delight for my eyes?]

When indeed? But here Baudelaire is slandering himself as he does all through the *Fleurs du mal* and the *Spleen de Paris*. Here lies his true subject, unbounded anywhere save by the limits of the human being himself. No work ever had a surer center, whence it always takes off, and which it never forgets, even at the peak of its flight. The purest aspiration, the richest nostalgia, the most sinisterly populated sewer, all is drawn with a sincerity so perfect that it surpasses the fragile perfection of a sentiment and attains the indestructibility of bronze. Doubtless every great work of art is an evasion, and for Baudelaire's nostalgia it was the supreme evasion, but only vouchsafed him into an absent world, the only world that his imagination was admitted to create wholly and to saturate with its riches. Everywhere else the action is that of certain El Grecos, and we cannot speak of evasion but of an ascension in which the poet willfully loads himself with the most dragging encumberments. No balloonist ever took off for so lofty a soaring laden with ballast, for his sincerity forbade him casting any away.

If Irenaeus may be accepted as a witness . . . the spiritual man, according to the Valentine teaching, was incapable of corruption by any course of life whatever. As gold, they said, when lying buried in the mud, does not lose the nature of gold, but remains distinct from mud, so the spiritual man, in whatever course of action he may be engaged, retains his spiritual nature and is incapable of deterioration.[7]

Baudelaire's case certainly lends a strange and powerful support to the Valentine heresy: think of the unfinished poem that was to have been inserted in the second edition of the *Fleurs du mal*:

> Anges revêtus d'or, de pourpre et d'hyacinthe,
> O vous, soyez témoins qu j'ai fait mon devoir,
> Comme un parfait chimiste et comme une âme sainte.
> Car j'ai de chaque chose extrait la quintessence.
> Tu m'as donné ta boue et j'en ai fait de l'or.

> [Angels clad in gold, purple, and hyacinth,
> O you, be witnesses that I did my duty
> Like a perfect chemist and like a holy soul.
> For of each thing I extracted the quintessence.
> You gave me your mud and I turned it into gold.]

But this spiritual incorruptibility does not protect the envelope from wear, and we find in *Mon Coeur mis à nu*:

I have nursed my hysteria with rapture and fright. By now my head swims continually, and today, January 23, 1862, I received a strange warning: I felt a wind brush past me from the wing of imbecility.

The end of *Fusées* sums up Baudelaire's still worldly thought.[8] After predicting the future of the world in terms that become truer day by day, he thus concludes:

As for myself, I sometimes feel a prophet's absurdity, but I know I shall never have the charity of a physician. Lost in this vile world, elbowed

[7] Mansel, *The Gnostic Heresies*, p. 196. Paul Bourget, in his *Sensations d'Italie*, has an interesting chapter comparing the case of some modern poets, especially Baudelaire, with this Valentinian heresy.
[8] The date of writing the *Fusées* is unknown; it was collected sometime before 1857.

by mobs. I am like a wearied man whose eye looks backward into the abyss
of time, on nothing but disillusion and bitterness, and forward on a storm
that holds nothing new, neither enlightenment nor sorrow. On the evening
when this man has stolen a few hours of pleasure from fate, then, lulled
in his digestion, forgetful, as far as possible of the past, content with the
present and resigned to the future, drunk with his aloofness and his elegance, proud of being less base than those who pass by, he eyes the smoke
from his cigar and says to himself: What do I care what becomes of all
these lives?

But five years pass. The *Fleurs du mal* have had a second edition.
Baudelaire stands at the height of his genius; nevertheless, a new
inclination shows itself. Of course he was ill, in debt, irrevocably alone
—yet there was something more.

"Consolation through the arts": thus Baudelaire defined the beneficent
power of the many forms of beauty. But the greater an artist, the more
surely comes a time when art ceases to hold him. The moment his work
begins to yield us an inexhaustible consolation, the artist is already
detached from it; and it no longer touches him, which shows that he
has attained a certain height and plenitude. If, as almost always happens
with those artists whom Baudelaire called "the Beacons," their feeling
has passed into form without spilling a drop of the divine liquor, then
the very perfection of their work undoes the bond, and the artist's
crowning proof of his supremacy as an artist lies in his very turning
away from art. He has accomplished his task here below too completely;
he has done with us and looks elsewhere. These haughty beings never
begin again, and if they do not fall silent, if their emotion, growing
constantly purer, stronger and richer, cannot be kept back, it finds vents
and utterance outside art itself. The world of forms is left behind in the
only way it may be, through having been in its time, the supreme world.

Something would be lacking from Baudelaire's greatness if the hostages
that he left in our hands had not become almost indifferent to him
before their time, if he had not written *Mon Coeur mis à nu*.

I once heard an ardent admirer of Baudelaire maintain that *Mon
Coeur mis à nu* overwhelms one simply because it shows Baudelaire had
nothing left to say, or that at least he had lost his power of expression,
and I admit that at first glance many passages seem to confirm this
view. *Mon Coeur mis à nu* is indeed all emotion from end to end, and
that is the secret of its extraordinary grip. But where some would see a
void of thought, I think that it is rather Baudelaire's tendency, increasing towards the end of his life, to give us nothing but the results, and
keep the searching and the working to himself. He slashes and no longer

weaves; and he seems then to have lost the middle ground of the spirit along with the others. I readily grant that Baudelaire had no great inner fertility, that he was even lean in this respect, but the essential thing about him is not the extent of his contact, but his ability to transmute everything touched. Every word in *Mon Coeur mis à nu* is an intimate summing up or a posted sentinel—a momento or a talisman. And then he probably seems impotent because he is dwelling on so very few themes. And here we must not forget that the old age of genius (and all tended to make Baudelaire an old man at forty) is above all retrenchment and rumination. The old age of a Christian genius could be nothing else in the very proportion of the sincerity of his Christianity, and for such a one after a certain point, nothing but salvation matters, and when we reproach him with an emptiness of thought, we speak the language of the intellect, which, gathered under a few heads that he has searched through, has nothing more to say to him. The wholly Christian tone of *Mon Coeur mis à nu* sets it apart even in Baudelaire's own work. Christianity's most absolute innovation is probably the idea that man attains his summits by yielding. The highest non-Christian wisdom, such as Marcus Aurelius', puts man's perfection in a certain tension, whose pride and clear awareness of self and the world, Christianity banished for humility, pity, and the healing dew of tears. Now, in this, Baudelaire was not wholly Christian until *Mon Coeur mis à nu*. Yet we stand debtors to his pride, to which we owe much that makes the *Fleurs du mal* what they are. But when this pride falls, as in certain unforgettable passages of *Mon Coeur mis à nu,* we see a soul at last unbound. This tone, so changed, submissive, and lowly, that no longer asserts, but implores, this modesty in desires and ends mean that Baudelaire really thinks of nothing but his mother and of paying off his debts. The God of the expulsion from the earthly Paradise gives way to the true Father, come down into the poet's daily life and mingling in all his preoccupations, an unfailing sign of growing faith.

> Pray every morning to God, the fountainhead of all strength and all justice, to my father, to Mariette, and to Poe as intercessors; pray them to give me strength for all my duties and to grant my mother a long enough life to enjoy my change of heart; work all day long, or at least as long as my strength lasts; trust in God, that is, in Justice itself, for the success of my plans; pray, every evening, afresh to God for life and strength for my mother and myself; divide my earnings into four parts, one for current expenses, one for my creditors, one for my friends and one for my mother; obey the principles of the strictest sobriety, of which the first is the suppression of every single stimulant whatsoever.

Baudelaire had no time to reach Pascal's "whole and sweet renunciation," nor his "Joy, tears of joy," but no one can read the above quoted end of *Mon Coeur mis à nu* without feeling that every day was bringing him closer, and now or never is the time to end with the evangelists: "Peace on earth and good will towards men."

Baudelaire and the Muse

by *Étienne Gilson*

Baudelaire is not one of those poets whose name, like Dante's or Petrarch's, is linked in our minds with that of a single Inspiration. There was no lack of women in his life but, although his art gained something from each one of them, none, probably least of all his dark-skinned Venus, wielded over his work the sovereign power of a Beatrice or a Laura. With Baudelaire one finds not so much a Muse as the small change of the Muse he was vainly seeking. For there is no doubt at all that he consciously and determinedly persisted in the search, and this desire should rivet our attention more especially because it is closely tied in with the fashion after which Baudelaire conceived his art.

If this poet's search for a Muse ended in failure, the failure was not total, and his lack of success had its compensation in the amazing lucidity of the witness he ceased not to bear of his own experiences. In this respect Baudelaire would be irreplaceable—had we not also had Richard Wagner. These men are not explained by their great predecessors: it is truer to say that, by the light of their confessions, we can spell out the story of Petrarch or of Dante. Nearer to us in time they have, besides their works, left behind them intimate letters, letters in which the torments of their unquiet hearts are described with a frankness very rare in classical manuscripts. Let us question them as to what they expected from the Muse they longed for. Men must have changed greatly since the fourteenth century if the psychology of the modern poet has nothing to reveal to us about the medieval poet. Anyhow, rereading Baudelaire is always a pleasure, and as poetry is here in question the pleasure is also profitable.

Setting aside his "sick Muse," "mercenary Muse"—and others of like kind whom Baudelaire himself did not consider true Muses—let us turn at once to his incomparable letter to an unknown woman. Some believe, I think mistakenly, that she was Marie Brunaud, who under her stage name Marie Daubrun was "the lovely witch" of "L'Irréparable," and from whom the poet at one time hoped for far more than aid to stifle the remorse of a soul "swallowed up by anguish." Théodore de Banville loved her too, and at one time was at odds with Baudelaire through a jealousy that was really pointless, and would still have been so had Baudelaire won from her the little which in the end was all he hoped for and which in fact he never did win. Supposing Marie really was this woman, Banville was a hundred miles from imagining what were the real feelings of his strange rival. Today we still find them hard enough to disentangle.

What exactly was the story? Baudelaire seems to have solicited her while she was posing for some artist or other, whereupon she declared she would not return. The poet experienced "a strange melancholy" upon learning that he had, unwittingly, brought her to this decision; he was startled by a new feeling that stirred within him. Baudelaire had told this young woman that he loved her, and she had answered that she loved another, one man alone, and that any further suitor would receive from her nothing but indifference or even contempt. Whereupon the poet's instant reply was that he would gladly be content with the crumbs from her table. After this supremely commonplace scene, however, his imagination went strangely to work: as he thought about it he despised himself, and Marie's refusal changed what had begun as quite commonplace lust into love.

To answer the question of what is the difference between lust and love, a complete reading of this long letter is essential. Every word in it invites comment. Despite the extreme difficulty felt by Baudelaire in expressing himself, we may also get from it certain indications of what happened.

To begin with, the poet has clearly taken a decision, the decision to make a choice, and in announcing that choice he sees it as irrevocable. "I have resolved to give myself to you forever." Why? Because their conversation had left him in a "new state," a state he is trying to describe. Ever since she had told him that she did not and never would love him because she loved another, Marie became "no longer merely the woman I want but a woman whom I love for her frankness, her passion, her freshness, her youth, and her folly." She has become beloved instead of merely lusted after, not because she loves him and he requites her love, but on the contrary because of the passion inspired in her by another. This paradox would make everything incomprehensible, if it did not actually provide the solution of a problem always presented by a feeling of this kind to the outside observer.

Little as the poet may have realized it, what now increases his longing, and may even transform it into love, is respect. Indubitably the passion felt by Marie for another man separates her completely from Baudelaire, but it adorns her also with a remoteness well fitted to exalt the imagination of a poet. Baudelaire now really wants to maintain an obstacle—to overthrow it by gratifying his desires would destroy his love. He tells us so in words that could hardly be clearer: "My loss is great since you have told me all: your decision was so clear that I instantly submitted. But you, Madame, have gained greatly in stature: you have inspired in me deep respect and honor. Remain always as you are now, and cling to that noble love which makes you so beautiful and so happy."

The element which from its very birth gives to a love of this kind a special character is here plainly visible. Baudelaire was certainly not the first suitor she had dismissed, nor was this probably his first experience. But he did not, like so many others, say to himself, "Lose one and find two." No doubt he had often talked like that in similar circumstances— but not today. Nor did he change into one of those trembling lovers who breathe out their sighs for twenty years, hoping that what has been refused today will at last be granted. Like the hero of Charles Morgan's *Portrait in a Mirror,* these men risk the discovery that what in the end they win is only a reflection of reality, that what they at last possess is not the thing they loved. Baudelaire is doing something very different: harshly dismissed by a woman, he grasps at the refusal that separates them and entreats her passionately to persevere in it. By thus entrusting to her keeping the "No" which transfigures her in his eyes, he shows surely his fear of a great loss if through kindness or weariness she allowed her "No" to weaken into "Yes."

What had he to lose? It is not to be believed that the poet renounces longing as well as possession. Indeed we can refine further and say that if we define desire as a will to achieve an object, the poet is hoping to keep the emotion whence desire is born, without keeping the desire to which it gives birth. To love without desiring is easier said than done. The man sees the beauty which the poet boasts of not desiring, and by this beauty he is moved. However chaste such love claims to be, the purity of an emotion is suspect in which the feelings, even if driven underground, are mixed with the most lucid acts of the reason. Exalted because inaccessible, the tangible cause of carnal emotion seems in some way to have become divine. Nothing is more striking in its repetition through the centuries than the tendency of such poets to talk the language of religion. Baudelaire is no exception: "You cannot halt my spirit as it hovers around your arms, your loving hands, your eyes in which your life dwells, your whole physical being. I know that this troubles you, but be at peace, you are the object of my worship, I could never defile you: I shall ever see you shining with the same brightness." It is the worship of a being of flesh, yet the poet adores this being as the pure source of his art.

All this combines to throw out our psychology, which loves to simplify everything and see it all clearly. Out of a passionate emotion that sprang from a chance meeting, the poet chooses to construct a spiritual quality so pure that it can outlive its cause: "I shall ever see you shining with the same brightness." Thus did the image of Laura, during the twenty years that followed their first meeting, remain in Petrarch's memory—as he saw her first at the hour of Prime in the Church of St. Clare in Avignon. What matter that she had since grown old and lost the flower of her beauty? The woman Petrarch never ceased to see, at whatever age she was, however old she became, remained always the only women he had ever loved, the Laura of that first meeting, inseparable from the overwhelming emotion which on the 6th of April, 1327, turned the little clerk of Avignon into one of the most perfect love poets the world has ever known. This too is why, following Dante and Petrarch with a cliché which in poets of their quality must have come from some inner compulsion, Baudelaire places the source of his physical emotion in the most spiritual part of the body: the eyes. He cannot help it. Once started on this path he must grind out in his turn a theme of love-poetry as well-worn as the spring—the birds and the flowers—but like them permanent, and commonplace simply because permanent. On this subject the poet of *Les Fleurs du mal* thinks and speaks like the simplest of novices. He has, in his turn, discovered that the power of the woman he loves dwells in her eyes: he has told her so and he repeats it:

> You give me life and energy, not so much because of your swift movements and the vehement side of your nature as because of your eyes, which perforce inspire the poet with an immortal love. I cannot express my love for your eyes, my delight in your beauty. You have two sorts of grace, contradictory yet harmonized in you: the child's and the woman's. Believe me when I cry from the bottom of my heart: you are an adorable being and I adore you.

Not a doubt of it! This river of clichés would be despairing if it did not, despite its love-sick student style, give us so many valuable pointers. Everything is there: the eternal permanence of a first emotion that will outlast the years, the etherealizing of the flesh into the pure spirituality of a glance, the device of the woman-child painted of old in Dante's Beatrice, that little girl of nine unassailably entrenched in the purity of her childhood, whose first glance pierced the poet's heart with a wound never healed. How many subtle tricks are used to assure the permanence of these fruitful emotions. The poet hopes that the refusal of the woman he loves will never be revoked, that he will always love her in the shining memory of their first meeting; he reduces her "adorable physical presence" to the pure spirituality of a glance; he is attracted by a woman's grace, and claims to love her with a stainless love which only the grace of childhood can inspire. One can hardly miss the hidden desire of transfiguration that determines these metamorphoses. What the body reveals to the poet is the soul, and what he asks of the flesh is spirit through the instrumentality of a beauty itself spiritual. Here we are back with Plotinus and Plato, or rather with that human experience which their doctrine did no more than embody in concepts: Aphrodite is beautiful because she shared in that intelligible beauty confusedly aimed at by lovers in their most passionate embraces. Here again it is impossible to do without Baudelaire's own statement:

> I love you, Marie, I cannot deny it; but the love I feel for you is that of a Christian for his God. Never give an earthly, still less a shameful, name to this disembodied and mysterious worship, this chaste and tender affection which links my soul with yours despite your determination. It would be a sacrilege. I was dead and you brought me back to life. Oh, you know not all I owe you! From your angelic glance I have borrowed unknown joys, your eyes have given to my soul the most perfect, the most exquisite happiness. Henceforward you are my only queen, my passion, my beauty; you are part of myself shaped by a spiritual essence. Through you, Marie, I shall become strong and great. Like Petrarch I shall immortalize my Laura. Be my guardian angel, my muse, my Madonna, and lead me on the road of Beauty.

On one of those days when the man and the artist reach the lowest point of their misery, Baudelaire had a chance meeting which his genius aspired to change from a mere unsuccessful amorous adventure into an inexhaustible source of poetic inspiration. What he wants Marie to be for him is precisely what Laura of old was for Petrarch. Neither Laura nor Marie, nor any other Muse, has any part in her election. Not only does the poet who chooses them ask nothing of them except to be, and to be what they are, but it does not even depend on them to be or not to be eternally chosen. Baudelaire explains this to Marie with a simplicity that is almost comic:

> I will wait for years, and when you see yourself loved perseveringly, reverently, with utter unselfishness, you will remember how cruel you were

in the beginning and you will admit how wrong this was. I am your prisoner: I must accept every blow inflicted by my idol. It pleased you to turn me away. It pleases me to adore you.

His idol! The tremendous word has been spoken, and it is indeed not merely one of those regular standbys of a poet's vocabulary, but also the most weighted with exact and authentic meaning. Marie is neither woman nor goddess, she is a false god. In other words, she is one of those objects of worship which as we know very well we have ourselves created, and in which, unable to forget entirely to what degree their divinity is our own work, we never fully believe. In Petrarch's eyes also Laura was supremely an idol. And yet—and here we seem close to the most mysterious element in these adventures of the heart and of the artist—there is between the two stories a difference at once deep and subtle. Laura, as we know from Petrarch himself, always refused to be his mistress, but she certainly did not refuse to be his Inspiration, and that is why she was his inspiration. It certainly looks as though the woman he loves must at least play the part for which the poet has cast her. That part is doubly dangerous: she alone can keep alight in his heart a flame without which the masterpiece cannot be created, but if the flame catches her, it is quite certain to be extinguished. Laura managed to play this part faultlessly: for twenty years she cherished spiritual intimacy, safeguarding herself by such severity as was necessary, and gaining for us the *Canzoniere*.

Baudelaire's admirers, on the other hand, owe precious little to Marie. Nothing could show us better how much the poet owes to his Muse, even if it matters little whom he chooses. For this time the marvellously clear-sighted Baudelaire deceived himself strangely. He believed that a Muse who refused to be a Muse was a possibility. Without a yielding of the spirit, however, the woman loved best and loved by the greatest of artists can hardly become his inspiration. Baudelaire at first thought he could do without this: you do not love me but I love you: the point is of no importance. He was self-deceived, but perhaps he was in fact less convinced than he boasted, for in this really inexhaustible letter (we can never be grateful enough to Marie for keeping it) he does say, "Give me an answering word I entreat, I beg of you, just one word." This "token of friendship," this "glance" which the poet implores are all small things enough, a bare minimum, but this minimum is a necessity. Petrarch received it from Laura, she was really his Muse. Baudelaire did not receive it from Marie, and he knew from the first that he never would: "If you only realized how much I love you. I throw myself at your feet: speak one word to me, only a single word. . . . No, you will never speak it."

Marie did not speak that word, and this is why she never became the Laura of this new Petrarch. The initial choice of a Muse is the sovereign decision of the poet and depends not at all on the woman he has chosen; but there is no such thing as a Muse in spite of herself. If he fails to win her consent, the artist can only submit: and this is what Baudelaire did. In spite of his oaths of eternal love, he neither "perseveringly loved" Marie, nor did he wait "for years" for a sigh from her in answer to his entreaties. In this very year, 1852, in which he swore an eternal love for the unwilling subject of his choice, Baudelaire replaced her by a willing candidate: too willing, indeed, to play for long the part of a Muse. But, as though this time he feared that the man might be sated at the expense of the poet, Baudelaire elected anonymity as a protection against the generous nature of Madame Sabatier.

What an odd business: this great artist, only just over the setback related above, sets out again to find himself a Muse. For he must have one at all costs. In a series of notes and letters of which every line and almost every word invite discussion, Baudelaire begins the cautious siege of a citadel which he might well have feared to conquer too easily —so often had it previously fallen! It might be added that in yielding to others this lady had only been able to give them what they expected from her, which was something entirely different from what Baudelaire wanted. Just reread that first anonymous letter which he begged her not to show anyone: "Deep feeling is modest and chooses concealment: the absence of a signature indicates a modesty that cannot be overcome. These verses were written in that dream state into which the image of their object often casts the writer. He loves her keenly though he has never told her, and will have for her *for ever* the tenderest feelings." Then follows the immortal poem, "A celle qui est trop gaie":

> Ta tête, ton geste, et ton air
> Sont beaux comme un beau paysage.
> Le rire joue en ton visage
> Comme un vent frais dans un ciel clair.
>
> [Your head, your gesture, your air
> Have the beauty of a beautiful landscape.
> Laughter plays on your face
> Like a cool wind in a clear sky.]

Let us not run the risk of psychoanalyzing, which would certainly prove a discouraging effort, but simply look at the *envoi*. The persistence of symptoms noted elsewhere is truly remarkable. This Baudelaire who hides his identity is no trembling lover, no gallant in search of a mistress, but a poet in search of a Muse. He does not desire Madame Sabatier, and if by the time she finally offered herself to him he still had not reached the stage of wanting her, it is in this fact that the reason lies hidden. From the very first Baudelaire wanted something from Apollonie Sabatier which would be lost by receiving her favors. What he expects to feel for her in the future he puts from the first into the past tense, as though the love she inspired escaped from the ordinary laws of time. As you listen to him speaking of this woman he has "keenly loved without telling her," whom he will love "forever," you realize that the poet has merely chosen a new Muse. The fidelity sworn by Baudelaire is all the more firmly guaranteed, because it does not bind in any way the weakness of his body, for his body remains out of the picture.

From Versailles comes another poem on May 3, 1853, followed on the 9th by yet a third, and with it a line of excuse for "this idiotic anonymous versifying which must seem terribly childish." But what can be done about it? Our poet is egoistic like a child or a sick person. "When I suffer I think of those I love. My thoughts of you are usually in verse, and when the verses are completed I cannot resist my longing to show them to their object. And yet I hide myself like one terrified of being laughed at." Once again the excellent Baudelaire has said it all in four sentences, and no one could have said it better. He values above all things this woman of whom he thinks in verse, against whose possible rebuff he protects himself by the ruse of anonymity, although he must in some fashion get into touch with her, that the spark may pass from her to him. In what transcendent sense is he an "egoist"? A little patience: he will soon tell us.

Meanwhile the letters continue to follow one another, becoming more and more urgent, and each one casting light on the obscure drama going on in the poet's heart. On February the 7th, 1854, he tells Madame Sabatier what he asks of her—which is simply to be there: "You do good without knowing it, even when you sleep, simply by being alive." But what good in particular? "Imagine if you will that at times, driven by some persistent torment, I find solace only in the pleasure of making verses for you, and that then I have to reconcile the innocent wish of showing them to you with the terrible fear of displeasing you. This is the explanation of my cowardice." But this man is not new to us who forgets his grief only in the pleasure of writing poetry for the beloved, and who loves namelessly to avoid either too generous a response to his love or the refusal of friendship. It was Dante who answered simply, when the friends of Beatrice asked him what happiness he found in loving her, "That of singing her praises."

It was the same with Baudelaire. After a night of joy and of misery the song inspired by the beloved image rises to his lips, purifies and redeems him. Even when he asks anxiously whether the women that poets love are befittingly "proud and happy in their beneficent work," that work still goes on. "I know not," he wrote on the 11th of February, 1854, "if the supreme delight will ever be granted me of revealing to you face to face all the power you have gained over me and the perpetual glow created in my mind by your image."

He had found the perfect description. All Baudelaire wanted was this creative "glow" to which he owes some of his finest poems, easily singled out by their especial beauty. We can well believe that no love was ever "more disinterested, more ideal, more utterly reverent." He asks of Madame Sabatier no more than the very least love could ask. His abnegation as a man is complete: but not so his abnegation as a poet, and Baudelaire is too utterly clear-sighted to deceive himself about this. He does not lust after Madame Sabatier, he is even so little jealous of her lovers that he congratulates her as he did Marie on the excellence of her choice. All this means nothing to him, but he makes her serve him after his own fashion—though for a different end, and by a more noble service. Once again his own words must be quoted: "Finally, to explain my silence and my fervor, a fervor that is almost religious, I must tell you that when my being is overwhelmed by the darkness of its native evil and folly, I dream deeply of you. From this thrilling and purifying revery some blissful gift of fortune is usually born. You are for me not only the most attractive of women, but the best loved and most treasured of superstitions. I am an egoist and I make use of you."

Once again Baudelaire discourages the commentator—all one can do is to invite the reader to listen to him. Madame Sabatier is in Baudelaire's mind what he calls a superstition because she really owes to him the power to give him what he is asking of her. And he is so well aware of this that one might even query whether he possessed the minimum of honesty necessary for a poet bestowing a Muse on himself. How comment upon this letter which ends by his sending her what he calls contemptuously a "miserable scrap"? This "scrap" is in fact the sheerly lovely hymn whose music has sung in men's memories ever since:

> A la très chère, à la très belle
> Qui remplit mon coeur de clarté, . . .
>
> [To the most dear, to the most beautiful
> Who fills my heart with a clear light, . . .]

"Forgive me," the poet ends, "I ask nothing more of you." How right he was! But Madame Sabatier wanted to give him more, and that was what spoilt it all. The sequel is well known. In 1857 *Les Fleurs du mal* was published—a collection whose title expresses perfectly the meaning of the whole story. Baudelaire sent Madame Sabatier a bound copy, thus officially bringing to an end an anonymity which had long worn rather thin. The Muse could no longer be ignorant what poet it was who had used her to serve his art. On the 18th August, 1857, plunged into a law suit, Baudelaire in the very letter telling her which poems were written for her, rages against "the wretches" appointed to judge him, for having dared to number among the incriminated poems two of those written for his beloved idol ("Tout entière" and "A celle qui est trop gaie"). The magistrates were indeed wide of the mark. They fancied they had to do with an immoral poet who was admitting the public into his confidence about his pleasures—and the worst of it was, everybody else believed it too. But everybody was wrong and it is best to accept Baudelaire literally when he tells us he was "struck dumb" by the young "sister" (or daughter?) of his idol, who asked him with a burst of laughter whether he was still "in love." He threw back the answer, proud, contemptuous, and definite. "The common herd are lovers, poets are idolaters."

It was a splendid phrase, and anyone who still fails to understand him is inexcusable. The cult of the poet for his idol is not the ardor of the lover for his mistress. No, that sort of ardor, however elevated, is excluded by Baudelaire as the very opposite of poetic love. Of all places into which entry is denied it, there is none with threshold more jealously guarded than the domain of great art. For the man who sings of his passion and puts into verse elementary physical emotions, Baudelaire felt nothing but supreme contempt. He wrote to Ancelle on the 18th of February, 1866, "As to 'feelings,' 'hearts' and other feminine trash, remember Leconte de Lisle's profound remark, 'All elegiacs are contemptible.'" This was probably the deepest cause of his lively animosity against Alfred de Musset. One of Baudelaire's greatest glories is precisely that, at grips with a devouring sensuality, he not only never confused it with his art, but actually conceived of poetic creation as the true means within an artist's power of getting free from it. In a way he deceived himself, for he was asking of art what only religion can give, but the mistake was noble and certainly not total. It explains of what "idolatry" the poet is speaking, and why the more clearly he tries to see into himself, the more he conceives of the link between him and his Muse as a sort of religious and all-absorbing devotion.

"They tell," he writes, "of poets who all their lives fixed their eyes upon one beloved image. I believe indeed (but I am biased) that fidelity is one of the signs of genius. You are more than the beloved image of my dreams, you are a *superstition*."

This poet is certainly haunted by the memory of Dante and Petrarch, whose worship of a single goddess protected them gloriously against the temptation of the facile elegy. And yet it is the poverty of this greatness that an image by itself would not work the miracle. The woman must be as real as the emotion she stirs. In short, there must be love, through which, human though it be, the man who asks and the woman who gives are looking only for the birth of a masterpiece.

Baudelaire knew that Madame Sabatier might cause for him some anxiety. He took pains to keep her in her part in the act: the part of goddess—a role to which she was not at all suited. On the 18th of August, 1857, five years after his first anonymous letter, he wrote, "When I do something good I tell myself: here is something to bring me nearer to her *in spirit*." The italics in the quotations are always his, and no man has ever told a woman more clearly and more persistently, "I do not desire you." It is not surprising, then, that when the goddess came down of her own accord from the pedestal, which she had found extremely boring, her worshipper could not meet her desires by managing to treat her as an ordinary woman. The experts, of whom I am not one, disagree about what happened; the best-informed actually state nothing happened at all. This is a possibility, although the famous letter of the 31st of August, 1857, could be interpreted in two ways. Anyway, if nothing did happen that day, it was certainly because Baudelaire, far from ever desiring that anything should happen, had taken infinite precautions to prevent it.

What does Charles Morgan's Nigel say in similar circumstances?

> Who was she whose flesh lay there? Though, beneath the dark, she had the outward form of her I loved, she was a stranger. To consume her body would be forever a spiritual adultery.

For Baudelaire, too, it seemed a profanation and a sacrilege. If something did prevent his committing this sacrilege, the very opportunity affected him as though it were the act. A Muse who offered him something he could easily find elsewhere took from him in the same act what he could get from none but her: and he had bravely struggled to persuade himself, despite appearances, that she would help him to preserve this treasure in all its purity. Nor need we accuse him of too much simplicity. Nothing proves that this amiable woman lacked the capacity of justifying Baudelaire's ambitions for her: she had perhaps a vocation of which she was very nearly worthy. Anyhow, the next morning Baudelaire awoke with tortured nerves and "the inexplicable moral discomfort" that he had brought away from his lady's house the night before. It was less "inexplicable" than he supposed. On the 30th of August he had a Muse, on the 31st he had her no longer, and the prospect of having her henceforward as a mistress was very far from consoling him.

Lying before him were two letters in which she offered herself "quite shamelessly" not only in dreams but "body, spirit, and heart." How could she have known that it was the body that was *de trop?* Complete as her error was, it really was venial and Baudelaire alone was responsible. The poet had made a mistake when picking his Muse: in his calculations he had neglected an important element: if Laura had not the right to figure in a Triumph of Virginity she was quite in place in a Triumph of Chastity. Madame Sabatier had never made the smallest claim to a place in either one or the other, and Baudelaire could hardly blame her for playing badly a part for which he had cast her but which she had never wanted, to which she was not suited. All that he could really blame her for was that he had made a mistake about her which she certainly did nothing to cause.

This, with peculiarly masculine injustice, he did not fail to do. But there is some excuse for him: he now realized that Madame Sabatier could never give him what he hoped for: she was instead making promises she was incapable of keeping. He had vowed her an eternal love, and there had been nothing to stop his being eternally faithful, since the mutual love of poet and of Muse is made eternal by the very fact that bodily fidelity plays no part in it. But it was the improbable fidelity of her body that Madame Sabatier was now promising, and the poet did not hide the fact that he counted no more on her fidelity than on his own: "In short I have no *faith* in you; your soul is beautiful, but after all it is the soul of a woman." Which meant, no doubt, that she was more indulgent towards the pleasures of a libertine than awake to the ambitions of a poet.

He certainly does not sound enthusiastic: but there is worse to come. For poor Baudelaire seems so harassed and worried that the question arises whether he really wants the fidelity he dare not believe in. Listen to him weighing and measuring: "Look at the confusion the last few days have thrown us into." First there is the lawful incumbent, Mosselman, "a worthy fellow, lucky enough to be still in love"—they might sadly upset him. And then there is the fear that both must have felt of the storm they would provoke. They knew, Baudelaire especially, that "there are knots hard to untie." This lover certainly lacks enthusiasm, but it is the poet within him who is on the watch. The great and determining objection is stated none the less clearly from being stated last: "And then, and then, a few days ago you were a goddess, helpful, beautiful, unattainable. Now you are only a woman."

How serenely cruel he is, how pitiless! Baudelaire does not yet know whether he has gained a mistress or for how long, but he knows very well that he has lost his Muse. His Inspiration is dead. She was his idol, but a profaned divinity is no longer sacred. She was his religion, but how can he go on believing when the unattainable ideal of which she was the symbol has turned into a reality of the most commonplace kind? "Never meet or never part" is the fine motto with which Madame Sabatier sealed her last letter. But did she really understand its solemnity? The "never meet" expresses the treason of his Inspiration, for "this positively means that it would have been much better never to have known one another, but that once together we should never part. Such a motto would be very funny on a letter of farewell."

This is really rather horrible, for the letter he is writing is actually the poet's farewell to the Muse he has just lost. Since we have come to know one another let us try never to part, but all the same it remains positively true "that it would be far better had we never met." However, the mischief is done. "Let what may happen, happen. I am a bit of a fatalist. But what I do know is that I have a horror of passion because I know it in all its falseness and the deeply loved image which has ruled over all my life's events is becoming too seductive." And one last touch towards the end of the letter, "Goodbye, my dear, dear beloved. I have rather a grudge against you for being too charming."

It would be an error surely to mistake for a man's physiological failure the psychological and moral recoil of a poet faced with such a lamentable conclusion of one of his finest artistic adventures. The reality is quite wretched enough without disparaging what are, after all, its noble elements. The type of love that his lady was generously offering was not what he needed to reach the high summits of poetry. Far from helping him, this storm of the senses could only hinder the one effort he had at heart, "that work through which a dream is turned into an artistic creation."

And this was something which Madame Sabatier cared nothing about, not because she lacked either heart or intellect but because she was totally unfamiliar with the problem with which Baudelaire was grappling. It is less surprising that she was lost in the maze than that in a confused sort of way she guessed its issue. Humiliated, wounded, frankly exasperated by Baudelaire's attitude, *she* did not see it as a physical weakness but as a refusal. This was certainly what enraged her and, after all, nobody can claim without absurdity to know better than she

did what it was that really drove them apart. And when she tries to
explain this sad affair, Madame Sabatier does not hesitate for a moment:
"My anger was perfectly justified. What was I to think when I saw you
running away from my caresses, except that you were dreaming about
that other whose black soul and face had come between us?" Was she
wrong? Most certainly, for it was her own soul, her own face as a radiant
Muse that had come between her and her poet. Still her mistake was an
intelligent one, for what she was offering to Baudelaire, Jeanne Duval
was far better able to give him. She had not really the physique for the
job of Baudelaire's mistress, but she did have for the job of his Muse—
for that, all she lacked was the soul. And so, offering the man the thing
he did not want, she deprived the poet of the one thing he did.

It must be said in all fairness to her that she saw quite clearly what
she should have been in order that her offer might be acceptable: you
have only to read the unhappy letter she promptly posted to her poet:
"Look, dear, shall I tell you my thought, a bitter thought and one that
hurts me a lot? I think you do not love me." Nothing could have been
more true, in the only meaning of the word love that she could understand. "You have no faith in me," she goes on, "but then you have no
love. What answer can you give: is it not perfectly clear?" Alas, it was
indeed. To the poet's appeal for the eternal feminine, the well-meaning
woman replied by offering him Apollonie Sabatier.

This affair, which ended as a sheer misunderstanding on both sides,
seems to have died quickly and left no great bitterness behind it. A
note from Baudelaire less than a year later saluting his lady as a "very
old pal"—or as a very old something a little less vulgar and a little more
affectionate than a pal—gives us a pretty good idea of what happened.
A Muse cannot become a pal, and this is why the small collection of
poems written for Madame Sabatier received only one further addition.

This collection stirs one's curiosity by appearing in *Les Fleurs du mal*
as a Petrarchan wedge of poems, but it would be an error to take for
imitation what is in reality a fresh repetition of an old story. His
moving "Confession" strikes the clear note of an experience, at that
date still unique for Baudelaire, of Madame Sabatier as a real woman
and no muse:

> Une fois, une seule, aimable et douce femme,
> À mon bras, votre bras poli
> S'appuya. . . .
>
> [Once, and once only, lovely and sweet woman
>   On my arm your polished arm
> Leaned. . . .]

These lines express only pity for her whose "hard trade it was to be a beautiful woman," and for the plaint which she who was naturally "too gay" had that night let her lips utter: "a dreadful confidence whispered in the heart's confessional." But read again "Tout entière," "Que diras-tu ce soir," "Le Flambeau vivant," "Réversibilité," and there you will see the real woman transformed into the Muse, the ideal object of the poet's worship, "Angel of happiness, joy, and light." "I am angel guardian, muse, Madonna," "Beloved goddess, pure and light-giving being," "Those eyes full of light lead me on." All these lines might have been written at Vaucluse: and if Baudelaire speaks of Apollonie Sabatier as Petrarch spoke of Laura, does it not mean that they both passed through the same experience? Nothing is more natural than that other verses written for Madame Sabatier should have been a straight borrowing from the prose of his letter to Marie. It has been claimed as proof of the poet's "subjectivity," and in one sense this is true, for in these affairs his primary interest is always his art. But it might also be viewed as a proof of the exact opposite: what he had offered to Marie was the office of his Muse, and the titles of honor bestowed on her in advance, if she would but accept, were surely possessed of right by Madame Sabatier during the seven years in which she played the part. In this case Baudelaire is surely notable for a striking objectivity.

There is one especially curious poem in *Les Fleurs du mal:* the "Franciscae meae laudes." No commentator, to my knowledge, has identified its inspiration. Written in the language and the rhythm of a medieval liturgical sequence, it at once evokes the picture of a time when love readily took on the aspect of a religion. And it was certainly with this intention that the poet selected so unusual a form to hymn a learned and pious milliner:

> Does not the reader feel, as I do, that the speech of Latin's last decadence —the dying breath of a strong man already transfigured and prepared for the life of the spirit—is of singular fitness to express passion as it is understood and felt by the world of modern poetry? Mysticism is the other pole of that magnet of which Catullus and his company of poets of animal union and bodily tension knew only the pole of sensuality?

Notice in the passage the barbed arrow loosed at the prince of Latin elegiac poets, and Baudelaire's own determination to lay under tribute the religious and spiritual outlook of the Middle Ages to find food for his art.

It is must important to notice how faithful Baudelaire was to this slight work. M. J. Moquet has pointed out that it is the only poem that finds a place in all three collections published by himself in 1857, 1861, and 1866. It certainly deserves this special affection, for even if it were less musically exquisite than in fact it is, it ought to be there. It is the perfect description of the ideal Muse as Baudelaire had conceived her. Whatever may have been her real name, or even if she was nothing but the creation of his fancy, the Francesca by whom his sins are forgiven, the divine vision that appears when storms of iniquity darken his path, who gives him back speech when his lips are sealed, is easily identified. She is the dream he has steadily pursued under the names of various women.

But where in truth did Reality abide amid those earthly things whose existence he declared was the slightest, or which, as he half believed, existed only in his dreams? To answer that, you must abandon art and turn to metaphysics. Baudelaire never did this, and when he asks the question, the answer he half glimpses is not at all simple. The preface of *Les Paradis artificiels* certainly affirms *en passant* the existential primacy of the dream over reality, and this latent Platonism is one of the deepest and most abiding tendencies of his thought. But when he asks, in *Petits Poèmes en prose*, "Which *is* real?" he is powerfully impressed by the tremendous complexity of the problem.

Both the Madame Sabatiers are real, but on different levels and in different ways. Both real, different from one another and yet the same: therein lies the mystery. The real Benedicta is indeed true sister of the eternal Beatrice, "in whom one breathed the air of the ideal, from whose eyes glowed out the longing for greatness, beauty, glory and all the stuff of immortality." It sounds like a translation of Petrarch. Like Madame Sabatier and so many other Muses, this ideal girl was too beautiful to live long. She died and the poet buried her, "sealed in a coffin of scented wood, incorruptible as the treasure chests of the Indies," or in such treasure chests as the *Vita Nuova*, the *Canzoniere*, the *Fleurs du mal*. The dead Beatrice, the dead Laura shine forth tranquilly from their tombs. Of different fashions and of a different era from Baudelaire's, these "wondrous women" did not in dying give birth to a vampire. No little creature was seen after the death of one of them, "singularly like the deceased," dancing frenziedly on her own tomb, exclaiming, with a burst of laughter, "I am the real Benedicta! Here I am, a 'nice sort of bitch.' And in punishment for your folly and your blindness you shall love me as I really am."

As she really is: but what exactly is she? Thinking about one of the others—for Madame Sabatier's wholly poetic bitchery could only be that of a fallen Muse—Baudelaire could see all the more clearly that

strange feminine polarity which was the continuing subject of his reflection. Because of it woman remained for him the most tempting of
artificial paradises. How was it that this "most natural well-spring of
the most natural pleasures" could pour into man's heart, along with
its muddy stream, that pure essence which the poet's heart alone can
distill from it? But that is not the surprising part of it. The strangest
thing of all is that the poet, not content to siphon off the spiritual
element from those disturbing emotions which pass from body to body,
wants to seize upon it, to let it no longer belong to "the other" but
himself try in some fashion to be transformed into it. Remember Baudelaire's profound remark to Marie, "You are the part of myself that a
spiritual essence has shaped." It seems as though the poet could only
become himself by absorbing the spiritual essence of a woman who,
becoming part of the masterpiece as she is part of the poet, is henceforward a necessary condition of his work. The poet's love for the Muse
is this very integration. The fact that this spiritual essence can be given
only in a body is for them both a professional risk, but to reach the
high peaks of art, risks must be run. This is suggested by the psychology
of the great poets, endlessly haunted as they were by concern over "the
eternal feminine."

This part played by the Muse in the lives of certain great artists
recurs so regularly that its significance cannot be denied. No doubt
there are women in the lives of all men, but even with creative artists
they are not all Muses. Picture the *Divina Commedia* without the luminous grace brought to it by Beatrice: this is easy—for you have only
to remember the *Inferno* and then imagine the *Purgatorio* and *Paradiso*
as they might have been if the poet, grown old, had not treasured
undiminished the passionate tenderness still awakened in him by the
lovely face of a child seen in his far-off youth. This is a question of his
art itself, of how his work would have been affected *as poetry* if he had
not so deeply absorbed the femininity of Beatrice. Nothing could be
more masculine than Dante's work, but the force of feeling that emerges
results surely from the fact that, even on its highest and most desolate
uplands, we breathe the atmosphere of that "Mundus Muliebris" of
which Baudelaire wrote, without which half of humanity would be
absent and the masterpiece would leave our thirst unslaked. This
woman's world is peopled indeed by bodies, and because he is a man the
artist's first contact with it is through his own body. To join it in order
to transcend it, at the constant risk of falling back into it, is the law of
a relationship which might be considered the very type of a dangerous
love affair if the reward were not sometimes so glorious. It is anyhow

an enterprise upon which some of the greatest poets have embarked. These sentimental journeys of so well-defined an order are not mere novels but depend upon a philosophy of art.

To think of Petrarch as a courtly poet is an odd illusion—even if in his bad moments he was just that. But try for a flash to imagine what he would have been if the clerk of Avignon had not met Laura! We should still have his *Africa,* which nobody reads, and his *Letters,* which are almost impossible to read. Perhaps we should even have the *Trionfi,* but most certainly not the absolute perfection of the most beautiful poems of the *Canzoniere.* It is the same with Baudelaire. He realized it, and the commonplaces into which he falls in his hours of aridity are enough to show us that he had good reason to be afraid. His descriptions in *Les Paradis artificiels* and, in a famous passage of the "Chagrins d'enfant" of the soft feminine atmosphere in which his youth was so long immersed have a hearing quite different from mere anecdote. He is asking of the emotional disturbances, which he cannot lose without diminishing the artist within him, that they introduce into the sensual form the purity of the idea—and this is the very secret of great art. He has said it himself. Dante's youthful passion for Beatrice still bathed with tenderness the most exalted of his poems, and Baudelaire begs of Marie and Madame Sabatier to give to his work that "distinction of accent," or, more profoundly, "that hermaphrodite quality without which the keenest and most virile genius remains, in regard to the perfection of his art, an incomplete being."

Certainly these second-class Muses were, even more than Beatrice, false images of the good, "who never fully keep their promises." You must reread "La Béatrice" to realize how this poet suffered. Mocked as a fool by those for whom Madame Sabatier served ends far other than the inspiration of a masterpiece, his real crucifixion was to witness the public prostitution of a Muse—and the sun not halted in its course by the crime—while she reckoned nothing of the eminence she refused, and of which he had hoped to find her worthy. Yes, Baudelaire knew it all, but as he roved after these empty idols he discovered some of his most lovely poems. And he knew that he could find them by no other path: "Woman is inevitably suggestive, she lives with a life that is not her own, she lives spiritually in the imaginations haunted and fertilized by her."

These reflections must be halted on the threshold of a profound mystery. To create life, a man needs a woman. To create the perfection of beauty, it may be that the man must also *be* the woman. Here "to be" excludes "to have," which is doubtless why the great artist guards himself so zealously from enslavement to a sensual passion that drags down instead of ennobling. He cannot allow himself to be exploited by her whom he exploits—to the point of being transformed into her to serve the ends of his art. The greater he is, the sooner he can dispense with her, but the nearer the work of which he dreams approaches the inaccessible summits of pure creation, the less he can do without her in its inception.

The "Jeanne Duval" Poems
in *Les Fleurs du mal*

by P. M. Pasinetti

At times that contemplator . . . would recite to her lines written in a language which she did not know.

Théodore de Banville, *Mes Souvenirs,* VII

When we take poems XX-XXXV (first ed.) of the *Fleurs du mal* as the Jeanne Duval group, as is often done, we do not claim an interest in biographical study. On the contrary, when we accept Baudelaire's own ordering of the book and we isolate an area in it, our assumption is that that ordering did not occur at the documentary level (as a man would order his journal for purposes of record) but at the level where the poet has already invented himself into character. He is the "speaker of the poem," and knows it. Such "invention" is possibly implicit in the very definition of literature; it seems to have been, at any rate, very much Baudelaire's way of looking at it. It is his way of looking at other writers, as would appear for instance in *Salon de 1846*: "Et vous, ô Honoré de Balzac, vous le plus héroïque, le plus singulier, le plus romantique et le plus poétique parmi tous les personnages que vous avez tirés de votre sein!"

Our other obvious assumption—that a study of imagery is a good way to start coming to grips with poems—could also be temptingly justified on Baudelaire's own premises. The imagery, the sensory material, would often yield easily to identification with "l'enveloppe amusante, titillante, apéritive, du divin gâteau." ("Le Peintre de la vie moderne," in *L'Art romantique*) ["the entertaining, titillating, appetizing wrapping of the divine cake." ("The Painter of Modern Life," in *L'Art romantique*)]. Even more (in the same passage and elsewhere) imagery seems to be felt by Baudelaire as the "body" of poetry, the medium toward the continuously

"The 'Jeanne Duval' Poems in *Les Fleurs du mal.*" From *Yale French Studies,* vol. I, no. 2 (Fall-Winter 1948). Reprinted by permission.

elusive revelation of the "divine essence." The images are, so to speak, the objects of the cult. And the importance of this situation could not be too strongly emphasized. Some of this poetry, as I shall try to suggest, is not only based on it; it is about it.

The images used to describe the "bizarre déité" are almost as recurrent as Homeric epithets. Baudelaire's well known craftsmanship seems to invest the very manner in which he handles his materials, the stones, the animals he has so persistently in mind (so that if we reread, e.g., *Fusées* XVII, we are on familiar ground). Intuitive as they may be in origin, in their application they recall the jeweller's poised and well-calculated craft; I use this trite simile to suggest also that they make the poem as single stones the jewel; they are applied with an eye to the whole piece. *Les Bijoux,* which opened the group in the first edition, exemplifies as well as anything this tendency to organize things around a central vision, and suggests, as we shall have occasion to repeat, the poet's preference for the kind of thing which can "faire tableau." The details of the description, subordinate to that inclusive pattern, are from the very start the rather familiar ones. Roughly speaking we have, on one side, the "monde rayonnant de métal et de pierre" ["radiating world of metal and of stone"], a world which is glittering but cold and hard. On the other hand, we have hints of another pattern, the invitation to voyage toward regions of voluptuous calm, typically based on sea allusion: "mon amour profond et doux comme la mer" ["my love profound and sweet like the sea"]. And, of course, animal imagery ("tigre dompté"). And above all, the general tone which is, as we suggested, remarkably one of "composition." The visual angle, the contemplative posture of the speaker, and the feeling of structural firmness which Baudelaire always gives, serve perfectly the manner of presentation of the central figure: moving in charming metamorphoses, she is making a show of herself, or is used as a show: "D'un air vague et rêveur elle essayait des poses." ["With a vague and dreamy air she tried on poses."] Action is, here and elsewhere, described: but action already shaped into posture, bent, so to speak, on itself as potential remembrance. The treatment of action in the light of memory is typical: we suspect already that acts achieve their highest significance only in the ritual of commemoration. The pattern of *Le Balcon,* to mention one, comes to mind ("Tu te rappelleras. . . ." "Je sais l'art d'évoquer. . . .").

It is also clear at once that the image of the mulatto girl has a function which transcends the love story, and that it does so in all its precious details: a halo of special significance is around each of them. And they are so concrete and so individually appropriate that abstract paraphrase becomes particularly inept. We have in the poems, of course, themes of

attraction and repulsion, soft warm and gelid detachment, longing and
ennui, pain and voluptuousness, but since these do not exist as polarized
abstractions (each pair being part of the same, indivisible impulse) they
can only be expressed through imagery, whose function they justify: the
conciliating function in coping with complexities. Typical is the con-
ciliation of immediate and distant; the near and tangible mainly serves
to excite longing. The central vision, the dark woman, is the tangible,
Parisian symbol of "là-bas." The possible illustrations of this pattern are
only too abundant; the slow motions of the calm blue seas provide the
underlying rhythm, and in the darkness of closed eyes and exotic perfume
the poet sees "se dérouler des rivages heureux" in the monotonous sun-
light (*Parfum exotique.*) There is a punctual, almost pedestrian appro-
priateness in the imagery used to express the longing toward exotic lands:
the woman's hair, in the famous baroque piece, is the "forêt aromatique";
the speaker's desires "partent en caravane" and "la bête implacable et
cruelle" of poem XXIV importantly suggests the oriental God, to be
appeased by precious though always insufficient offerings (cf. also *La
Chevelure,* last stanza.) The idol is unappeased, unattainable, also frigid;
the mineral imagery of *Les Bijoux* occurs again and again (cf. second part
of Sonnet XXVII).

The pattern of contemplation established at the start is further stylized
in a certain use of animal images. *Le Chat* is pretty, and rather predict-
able. The use of the serpent, I feel, shows more complexity. It is introduced in the sonnet "Avec tes vêtements . . ." by the slow, dance-like
motion of the woman; and the image is reworked in a special poem, the
following *Serpent qui danse.* The serpent is exotic and secret, it partakes
of the "nature étrange et symbolique/Où l'ange inviolé se mêle au sphinx
antique"; in its immediately descriptive function, the image is elaborated
upon to the point of establishing connections between the serpent's skin
and the woman's "vêtements ondoyants et nacrés"; and much of the usual
imagery connoting cold and unattainable indifference is adopted (the eyes
are "bijoux froids" etc.)

We cannot help observing, however, the subtle and precise qualification
that the place of the serpent in the picture implies; it is not so much the
idol, to which appeasing gifts are vainly offered, as the object, the instrument of the magic performance:

> Comme ces longs serpents que les jongleurs sacrés
> Au bout de leurs bâtons agitent en cadence.

> [Like those long snakes which sacred jugglers
> At the end of their sticks rythmically swing.]
>
> ("Avec tes vêtements")

Also, in the second "serpent" poem, the sea imagery is relevant. Until then it had been more typically used to imply a dream of unattainable warmth, longing toward "île paresseuse," or annihilations, dark "gouffre" (even her hair was "ce noir océan"). Here it serves as a vision of activity, in a rhythm of unusual vivacity:

> Comme un navire qui s'éveille
> Au vent du matin,
> Mon âme rêveuse appareille
> Pour un ciel lointain.

> [Like a vessel that awakes
> At the morning breeze,
> My dreamy soul sets sail
> Toward a distant sky.]
> ("Le Serpent qui danse")

It is "lointain" to be sure, but it does sound different from the sky we imagine over the

> . . . rivages heureux
> Qu'éblouissent les feux d'un soleil monotone

> [. . . fortunate shores
> Dazzled by the fires of a monotonous sunlight]

of *Parfum exotique* or from the "immensités bleues" of poem XXIV. The image of the "navire" in the morning creates quite a perceptible difference; and it is tempting to think what the word "navire" was liable to evoke in Baudelaire's mind. In the splendid passage in *Fusées* XXII his vision of the "navire" is given as the very type of the poetic image.

I am not trying to force this series of poems into a too well formulated scheme. It seems clear, however, that at this more or less central point of the group, the quality of the vision changes. At least, there is shift in emphasis. In particular I would describe this as an increased awareness of the fact that the speaker's contemplation is an image of the poetic act. And I would suggest that consequently the vision of the woman and of the poet bent toward her in long monologue is more and more characteristically placed in a light of recollection: recollection being Baudelaire's typical mode of the artistic evocation.

In the *Bijoux,* by way of example, we had already noticed how the composition tended to "faire tableau"; now the "tableau" is placed more evidently at what Wordsworth would call "a distance that was fit"; and the even more important thing is that memory becomes not only the method but also the theme of the poetry. In Baudelaire, and we have here the support of some of his most famous passages of criticism, recollection can be said to constitute the proper form of the imaginative vision.

The important stanzas 7 and 8 of *Une Charogne* are a case in point. The moment has been preceded by a gradual shifting from images of death and decomposition to images where the dead body is seen more and more as an inchoate, anonymous mass, suggesting, rather than the dead, the blind, the unnamed, the prenatal. Finally "tout cela" in the crucial passage acquires a rhythmic movement which several types of visual and auditive images contribute to suggest, and "enflé d'un souffle" achieves no less than the meaning of a parable of artistic creation from memory:

> Les formes s'effaçaient et n'étaient plus qu'un rêve,
>   Une ébauche lente à venir,
> Sur la toile oubliée, et que l'artiste achève
>   Seulement par le souvenir.

> [The shapes became blurred and were then but a dream,
>   A sketch slow to come off,
> Forgotten on the canvas, and completed only
>   In the artist's memory.]

> ("Une Charogne")

The lines 2 and 4 should begin indented, as here printed.

In other words we have, here and elsewhere, the pattern of past event and present evocation, the ritual of recollection which equates the stylizing, purifying and, indeed, commemorative function of art.

Le Vampire in this respect is a sort of ironic counterpart to what seems to me the basic theme of *Une Charogne* and of much that follows it. It adopts some of the same imagery ("comme aux vermines une charogne"). In the last stanza of the poem, the identification of the speaker with the "vermine qui vous mangera de baisers" of *Une Charogne* is, if we keep that vision in mind, as we cannot help doing, rather more than a hint.

The theme of recollection through art or, more generally, that of artistic creation, can naturally be seen in imagery of light and darkness: the imagery with which birth and nonlife are associated in the subconscious patrimony of all people. Roughly speaking, art would be seen as the process of rescuing the image from chaotic darkness and oblivion: its illumination and ordering into beauty and remembrance. *Les Ténèbres* (first sonnet of *Un Fantôme*) is the nearest thing to a close adherence to that scheme. The speaker is in unfathomable depths of despair and darkness; and the analogy with a chaotic state from which creative power is painfully absent is supported by a comparison with the predicament of an artist. The art is painting, as in *Une Charogne,* as in some of the titles of the final poems of this cycle (*Le Cadre, Le Portrait*) and as in some of the most impressive pieces of Baudelaire's criticism (where, through his notations on painting, we are accustomed to read, as though on a palimpsest, his ideas on poetry.)

> Je suis comme un peintre qu'un Dieu moqueur
> Condamne à peindre, hélas, sur les ténèbres. . . .
>
> [I am like a painter whom a mocking God
> Condemns to paint, alas! on shades of night. . . .]
> ("Un Fantôme")

Finally the memory appears, made of grace and splendor, recognizable "à sa rêveuse allure orientale," and the exclamatory conclusion is: "C'est Elle! Noire et pourtant lumineuse."

This suggests, also, the ambiguous complexity of the light-darkness pattern. Appropriately, there is continuous exchange between the two states. Some of the light imagery (temperate, warm light to be sure) throughout these poems has suggested, rather than a burst of creativity, nostalgia toward the inarticulate calm of the lazy islands. There is such a thing as annihilation *and* peace. And, on the other hand, if darkness indicates chaos, there is the luminous attractiveness of that chaos, the ambivalence toward the "gouffre," the fascination of unrescued darkness, which "la belle ténébreuse" herself, as a matter of fact, has often been there to symbolize.

What makes the "gouffre" of *De Profundis* really horrible, then, is the awareness of it. So that in the last stanza of that sonnet the poet envies

> . . . le sort des plus vils animaux
> Qui peuvent se plonger dans un sommeil stupide.
>
> [. . . the fate of the vilest beasts
> Which can plunge into a stupid sleep.]
> ("De Profundis clamavi")

Now, the complexity of Jeanne's image is also in the fact that she exemplifies the capability of such a "sommeil stupide." That makes her irritatingly enviable and contemptible. Contemptible, because if on the

biographical level this simply means Jeanne Duval talking to Banville
about Monsieur Baudelaire, "ses meubles, ses collections, ses manies,"
in the final poem of the section it makes her the "être maudit, à qui, de
l'abîme profond/Jusq'au plus haut du ciel, rien, hors moi, ne répond!"
Damned; unrescued; the poet is her only hope of rescue. The final line
is possibly the most detached and glorious vision of the series; there for
a moment a kind of total liberation in the image seems achieved:

> Statue aux yeux de jais, grand ange au front d'airain!

> [Statue with jet-black eyes, great bronze-browed angel!]
> ("Je te donne ces vers")

It is the supreme moment of a development long prepared, more intensely
so in the last contemplations. These are sonnets. With his sense for the
"forme juste" Baudelaire chose this, with its possibilities of epigraphic
finality. There is here a sort of recapitulation of the known motifs:
jewels, metals, "nudité," animal gracefulness, the theme of memory, a
metaphorical sea-voyage in the splendid opening:

> Je te donne ces vers afin que si mon nom
> Aborde heureusement aux époques lointaines. . . .

> [I give you these verses so that my name,
> If it happily should land on distant ages. . . .]
> ("Je te donne ces vers")

And, as we have observed, the commemorative function of poetry, its
ability to rescue from Time ("noir assassin" etc.) is openly suggested.

I do not wish to stress the unity of this group and force it into a too
well classified pattern; but I feel it is legitimate to say that from the early
suggestions of the "tableau" pattern, through, for instance, the serpent
image (where the woman is seen as the object on the magician's baton)
to this concluding part, there is an overall movement toward some sort
of revelation: expressed abstractly, this would be the revelation of the
poet's true position before the woman, his superiority and, in a sense,
his deeper curse. As artist, he is the magician ("Je sais l'art d'évoquer
. . ."), the owner of the secret language. This is *his* counterpart to the
"bizarre déité," to the "sorcière," to her mysteries which in the last
analysis are of his own creation, because she is not aware of them. So that
the relationship becomes one of reciprocal secret, the poet's painful
advantage being that he is aware of the predicament, renouncing as he

does the animal's dumb inarticulateness. That there are underlying religious analogies, Baudelaire's imagery often implies. When we started these notes by calling the images the object of the cult, his passage on prayer (*Fusées* XVII: "Le chapelet est un médium, un véhicule" [The beads are a medium, a vehicle"], etc.) was in our mind.

It is a terrible cult, because the "idea behind," the supreme beauty, the divine essence, is bound never to be expressed; but then, on the other hand, if it were achieved, the spoken word would be appeased in utter and still contemplation. (The "ciel lointain," the "calme" etc., inasmuch as they are objective correlatives of that revelation of peace, can exist on the page because they cannot be reached; and art springs characteristically from longing and regret, the two recurrent types of the visionary attitude.) All that the poet can do, then, is to perform again and again the act of desire, the prayer; and perform it well. Baudelaire's preoccupation with the craft of poetry, and also the very recurrence, the very monotony of his images, acquire in this light their full moral and ritualistic meaning.

Baudelaire

by John Middleton Murry

Perhaps no word has been more prolific of literary misunderstandings in the last half-century than the word decadence. Critics with the best will in the world, which is the will for exact description, have called writers decadent. The unfortunate writer has been damned by a definition that no one had troubled to understand. In the general mind to be decadent is to be impure, immoral, or, in the now more frequent and really more damaging phrase, to be "unhealthy." Many poets were branded as decadents in the nineteenth century. All of them suffered by the name; some deserved to suffer, and some did not. Charles Baudelaire, who was the first and greatest of the line, suffered most and deserved it least. He suffers still, because every critic who is convinced of his high excellence as a poet and is anxious to elucidate it is driven to dwell on the element of decadence in the man and his work. The word is as necessary to the understanding of Baudelaire as a particular instrument to a surgeon for a particular operation.

Decadence is essentially a word of the historian who applies it to those periods in the history of a society when its old institutions are breaking down and being obscurely replaced by new; to ages when the transition is being made from one social ideal, one social fabric, to another. The word can be applied to literature, or art in general, in one of two ways. It can be used historically to distinguish the literature that is created during an age of decadence, or it can be used metaphorically to describe the literature of a period of transition between two literary ideals. These meanings are utterly different, yet the word is generally made to carry them both at the same time, as though a literary decadence were the necessary concomitant of a social decadence. Worse still, to the vagueness created by the fusion of these two meanings has been added a misty recollection of orgies under the Roman Empire.

A tincture of fiddling Nero, Caligula, and Elagabalus gives a piquant flavor to the bolus of haziness. Writers and artists are called "decadent" by people who mean that they are merely bad artists, or artists who deal with "unhealthy" subjects. Thus a valuable word is ruined because it is used to save people the trouble of thinking.

It may be true, though it remains to be proved, that the literatures of all periods of decadence have certain elements in common; it is certainly untrue that the literature of such a period is necessarily inferior as literature (indeed Nietzsche argued, very plausibly, that the veritable heights of literature can be attained only in an age of decadence). In the case of Baudelaire it is extremely necessary that we should be clear in what sense the epithet decadent is used when it is applied to him. Baudelaire is the poet of an historical decadence; he is not in any useful sense of the word a decadent poet. On the contrary, he was one of the greatest and most assured poets that France has produced. As a poet, he was strong, masculine, deliberate, classical; not a puny successor of great men, but the heroic founder of a line; and the peculiar quality of his work derives from the interaction of these two very different factors, the decadence of the age in which he lived and his own poetic strength and determination. Not that his choice of subject may not sometimes be called perverse; but the perversity of his work is the least important, the least relevant, and, to the unbiased reader, the least noticeable of its qualities. It is easy for any poetaster to be perverse; it is extremely difficult for a poet to be perverse in Baudelaire's way. For Baudelaire was not a furtive dabbler in unclean things; he was the deliberate and determined poet of an attitude to life to which we cannot refuse the epithet heroic. The driving impulse of his work was not a predilection, but a conviction.

Baudelaire was convinced that the age in which he lived was a decadence, and we who know it not only by his own passionate protest against it, but by Balzac's romantic anatomy of its corruption, must acquiesce in his conviction. The old aristocratic order had fallen; there was no new democratic order to supply its place: in the interval arose, like a growth of weeds on the site of a demolished building, as the sole principle of spiritual and social order, that reverence for wealth for its own sake which distinguished nineteenth century France. Guizot's "Enrichissez-vous" marked a social nadir. It was the age of rampant industrialism and violent and abortive revolution; of the hideous and uncontrolled eruption of the great cities; of all the squalor of a victorious and hypocritical materialism. Against this tyranny Baudelaire conceived it his duty to protest, not merely by the poetic utterances of cries of revolt but by the actual conduct of his life. The French romantic movement as a whole was animated to some extent by a spirit of protest against the sordidness of the age; but Baudelaire belonged to a curious section of the movement which had very little in common with romanticism as we generally conceive it now. His affinities were with the disciplined and contemptuous romanticism of Stendhal and Mérimée. This romanticism was rather a kind of sublimated realism, based upon an almost morbid "horreur d'être dupe"—romantic in its aspiration away from the bourgeois society which it loathed, realistic in its determination to accept the facts as they were. It was romantic also in its conception and elaboration of the attitude which it considered inevitable for the chosen spirits who would not bow the knee to Baal.

It is important to grasp these two intimately woven strands of realism and romanticism in Baudelaire and his two predecessors. This strange but natural combination plays a great part not in the literature of France only, but in that of Europe as a whole during the last century. A single thread runs through the work of Stendhal, Mérimée, Baudelaire, Nietzsche, and Dostoevsky; in spite of their outward dissimilarity and the great differences between their powers, these men are united by a common philosophical element which takes bodily shape in their conceptions of the hero. They are all intellectual romantics, in rebellion against life, and they imagine for themselves a hero in whom their defiance should be manifested. The three Frenchmen had in common, and put into actual practice, the ideal of "le Dandy." "Le Dandy" is an imperturbable being above the law, inscrutable, contemptuous of the world, silent under the torments which it inflicts upon his sensitive soul, continually experimenting at his own risk with morality, exercising a drastic discipline upon himself, and adopting, as a symbol of his inward discipline, that elegance of outward appearance which we generally associate with the word "dandy." On the one side the conception of the Dandy touches the romantic literary ideal of the poet in his "ivory tower," on the other it reaches out in anticipation towards the superman of Nietzsche and the still subtler and more impressive antinomian hero of Dostoevsky's novels. In both these forms it influenced Baudelaire's life as a man and activity as a poet.

From this angle it is perhaps easier to understand and analyze the almost massive impression of unity we receive from so small a work as Baudelaire's. A volume of poetry, a volume of prose (of which fully one-third is a paraphrase of De Quincey's *Opium Eater*), two volumes of scattered criticism, chiefly of painting, three volumes of translation from Poe—these are the complete works of Baudelaire. What is really original in them could easily be contained in three pocket volumes. Yet the abiding impression made by them is one of solidity. This is in the main because the inspiration is single and the foundations firm and invariable. As an artist Baudelaire works from a single center; his attitude to life and his attitude to art lend each other aid and confirmation. Even his vices as a poet have the merit of being deliberate, and of contributing to the total effect at which he aimed. They are the vices proper, one might almost say essential, to his achievement. When Baudelaire is rhetorical, his rhetoric is never entirely empty; it has a dramatic propriety and significance in the mouth of the "âme damnée," the rebellious angel hurling defiance at the powers of heaven. When he indulges his desire to astonish, he is asserting his immunity from conventional fears. Both these vices, it is true, betray in Baudelaire's mind some confusion between the laws of heroism in life and in art. They are not the less vices because they are intelligible. Nevertheless, it does make a difference that they are not irrelevant. A writer's weaknesses are to some extent condoned when they are seen to be the condition of his strength.

It is Baudelaire's chief distinction that, in spite of these one or two failures, he made a successful and undeviating effort to translate his ethical attitude toward life into a purely poetical gesture. He might so easily have been a poet of the confessional, pouring out his wounded soul in lyrical "cris de coeur"; but his Dandyism helped him to a more truly poetic conception of his task. The fox might be tearing at his vitals, but there must be, if not a smile, an inscrutable expression of Spartan impassivity on his face. The self-sacrifice demanded of him by his moral creed coincided with the self-sacrifice demanded of him as a poet. That the original impulse was partly moral discounted nothing of his achievement, for he was in the fortunate position of one whose effort in life seconded his endeavors in art; and if he more often formulated his purpose in ethical terms, it was more because he was enough of a romantic to prefer the hero of life to the hero of art than because he was unable to envisage it as a poetic problem alone.

> Many others than myself [he writes in *L'Art romantique*], have taken care to underline the fatal consequences of an essentially personal genius; and it might well be also, after all, that the finest expressions of genius, elsewhere than in the pure heavens . . . could only be reached at the price of an inevitable sacrifice.

Still, in spite of this unequivocal declaration of faith, it would be a mistake to suppose that Baudelaire admitted any clear distinction between his Dandyism and his poetry. Though he saluted the artistic heroism of Flaubert when *Madame Bovary* appeared, he did not particularly admire it; much less would he have admired the attitude of

Cézanne towards his painting or Hardy toward his poetry. He would
have found them lacking in gesture.

Here again Baudelaire was fortunate. The desire for a gesture is not
so dangerous in French poetry as it is in English. Traditional French
prosody, and above all the prosody of the alexandrine, is a perpetual invitation to rhetoric, just as the blank verse prosody of Milton sooner or
later compels the English poet who adopts it to become more tremendous
than he wants to be; but whereas the Miltonic prosody is an aberra-
tion from the true English tradition, the prosody of the French alexandrine is the tradition itself. Wordsworth said of the English sonnet that
in Milton's hands "the thing became a trumpet"; the French poet's
difficulty with the alexandrine has always been to prevent the thing
from becoming a trumpet. Luckily Baudelaire wanted a trumpet—one
might almost say he wanted a cavalry bugle. The alexandrine was made
for a man possessed by the burning desire to send his challenges ringing
up to heaven. Had it not been that his Satanic defiance was moderated
by a Satanic sense of "comme il faut," Baudelaire might have gone the
way of Victor Hugo and largely wasted his lesser genius in a mere fury
of blowing.

Baudelaire's power of concentration saved him from rhetorical dis-
aster. In the matter of prosody he willingly accepted the severest limita-
tions. He made no technical innovations himself, and he rejected some
of those which Victor Hugo had made before him. He saw that for him
it was much more important to blow a few blasts that were piercing than
many that were merely loud; and he early set himself to the task of finding an equivalent in pure poetry to his detestation of the world and
his defiance of the powers that ordained it. He sought the equivalent by
making his poetry as metallic in sound and suggestion as he could; he
would change the psychological oppression of life into a plastic oppression. To make concrete the immaterial is, of course, a familiar process
of the poet's activity, and the effort lies at the source of all metaphor. But
Baudelaire went far beyond this phase; he made it his deliberate aim to
expel all elasticity from his verse, all bright and ethereal perspectives
from his vision. He built himself a house of metal and went from room
to room, shutting, bolting, and barring all the magic casements. The
surface of his vision and the texture of his verse should alike be hard
and impenetrable; thus he would render in poetry his sense of the
stifling oppressiveness of life. He would meet steel with steel.

His methods of achieving his end were manifold. The most obvious
and the most successful is his endeavor to reduce all living things to a
condition of immobile solidity. There is a curious example of this in
the "Rêve parisien," where the poet dreams of a symbolic landscape:

Je savourais dans mon tableau
L'enivrante monotonie
Du métal, du marbre et de l'eau.

[I relished in my picture
The intoxicating monotony
Of metal, marble and water.]

Even at the outset only one-third of his universe—the water—has any chance of moving; within a half-dozen lines he has (literally) petrified even that third.

Et des cataractes pesantes
Comme des rideaux de cristal
Se suspendaient obéissantes
À des murailles de métal.

[And heavy cataracts
Like curtains of crystal
Hung obediently
To walls of metal.]

Here Baudelaire has indulged his obsession at the cost of an artistic blemish; his stately pleasure-house needed the movement of water to make the contrast of his motionless marble more intense and oppressive. In a poet so scrupulous of his plastic effects the blunder and the underlying motive are the more striking. But in Baudelaire the strangest things are turned to stone and brass; he speaks of a woman's "granite skin" in one poem, and in the next, "Slowly I sharpened the dagger on my heart." The beautiful Dorothea, his mulatto Venus, is "belle et froide comme le bronze." His dreamland of happiness is "A true land of Cockaigne, where all is rich, neat and shiny, like a beautiful conscience, a magnificent set of kitchen utensils, a splendid goldsmith's shop, a multicolored jewelry." It is not necessary to accumulate examples; one has but to open *Les Fleurs du mal* at random to find them. Baudelaire makes solid everything he can. His very ideal of Beauty is an absolute immobility; Beauty itself declares:

Je hais le mouvement qui déplace les lignes
Et jamais je ne pleure et jamais je ne ris.

[I hate motion which sets lines awry
And never do I cry and never do I laugh.]

We are not surprised that Beauty should define itself in terms exactly descriptive of the inscrutable Dandy; nor even that an immobile Beauty should be a symbol of the poet's oppression by an adamantine and inexorable world. In Baudelaire's vision of the cosmos, as we have said, steel is opposed to steel. The oppressor and the oppressed are equally ruthless, equally immobile, equally conscious, and equally beautiful. Only the poet-hero knows the Adversary, but to know him is to salute the splendor of his majesty.

> Etre maudit à qui, de l'abîme profond
> Jusqu'au plus haut du ciel, rien hors mot ne répond! . . .
>
> [Cursed being to whom, from the deepest abyss
> Up to the highest sky, none but I reply! . . .]

To this Moloch of existence the poet sacrifices himself in an ecstasy which is concealed beneath a mask of bronze. In harmony with the clangor of this meeting of metallic opposites, Baudelaire conceived himself as working like a smith at an anvil on the very words of his poems, hammering and shaping them till they rang with steely resonance. It is something more than a metaphorical flight when he speaks of

> mes vers polis, treillis d'un pur métal,
> Savamment constellé de rimes de cristal.
>
> [my polished lines, trellis made of a pure metal,
> Skillfully studded with rhymes of crystal.]

This is not fancy, but a precise description of them; they are tempered: and even if the poet had not himself given the hint, one might without any violent exercise of the imagination have compared them to swordblades, cunningly damascened.

Within this metallic resonance which is the large and general characteristic of Baudelaire's poetry we may distinguish many variations and undertones; or rather we may say that in one continuous and predominant physical sensation—for Baudelaire's verse is physically oppressive—we can detect various separate pulses. Of these the most remarkable might be called an exacerbation of the image. It appears in many forms: in some it is used to give to a vague emotion the acuteness of a physical sensation, as in

Ces affreuses nuits
Qui compriment le coeur comme un papier qu'on froisse

[These ghastly nights
Which oppress the heart like paper being crumpled]

Sometimes it is a peculiar variation of the dominant endeavor after solidity which has already been discussed. Thus he writes of the beautiful Dorothea:

Ta gorge qui s'avance et qui pousse la moire,
Ta gorge triomphante est une belle armoire
  Dont les panneaux bombés et clairs
Comme les boucliers accrochent des éclairs.

[Your jutting breast which heaves the moires,
Your triumphant breast is a lovely treasure chest
  Whose panels, swollen and clear,
Like bucklers catch lightnings.]

The varieties are, indeed, too many to be separately defined; but a small collection of examples will show some of the curious tones that Baudelaire extracted from this singular instrument:

Le ciel! couvercle noir de la vaste marmite
Où bout l'imperceptible et vaste humanité. . . .

[The sky! black lid of the vast pot
In which imperceptible and vast mankind boils. . . .]

Coeur racorni, fumé comme un jambon. . . .

[Hardened heart, smoked like a ham. . . .

La nuit s'épaississait ainsi qu'une cloison. . . .

[Night grew thicker like a partition wall. . . .]

Sous le fardeau de ta paresse
  Ta tête d'enfant
Se balance avec la mollesse
  D'un jeune éléphant. . . .

[Under the burden of your indolence
Your child's head
Swings with the soft gesture
Of a young elephant. . . .]

Le plaisir vaporeux fuira vers l'horizon
Ainsi qu'une sylphide au fond de la coulisse. . . .

[Vaporous pleasure will take flight to the skyline
Like a sylph behind the scenery on the stage. . . .]

Quand, ainsi qu'un poète, il [le Soleil] descend dans les villes
Il ennoblit le sort des choses les plus viles. . . .

[When, like a poet, it [the sun] descends into the cities,
It ennobles the fate of the vilest things. . . .]

Some of these attempted effects may be traced to the desire to astonish which is permitted to the Dandy on the condition that he himself betrays no astonishment. But the explanation would certainly not cover them all, even if the desire to astonish were not closely related to the desire to compel a response, which is not lawful only but essential to the poet. Some of them are curiously beautiful; they have a novel and bizarre beauty that lingers in the mind. The Dandy is not only looking steadily at facts; he is extracting from them some quaint and vivid essence that escapes the duller or more cowardly eye. His world may be hard, repellent even, but it is full of a number of interesting things.

Nevertheless, the importance of these quaint vistas opening on to things grotesque or beautiful must not be exaggerated. Baudelaire's exacerbation of the image was destined to play a considerable part in the subsequent evolution of French poetry, and, at the second hand, of our own; but he himself used it sparingly, as one aware that the method was scarcely on a scale with the large effect of solidity at which he aimed. His main road of escape from his iron-walled world lay elsewhere, and was as ample as the prison-house was huge. His symbol of deliverance was the sea. The sea appears as often in his poetry as the metals themselves. It was for him a terrestrial infinite that led "anywhere out of the world"; and even in that famous and beautiful poem "Le Voyage," the last of *Les Fleurs du mal,* when the voyagers have returned with their mournful message that in every corner of the world "the eternal bulletin" is the same, the poet calls to Death as the great ship's captain. After the failure of all voyages, a voyage remains: Toward Death.

Doubtless, in the constant recurrence of the vision and imagery of the sea throughout Baudelaire's poetry, we may detect the profound impression made upon him as a young man by the voyage on which his perturbed parents sent him to cure his passion for poetry. But the sea is, after all, only a symbol; if he had not found the sea to express his intentions he would have found something else; hardly anything, however, that would have served him so well, or have made so universal an appeal. Even those who know nothing of Baudelaire's disdains and detestations, and would dismiss his attitude of rebellion as a mere theatricality, cannot fail to respond to his recurrent imagery of the sea. We may call it a simple or a naïve emotion that finds in a "splendid ship with white sails crowding" the perfect symbol of the freedom and happiness that are hidden beyond our mortal horizon; it is a profound emotion, and, what is more, an emotion peculiarly of our time. An age of industrialism drives men to treasure the symbol of the sea and its ships. Baudelaire made a magnificent use of this great modern commonplace. "Grand style: rien de plus beau que les lieux communs," he notes in his "Journal," where we also find this delicate statement of the fundamental theme:

> Those beautiful tall ships, imperceptibly swinging and rolling along on tranquil waters, those robust ships with their idle and nostalgic air, do they not say to us in a mute tongue: When do we set out for happiness?

The image appears in an innumerable variety of forms and contexts. Music is a sea opening on to he knows not what freedom:

> Je mets à la voile
> La poitrine en avant et les poumons gonflés
> Comme de la toile.
>
> [I unfurl the sails
> My breast thrown forward and my lungs swollen
> Like canvas.]

The lovely Dorothea sails along his memory like a ship. Again, "notre âme est un trois-mâts cherchant son Icarie." Every desire for the illimitable, every hope that some final freedom lay behind the brazen wall of circumstance, took concrete form in this image. If in a rare moment his fascinated loathing of the octopus city gives place to a delighted contemplation, it is because the beloved vision has interposed between him and the reality. "Les tuyaux, les clochers," have become "ces mâts de la cité." Here finally are two passages from the *Poèmes en prose;* placed side

by side they render exactly the quality of significance which the sea and the ships possessed for the poet's mind:

> I alone was sad, inconceivably sad. Like a priest from whom his god would be torn away, I could not without heart-rending bitterness tear myself away from that monstrously seductive sea, from that sea so infinitely varied in its frightening simplicity, which seems to contain itself and to represent by its playful whims, its wrath and its smiles the moods, the agonies and the ecstasies of all the souls which have lived; which now live and which some day will live.
>
> ("Déjà")

> A port is often a lovely sojourn for a soul wearied by life-struggles. The expanse of the sky, the mobile architecture of the clouds, the changing hues of the sea, the scintillating flashes of lighthouses make a prism marvelously fit to entertain the eyes without ever tiring them. The slim shapes of ships, with their intricate rigging, harmoniously swinging with the swell, serve to keep alive in the soul the love of rhythm and beauty. And even more, there is a mysterious and aristocratic pleasure, for him who no longer entertains any curiosity or any ambition, to lie down in the belvedere or to lean on the mole and to contemplate all those motions of those who leave and of those who return, of those who still have the strength to will, the desire to voyage or to get rich.
>
> ("Le Port")

The sea is life, and the ship that rides over it is that triumphant, impossible beauty which haunts the mind with the promise that by its power the terrors of life may be overcome. It is only a dream, as Baudelaire knew well, but he dreamed it continually.

For Baudelaire was truly an "âme damnée," because he was in love with an ideal. The fox of disillusion and disgust really tore at his vitals. Like Ivan Karamazov, he persisted in his determination to give God back the ticket; because his sensitiveness was such that the degradation and misery of life left him no peace. Ennui and spleen had "magnified themselves into divinities"; they were not petulant and momentary outbreaks of emotionalism, but constant factors of his being. To maintain himself he adopted an attitude, he became Satanic after the pattern of the Miltonic Satan, whom he considered the perfect type of manly beauty; and in the parallel world of art he sought to transform the reactions of his sensibility into the elements of a cosmos of his own making, a little universe that should produce in us the emotions that had tormented him in the world of everyday. Sometimes the original emotions show through the mask he wore; not through any artistic failure on his part, for no man was ever more resolute in his determination to sacrifice himself to his achievement, but because in the later work in prose he was intentionally loosening the rigor of his artistic creed. He was looking for a more precise equivalence to his feeling. In the texture of the *Poèmes en prose* we can distinguish the separate threads of emotion which are lost in the stiff brocade of *Les Fleurs du mal*. The prose is more lightly and in a sense more delicately woven; the unity of effect which the little pieces give derives more from complicated harmony than from the resonant unison which marks the poetry. In his prose Baudelaire is content to be ironical, compassionate, lyrical, and symbolic by turns; each piece has the contour of a single mood, together they have the complex solidity of an attitude. There, if we look, we may find as much of Baudelaire the man, as much of his human sensibility, as we shall ever find; there his pity, his irony, his dreams have their original quality, their individuality is not submerged. And there we discover an exquisite compassion and sympathy with the oppressed, of which we may be sure none of those who denounced his immorality was ever remotely capable; and even now few people know that it was Baudelaire who wrote in "Les Veuves" one of the most compassionate phrases in all literature:

> Have you sometimes observed widows on those solitary benches, poor widows? Whether they wear black or not, they are easy to recognize. Besides, always in the mourning of the poor, there is something lacking, an absence of harmony which makes it all the more heartbreaking. *They are compelled to be niggardly even on sorrow.* The rich men display theirs complete to the last item.

"They are compelled to be niggardly even on sorrow." No wonder the inventor of this phrase gave toys to the waifs of Paris and watched them "steal away like cats who take the bit you give them far away to eat, having learned to mistrust men," and recorded with a delicate precision the plans four little children were making for their lives; or that the most cynical of all his cynicisms about love is the story, "Les Yeux des pauvres." The poet and his mistress are sitting outside a new and splendid café. Suddenly he is aware of a poor man holding two tiny children by the hand; all three are staring, "extraordinarily serious," with large and fascinated eyes into the café:

> Not only was I moved by that family of eyes, but I felt a little ashamed of our glasses and of our decanters, bigger than our thirst. I turned my look toward yours, my dear love, to read *my* own thoughts in them; I plunged into your lovely and strangely soft eyes, in your green eyes, inhabited by Caprice and inspired by the Moon, when you said to me:

"Those people are unbearable, with their eyes open wide like carriage doors! Could you not beg the café owner to send them away?"

So difficult it is to understand one another, my dear angel, and so incommunicable is thought, even between people who love each other!

This suppressed yet passionate sympathy with the sufferings of the poor is one of the deepest strains in Baudelaire's nature; it helps to give to his ennui and his spleen the decisive, creative force which a passing mood of disenchantment could never have. Unlike Verlaine, Baudelaire is a constructive poet; he works from a constant center and builds on a firm foundation. It was easy for Verlaine to react against his first admiration for Baudelaire and say, "Prends l'éloquence et tords-lui son cou." He had very little to be eloquent about; but Baudelaire's moods have all the force of convictions, they have the backing of an accumulation of unforgotten injuries. Even when he is deliberately striving to express a mood, the effect is massive and overwhelming. To compare with Verlaine's plaintive songs his "Chant d'automne":

> Bientôt nous plongerons dans les froides ténèbres;
> Adieu, vive clarté de nos étés trop courts!

> [Soon we shall plunge into cold darkness;
> Farewell, vivid light of our too short summers!]

is to apprehend "the difference between poetry of an eternal intensity and poetry that is merely beautiful." The grave austerity of "Recueillement" belongs to the same rare order of achievement, the highest of which French poetry is capable:

> Sois sage, ô ma Douleur, et tiens-toi plus tranquille.
> Tu réclamais le soir; il descend; le voici.

> [Be good, O my Sorrow, and keep more still.
> You clamored for the evening; it comes down; here it is.]

There were one or two enthusiastic critics who welcomed the appearance of *Les Fleurs du mal* with references to the great name of Dante. They were generous; but their instinct was sound. Baudelaire stands to Dante in a relation not unlike that of Keats to Shakespeare.

We need not describe in detail the misery of the poet's life. Behind his mask he waged an incessant but a losing battle against a strange paralysis of the will. Only in the last two years, during which his letters to his mother and the fragments of his intimate journal have been published, has it been possible to appreciate his sufferings. Even now much of his life remains mysterious; but enough is revealed to show how striking are the points of resemblance between him and Dostoevsky. The two men were born in the same year. Certainly Baudelaire's powers were less than those of the Russian, but had Dostoevsky died when Baudelaire did, in 1867, he would have left only *Crime and Punishment* of his greater novels. Baudelaire did not live to push his exploration into the possibilities of rebellion so far. But Dostoevsky would have found in him all the material for one of his inscrutable heroes. This heroic side of Baudelaire, his prolonged and passionate attempt to live up to his own conception of heroism, is the part of his private life which most excites our curiosity, for it has a direct bearing upon his work as a poet. We may take his actual existence in the underworld for granted, as we take Dostoevsky's; it is his endeavor to establish himself in a place midway between the "âme supérieure" of his compatriot Stendhal and the Stavrogin of Dostoevsky that needs illumination. In his journals we catch only fitful glimpses of his immense exercise of will. We grasp at odd, fragmentary phrases like "Self-purification and Anti-Humanity" (written in English and in capitals), or "Être un grand homme et un saint pour lui-même, voilà l'unique chose importante," or this—with its curious anticipation of an uncanny scene in *The Possessed*—"The dandy must aspire to be continuously sublime; he must live and sleep before a mirror." And how unexpected to those who persist, like Mr. Arthur Symons in his recent study, in seeing in Baudelaire only a Swinburnian singer of "strange sins," will this be! "There can only be any true, that is to say, any moral, progress in the individual and through the individual himself." Yet all these professions of faith are perfectly consistent. Baudelaire's pursuit of the ideal of the rebellious angel called for a rigorous self-discipline and aimed at an ethical victory; but it also demanded enormous courage and physical endurance. The isolation of the man who adopts an individualist morality is complete; he cannot expect sympathy or even understanding. Even a friend and admirer like Théophile Gautier confessed that he knew nothing about Baudelaire the man. We see the evidence of the tortures which he suffered from his spiritual loneliness in the almost hysterical way in which he clung to the affection of his mother and of Jeanne Duval, to both of whom he was, and knew he was, quite incomprehensible.

"One cannot live in rebellion," said Ivan Karamazov. Just as Baudelaire used the symbol of the sea in his poetry for a way of escape from the adamantine world he had made, so in his life he was haunted by the thought that a simple domesticity might liberate him from the oppression and fascination of Paris. He will live in suburban rusticity with Jeanne at Neuilly in a quiet little "home"—it is the English word he uses; and nothing is more pathetic than his hysterical attempts to escape to his mother's villa in Honfleur. Again and again the plans are made, the day fixed. In vain. A month or more of silence precedes the inevitable letter, with its pages of feverish explanation why it was impossible. When he did break away from Paris, it was only to be drawn into the vortex of another great city; and when at least he made the journey from Brussels to Honfleur his mother herself brought him, for he was paralyzed and speechless.

So, too, in his inward consciousness he dreamed of a way of escape by belief in God. In his moments of doubt of his own endurance came the thought that there still might be an explanation of all that was intolerable to him in life: the veil of the mystery might be lifted. We have for evidence the pitiful prayers which are scattered through his Journal, and the appeal with which he ends "Mademoiselle Bistouri:"

> The city swarms with innocent monsters.—Lord, my God! you the Creator, you, the Master; you who made Law and Liberty; you, the Sovereign who permits, you the Judge who forgives; you who are full of motives and of causes, and who perhaps put into my spirit the taste for horror so as to convert my heart, like the cure at the end of a blade; Lord, take pity, take pity upon the madmen and the madwomen! O Creator! can there exist monsters in the eyes of Him alone who knows why they exist, how they *have become monsters* and how they could *have not become* such?"

"Healing at the point of the knife." Baudelaire was never to believe it wholly, but it was a possibility which haunted him. Perhaps it weakened his resolution; certainly it was a cause of that paralysis of the will— the faculty by which he chiefly lived—which most afflicted him in his later days. The poignant notes in his Journal, "Immediate work, even if bad, is preferable to revery," his repeated references to "the sentiment of the abyss," give us an inkling of what he endured.

Baudelaire was a great poet of a decadence. In other words, he was a great modern poet; for the decadence which shaped him by compelling him to revolt against it was the "civilization of industrial progress" which has endured from his day to our own. Baudelaire confronted the reality like the hero he strove to be; he had the courage both of his attitude and his art, and the result of his unremitting exercise of will in transforming his keen emotions is a poetic achievement that makes a single and profound impression upon our minds. Baudelaire, true to the practice of the great poet, had crystallized his experience; he had accumulated a weight of conviction to endorse his emotions. "In certain, almost supernatural, moods of the soul, the profundity of life is revealed entire in the sight, however ordinary it may be, which lies under our eyes. It becomes its very symbol." We have tried to elucidate the quality which Baudelaire discerned in "the depth of life" and to disentangle some of the methods by which he sought to convey it to posterity. He was indeed the poet of rebellion; but the resolution of his defiance was subtly modulated by doubts and dreams which he would entertain and cherish for a while and then dismiss with an ironical contempt for his own unworthy weakness. Underneath his steely surface lay an infinity of sensitive responses. We could have deduced it; deep resentments are born only of deep wounds, and the solidity of permanent poetry is the work only of the most delicate fingers. But the finest artist seldom permits the precise quality of his personal response to appear. He makes his sacrifice to his own universality. It is for us to detect where most the man shows through the texture of his work; and we may decide that Baudelaire reveals himself nowhere more plainly than in these two last stanzas of "L'Irréparable":

> J'ai vu parfois au fond d'un théâtre banal
> > Qu'enflammait l'orchestre sonore,
> Une fée allumer dans un ciel infernal
> > Une miraculeuse aurore;
> J'ai vu parfois au fond d'un théâtre banal

> Un être, qui n'était que lumière, or et gaze,
> > Terrasser l'énorme Satan;
> Mais mon coeur, que jamais ne visite l'extase,
> > Est un théâtre où l'on attend
> Toujours, toujours en vain, L'Etre aux ailes de gaze.

> [I have sometimes seen, on the stage of a banal playhouse
> > All alit with the sonorous orchestra,
> A fairy, in an infernal sky, light
> > A miraculous dawn;
> I have sometimes seen, on the stage of a banal playhouse

> A being, all light, gold and gauze,
> > Vanquishing huge Satan;
> But my heart, never visited by ecstasy,
> > Is a theater where forever is awaited,
> Ever, ever in vain, the Being with wings of gauze.]

Apropos of Baudelaire

by Marcel Proust

MY DEAR RIVIÈRE,

I am unfortunately prevented by a serious disease from giving you a study, or even a mere article, on Baudelaire. Let me be content with a few remarks since I can do no more. I regret it all the more keenly as he is in my estimation, along with Alfred de Vigny, the greatest poet of the nineteenth century. By that I do not mean that, if the most beautiful poem of the last century had to be selected, it should be looked for in Baudelaire. I doubt that a poem equalling Hugo's "Booz endormi" could be found in *Les Fleurs du mal,* that sublime but sardonic book, in which piety sneers, in which debauchery makes the sign of the cross, in which Satan is entrusted with the task of teaching the most profound theology. A whole era of history and of geology unfolds there with an uninterrupted and unchecked amplitude, from

> La Terre encor mouillée et molle du déluge
>
> [The Earth still soft and moist from the flood]
> (Victor Hugo, "Booz endormi," *La Légende des siècles)*

down to Christ:

> Un roi chantait en bas, en haut mourait un Dieu.
>
> [Down below a king sang, above a God expired.]
> (Id., Ibid.)

That vast Biblical poem is in no way dryly historical; it is at all times vivified by the personality of Victor Hugo objectified in Booz.

"Apropos of Baudelaire." From *La Nouvelle Revue Française* (June, 1921). Translated by Lois A. Haegert. Copyright 1927 by Gallimard. Reprinted by permission. A letter to the critic Jacques Rivière, then director of *La Nouvelle Revue Française.*

When the poet writes that women gazed at Booz more than any young man, it is either in order to recall recent good fortunes he had enjoyed or to invite new ones. He is trying to convince women that, if they have any taste, they will love the old bard and not a youngster. All that is expressed in the freest and noblest syntax. Not to mention very famous lines on the eyes of the young man compared to those of the old man (the latter's naturally being preferred). What familiarity does Hugo display in that same stanza to bend logic to obey the laws of French verse!

> Le vieillard, qui, revient vers la source première,
> Entre aux jours éternels et sort des jours changeants.
>
> [The old man, returning toward the pristine spring,
> Enters upon eternal days out of the changeful ones.]
> (Id., Ibid.)

In prose a writer naturally would have begun with "sort des jours changeants." But he is not afraid of inserting at the end of the line, where they acquire nobleness, very trivial phrases:

> "Laissez tomber exprès des épis," disait-il.
>
> ["Drop some ears on purpose," would he say.]
> (Id., Ibid.)

All along, that grandiose historical poem is supported by personal impressions and lived moments. In such a personal impression experienced by the poet, and not in the Bible, lies no doubt the origin of the admirable lines:

> Quand on est jeune, on a des matins triomphants;
> Le jour sort de la nuit comme d'une victoire.
>
> [When one is young, mornings are triumphant;
> The day out of the night emerges as from a victory.]
> (Id., Ibid.)

The most indivisible thoughts are conveyed with the required degree of fusion:

> Voilà longtemps que celle avec qui j'ai dormi,
> O Seigneur! a quitté ma couche pour la vôtre,

Et nous sommes encor tout mêlés l'un à l'autre,
Elle à demi vivante, et moi mort à demi.

[Long ago already the one with whom I lay,
O Lord! has left my bed for yours,
And still we both are blended with each other,
She being half alive and I being half dead.]
(Id., Ibid.)

Even in the simplest lines the nobleness of the syntax never falters:

Booz ne savait pas qu'une femme était là,
Et Ruth ne savait pas ce que Dieu voulait d'elle.

[Booz was not aware of a woman being there,
And Ruth was not aware of God's designs for her.]
(Id., Ibid.)

And in the following lines, the poet's art to produce an impression of lightness, through the repetition of "l"s, is beyond compare:

Les souffles de la nuit flottaient sur Galgala.

[The breath of night was hovering on Galgala.]
(Id., Ibid.)

Alfred de Vigny did not proceed otherwise. In order to instill an intense life into that other Biblical episode, "La Colère de Samson," Vigny objectified himself into Samson, and it was because his jealousy had been aroused by Madame Dorval's friendship for certain women that he wrote:

La femme aura Gomorrhe et l'homme aura Sodome.

[Woman will have Gomorrah and man Sodom.]
(Vigny, "La Colère de Samson")

But Hugo's magnificent serenity which enables him to lead "Booz endormi" down to the pastoral image at the end,

Quel Dieu, quel moissonneur de l'éternel été,
Avait, en s'en allant négligemment jeté,
Cette faucille d'or dans le champ des étoiles,

[What God, what harvester of an eternal summer,
Had, on leaving, nonchalantly thrown
That golden scythe in the field of the stars,]
(Victor Hugo, "Booz endormi")

that serenity which majestically unrolls the poem does not equal the extraordinary tension in Vigny's. Likewise, in his calm poems, Vigny remains mysterious and we do not explore the source of his calm and of his ineffable beauty. Victor Hugo always magnificently does what is to be done. No image could be more precise than that of the crescent. The very lightest motions of the air, as was just noticed, are superbly rendered. But there again the manufacturing as it were, the manufacturing of the impalpable, is visible. Thus at the very moment when mystery should shroud everything, no impression of mystery is received. In contrast, could one say how mysterious lines such as these, taken at random in "La Maison du Berger," have been made:

Dans les balancements de ta tête penchée . . .
Et dans ton pur sourire amoureux et souffrant

[In the swinging of your leaning head . . .
And in your pure smile, loving and dolorous]
(Vigny, "La Maison du Berger")

or

Pleurant comme Diane au bord de ses fontaines,
Ton amour taciturne et toujours menacé

[Weeping, like Diana at the edge of her springs,
Her taciturn and ever threatened love]
(Id., Ibid.)

Many lines in Baudelaire's "Balcon" produce a similar impression of mystery. But that is not the most striking feature about him. Next to a volume like *Les Fleurs du mal,* Hugo's immense work appears vague, soft, devoid of accent. Hugo never ceased talking about death, but with the detachment of a greedy eater and of a man who passionately enjoys life. It may be, alas! that only he who contains approaching death in him, who like Baudelaire is threatened with aphasia, can reach the lucidity in true suffering, the religious strains which move us in the Satanic pieces:

Il faut que le gibier paye le vieux chasseur. . . .
Avez-vous donc pu croire, hypocrites surpris,
Qu'on se moque du maître et qu'avec lui l'on triche,
Et qu'il soit naturel de recevoir deux prix,
   D'aller au ciel et d'être riche.

[The old hunter must be repaid by the game caught. . . .
Could you ever believe, hypocrites now exposed,
That the master may be mocked and cheated,
And that two prizes may be naturally expected,
   To go to heaven and to be rich?
                          (Baudelaire, "L'Imprévu")

It is necessary perhaps to have endured the mortal weariness which precedes death, in order to write the delightful line on death which Victor Hugo never would have found:

Et qui refait le lit des gens pauvres et nus.

[And who does the beds of the poor and the naked.]
                          (Baudelaire, "La Mort des pauvres")

If he who wrote that line had not yet experienced the mortal craving that "his bed be redone," that verse must have been dictated to him by an anticipation of his unconscious, a prompting of fate. That is why I cannot quite endorse the opinion of Paul Valéry who, in an admirable passage in *Eupalinos,* opposing a bust deliberately chiselled by an artist to one unconsciously sculpted through the ages by the sea indenting a rock, has Socrates speak thus: "Enlightened and lucid acts," says Valéry under the mask of Socrates, "shorten the course of nature. And it may be said in all security that an artist is worth a thousand centuries, or a hundred thousand, or even more." But I would reply to Valéry: "Those harmonious and premeditating artists, if they represent a thousand centuries when compared to the blind work of nature, do not by themselves, like Voltaire for example, constitute an indefinite time relatively to some sick man, a Baudelaire, better still a Dostoevsky, who, in thirty years, between their epileptic and other fits, create something of which not a single paragraph could have been accomplished by a whole line of a thousand artists in fine health."

Socrates and Valéry interrupted me as I was quoting the lines on the poor. No one has written on the poor with more genuine tenderness than Baudelaire, that "dandy," did. The praise of wine might not be approved by the tenants of a good antialcoholic hygiene.

À ton fils je rendrai la force et la vigueur
Et serai pour ce frêle athlète de la vie
L'huile qui raffermit les membres du lutteur.

[To your son I shall restore strength and pink cheeks
And to the frail athlete of life I shall be
The oil to give new vigor to wrestlers' muscles.]
(Baudelaire, "L'Âme du vin")

The poet might retort that the wine is speaking there, not he. In any case, the poem is divine. How admirable the style is ("tombe et caveaux"). What human cordiality, what a sketch of the vineyard! The poet often recaptures that popular vein. The sublime lines on public concerts are well known:

ces concerts, riches de cuivre,
Dont les soldats parfois inondent nos jardins,
Et qui, par ces soirs d'or où l'on se sent révivre
Versent quelque héroïsme au coeur des citadins.

[Those concerts, rich in brass,
With which soldiers at times flood our parks,
And that, on those golden evenings which revive us,
Pour some heroism into the hearts of town dwellers.]
(Baudelaire, "Les Petites Vieilles")

It may seem impossible to go beyond that. Yet Baudelaire was able to heighten that impression still further; he endowed it with a mystical significance in the unexpected finale in which the strange bliss of the elect closes a sinister piece on the "Damnés":

Le son de la trompette est si délicieux,
Dans ces soirs solennels de célestes vendanges,
Qu'il s'infiltre comme une extase dans tous ceux
Dont elle chante les louanges.

[The sound of the trumpet holds such delights,
On those solemn evenings of celestial grape gathering,
That it invades like an ecstatic philter all those
Whose praises it celebrates.]
(Baudelaire, "L'Imprévu")

It may well be surmised that here, to the impressions of the Parisian loiterer that he was, was added the memory of the passionate admirer of Wagner. Even if the young musicians of today were right, which I refuse to believe, in negating Wagner's genius, such lines would prove that it hardly matters whether judgments offered by a writer on the works in another medium are objectively correct or not; the writer's admiration, even if unfounded, inspires him with useful reveries. I for one, who admire Wagner highly, well remember that, in my childhood, at the Lamoureux concerts, the enthusiasm which should be reserved for genuine masterpieces such as *Tristan* or *Die Meistersinger* was indiscriminately "aroused" by insipid pieces like the song to the star or Elizabeth's prayer in *Tannhäuser*. I may err in my musical taste. . . . But the college boys around me who endlessly and noisily applauded shouted their admiration like madmen or like politicians. No doubt as they came home, there sparkled before their eyes a starry night which the poor song could not have conjured up if, instead of being signed Wagner, then at the peak of his fame with the young, it had bore the unexciting name of Gounod. . . .

Baudelaire is incomparable in his relatively shorter poems, such as "La Pipe." Longer poems, even "Le Voyage," open splendidly:

> Pour l'enfant, amoureux de cartes et d'estampes
> L'univers est égal à son vaste appétit.
> Ah! que le monde est grand à la clarté des lampes!
> Aux yeux du souvenir que le monde est petit!
>
> [To the child, in love with maps and prints,
> The universe equals his vast appetite.
> Ah! how wide is the world by lamplight imagined!
> How small it is when seen with memory's eyes!]
>   (Baudelaire, "Le Voyage")

But then they seem to need the support of rhetoric. This one, like many another long poem by Baudelaire, such as "Andromaque, je pense à vous" ("Le Cygne"), almost falls flat. It ends with the line:

> Au fond de l'Inconnu pour trouver du nouveau,
>
> [Into the deep unknown to find something new,]
>   (Id., Ibid.)

and "Le Cygne" with:

> Aux captifs, aux vaincus, à bien d'autres encor.

> [To the captive, to the vanquished, to many others still.]
> (Baudelaire, "Le Cygne")

Such simple endings may well be calculated. Yet one senses that something has been cut short, the breath may have been short.

Still no poet more surely possessed the gift of renewing a poem in its very middle. At times it is by an abrupt change of tone as in the Satanic piece already quoted which begins "Harpagon qui veillait son père, agonisant" and ends with "Le son de la trompette est si délicieux. . . ." An even more striking example, admirably rendered by Gabriel Fauré in one of his melodies, is the poem opening

> Bientôt nous plongerons dans les froides ténèbres.

> [Soon we shall plunge into the cold darkness.]
> (Baudelaire, "Chant d'automne")

All of a sudden, with no transition, it continues on another tone with lines which, in the poem itself, are naturally sung:

> J'aime de vos longs yeux la lumière verdâtre.

> [I love the greenish light of your eyes.]
> (Id., Ibid.)

At other times the piece is interrupted by a precise action. At the very moment when Baudelaire exclaims: "My heart is a palace . . ." suddenly and without its being stated, he is overtaken with desire; the woman forces him to renewed enjoyment; the poet, at once intoxicated by the delights thus offered and thinking of the morrow's weariness, exclaims:

> Un parfum nage autour de votre gorge nue! . . .
> O Beauté, dur fléau des âmes, tu le peux!
> Avec tes yeux de feu, brillants comme des fêtes,
> Calcine ces lambeaux qu'ont épargnés les bêtes!

> [A fragrance swims around your bare throat! . . .
> O Beauty, harsh courage of souls, it is your will!
> With your fiery eyes, sparkling like beasts,
> Burn to ashes these shreds spared by wild beasts!]
> (Id., "Causerie")

There are to be sure a few long poems which, exceptionally, are to the very end controlled unfalteringly, such as "Les Petites Vieilles," dedicated, probably because of that achievement, to Victor Hugo. But that very beautiful poem leaves, like some others, an impression of cruelty which is painful. It is in principle possible to understand suffering and not be kind; but I doubt that Baudelaire meant purposely to be cruel when he blended irony with pity in his portrayal of those old women. He was anxious not to let his pity appear; it was enough for him to extract the "character" of such a sight, so that some stanzas emerge with an atrocious and wicked beauty:

> Ou dansent sans vouloir danser, pauvres sonnettes. . . .
> Je goûte à votre insu des plaisirs clandestins.
>
> [Or they dance without wanting to, poor doorbells. . . .
> I relish, without your knowing it, clandestine pleasures.]
> (Id., "Les Petites Vieilles")

My conjecture would mainly be that Baudelaire's line was so vigorous, so firm and beautiful that it lured the poet to overstep some bounds without realizing it. He wrote on those unfortunate little old women the firmest lines anywhere in French without thinking of softening his language so as not to lash those dying creatures any more than Beethoven, when composing his Symphony with choirs, understood that the notes he was writing were not always made for human throats, were not audible to human ears, and would always sound as if not sung right. The very strangeness which, to me, renders Beethoven's last quartets so enrapturing makes it impossible for certain persons to listen to them, unless they are transposed for piano; these persons are certainly not deaf to the divine mystery of these quartets, yet they set their teeth on edge. It is up to us to extract whatever sorrow inhabits those little old women,

> Débris d'humanité pour l'éternité mûrs.
>
> [O wrecks of humankind ripe for eternity.]
> (Id., Ibid.)

The poet, rather than express that sorrow, tortures us with it. He leaves us with a gallery of extraordinary caricatures of old women, comparable to Leonardo's caricatures, portraits of unequalled greatness and devoid of pity:

Celle-là, droite encor, fière et sentant la règle,
Humait avidement le chant vif et guerrier;
Son oeil parfois s'ouvrait comme l'oeil d'un vieil aigle;
Son front de marbre avait l'air fait pour le laurier!

[That one, still very straight, proud and like a ruler stiff,
Avidly sniffed the lively and warlike song;
Her eye at times opened like that of an aged eagle;
Her marble brow seemed made to be crowned by laurel.]

(Id., Ibid.)

That poem, "Les Petites Vielles," is among those in which Baudelaire shows his knowledge of antiquity. It is equally noticeable in "Le Voyage," in which the story of Electra is mentioned as it might have been by Racine in one of his prefaces. The difference is that, in seventeenth century prefaces, the authors resort to those allusions in order to answer a charge. We cannot help smiling when we are shown the whole of antiquity testifying, in the preface to Racine's *Phèdre,* that the author "composed no tragedy in which virtue was more conspicuously put forward than in that one; the slightest faults are severely punished. The thought of crime inspires as much horror as crime itself; the weaknesses of love are treated as true weaknesses; and vice everywhere is depicted in colors which cause its hideousness to be hated." Racine, that skillful pleader, regrets at once that he does not have Aristotle and Socrates as his judges, for they would recognize that his theater is a school in which virtue is no less well taught than in the philosophers' schools. It may be that Baudelaire is more sincere when, in the opening poem addressed to the reader, he addresses him as

Hypocrite lecteur, mon semblable,—mon frère!

[Hyprocrite reader, my fellow-being—my brother!]

(Id., "To the Reader")

To one who keeps in mind the difference between the two ages, nothing appears so Baudelairian as *Phèdre,* nothing is worthier of Racine or even of Malherbe than *Les Fleurs du mal.* Even the difference between the two ages and their styles did not keep Baudelaire from writing like the classical French writers:

Car c'est encor, seigneur, le meilleur témoignage
Que nous puissions donner de notre dignité . . .

[For it is still, O Lord, the best testimonial
Which we may give of our dignity. . . .]
(Id., "Les Phares")

O Seigneur, donnez-moi la force et le courage. . . .

[O Lord, bestow upon me the strength and the courage. . . .]
(Id., "Un Voyage à Cythère")

Ses bras vaincus jetés comme de vaines armes,
Tout servait, tout parait sa fragile beauté.

[Her defeated arms thrown like vain weapons,
Everything served and adorned her frail beauty.]
(Id., "Femmes damneés")

Those last lines, it is remembered, describe a woman whom another woman has just exhausted with her caresses. But would Racine resort to a different language if he portrayed Junie facing Nero? When Baudelaire is inspired by Horace, again in one of the poems which take place between two women, he does better than his model. Instead of "dimidium animae meae," which one is bound to imagine he must then have had in mind, he will write "mon tout et ma moitié." Incidentally, it must be admitted that when Victor Hugo wanted to quote from the ancients, he did so with the all-powerful freedom, the masterly imprint of genius: such is the case in the wonderful piece which ends with

Ni l'importunité des sinistres oiseaux

[Nor the importune and sinister birds]
(Victor Hugo)

almost literally "importunique volucres."
I am using very truthfully the phrase "Baudelaire's classicism," with scrupulous eagerness not to betray what the poet intended or prove overingenious. For I cannot help finding overingenious, and outside the Baudelairian truth, the contention of a friend of mine that

Sois sage, ô ma douleur, et tiens-toi plus tranquille.

[Be good, O my Sorrow, and hold yourself more still.]
(Baudelaire, "Recueillement")

is nothing but the

> Pleurez, pleurez, mes yeux, et fondez-vous en eau,
>
> [Weep, weep, O my eyes, and melt into water,]
> (Corneille, *Le Cid*)

from Corneille's *Le Cid*. The lines of the Infanta in the same play on the "respect de sa naissance" might appear to be a fitter parallel, although such parallels remain very exterior. The poet's hortatory address to his own sorrow has not much in common with a Cornelian apostrophe. Rather it is the restrained, quivering language of someone who shivers for having cried too much.

The feelings we just described—for suffering, death, and humble fraternity—rank Baudelaire as the man who wrote best on the humble people and on the beyond, if Victor Hugo is the poet who wrote most abundantly on them. Hugo's capitals, his dialogues with God, his thundering brass cannot match what poor Baudelaire found in the suffering intimacy of his body and of his heart. Baudelaire's inspiration owes nothing to Hugo. The one of the two poets who might have been the sculptor of a Gothic cathedral is not Hugo with his fake medievalism, but Baudelaire, the impure devout, the kneeling, grimacing accursèd casuist. Yet if their strains on death and on the poor are thus unequal and if the string of Baudelaire's lyre is more tense and vibrating, I should not submit that Baudelaire towers above Hugo in the delineation of love. To the lines in "Femmes damnées,"

> Et cette gratitude infinie et sublime
> Qui sort de la paupière ainsi qu'un long soupir,
>
> [And that infinite and sublime gratitude
> Which the eyelid heaves like a long sigh,]

I prefer Hugo's lines:

> Elle me regarda de ce regard suprême
> Qui reste à la beauté quand nous en triomphons.
>
> [She looked at me with that supreme gaze
> Which remains in beauty even while vanquished.]
> (Victor Hugo, "Elle était déchaussée," *Contemplations* I, xxi)

Love, besides, is very different in the two poets. Baudelaire's inspiration was in truth drawn from no other poet. His world cuts off strange sections in time, letting only a few notable days appear. That explains the frequent phrases such as "if some evening," and others. As to Baudelaire's furniture, let it serve as a lesson to our elegant ladies of the last twenty years, who would not consent in their "mansions" to the slightest lapse of taste. They strove hard to reach an imaginary purity of style; let them reflect that our poet could be the greatest and the most artistic of writers, yet painted only beds with folding curtains, halls similar to hothouses ("Une Martyre"), beds impregnated with light fragrance, couches as deep as tombs, shelves with flowers, lamps which burnt only for a while, so that only the embers in the fireplace threw any light. That Baudelairian world is fitfully visited and enchanted by a fragrant breath from afar, either through reminiscences (as in "La Chevelure") or directly, through those porticoes which often recur in Baudelaire, "ouverts sur des cieux inconnus" ("La Mort") or

> Que les soleils marins teignaient de mille feux.
>
> [Which ocean suns dyed with a thousand fires.]
> (Baudelaire, "La Vie antérieure")

I said that Baudelairian love differs widely from love according to Hugo. It has its peculiarities and, where it is not secretive, it appears to hold especially dear in woman—the hair, the feet, and the knees:

> O toison moutonnant jusque sur l'encolure. . . .
> Cheveux bleus, pavillons de ténèbres tendus.
>
> [O fleece down to the neck pressing its waves . . .
> Blue hair, tents out of darkness woven.]
> (Id., "La chevelure")

> Et tes pieds s'endormaient dans mes mains fraternelles. . . .
>
> [And your feet in my fraternal hands were lulled to sleep:]
> (Id., "Le Balcon")

> Et depuis tes pieds frais jusqu'à tes noires tresses
> [j'aurais] Déroulé le trésor des profondes caresses.
>
> [And from your cool feet up to your black tresses,
> [I would have] Unrolled the treasure of deep caresses.]
> (Id., "Une Nuit que j'étais.")

Of course between the feet and the hair, there is the whole of the body. Baudelaire must have cherished the knees, from his repeated allusions to them in his poetry:

Ah! laissez-moi, le front posé sur vos genoux. . . .

[Ah! Allow me, my forehead laid on your lap. . . .]
(Id., "Chant d'Automne")

Dit celle dont jadis nous baisions les genoux

[Says she whose knees we used to kiss]
(Id., "Le Voyage")

Still that manner of unrolling the treasure of deep caresses is rather special. And love according to Baudelaire must be touched upon, if we leave out what he chose not to say, what he occasionally and at the most hinted at. When *Les Fleurs du mal* appeared, Sainte-Beuve naïvely wrote that those poems, once gathered together, produced an altogether different impression. That impression which seems a favorable one to the critic of the *Lundis* was grandiose and terrifying for any one who, like men of my own age, had known the volume only in its expurgated edition. We well knew, of course, that Baudelaire had composed "Femmes damnées" and we had read those poems. Several other poets had thus had their own secret publication. Who has not read two volumes by Verlaine, as poor as "Femmes damnées" is beautiful, entitled *Hommes, Femmes*? Schoolboys pass on to each other works of sheer pornography which they believe to be by Alfred de Musset. I have never thought of finding out whether the attribution is in any way founded. Not so with "Femmes damnées." When we open a Baudelaire volume which reproduces the original edition faithfully, those who are not aware of it are amazed to see that the most licentious, the rawest of the pieces on Lesbian loves are to be read there; in his genial innocence, the great poet had granted as much importance to the piece on Delphine and Hippolyte in his volume as to "Le Voyage" itself. I would not go so far as to subscribe absolutely to the judgment which I heard Anatole France utter, that the long poem on "Femmes damnées" was the most beautiful that Baudelaire had written. There are sublime lines in it, but beside those, others are irritating such as

Laisse du vieux Platon se froncer l'oeil austère.

[Let old Plato's austere eye frown]
(Id., "Lesbos")

André Chénier said that after three thousand years Homer was still young. But how much younger Plato is! Baudelaire's line on him is that of an ignorant schoolboy, and all the more surprising as Baudelaire

had a philosophical turn of mind, and was fond of making a Platonic
distinction between form and the matter invested by form:

> Alors, ô ma beauté, dites à la vermine
>   Qui vous mangera de baisers
> Que j'ai gardé la forme et l'essence divine
>   De mes amours décomposés!

> [Then, O my beauty, whisper to the worms
>   Which with kisses will eat you,
> That I have retained the form and the divine essence
>   Of my decomposed loves!]
>   (Id., "Une Charogne")

Or else

> Réponds, cadavre impur . . .
> Ton époux court le monde et ta forme immortelle

> [Answer, impure corpse . . .
> Your husband runs free and your immortal shape. . . .]
>   (Id., "Une Martyre")

Unfortunately, as soon as the reader has had the time to drown his
rancor in the lines which follow, which rank among the finest ever
written, the poetical form adopted by Baudelaire will, after five more
lines, bring again

> Laisse du vieux Platon se froncer l'oeil austère.

The same five line stanza produces the loveliest effects in "Le Balcon":

> Les soirs illuminés par l'ardeur du charbon.

> [Evenings illuminated by the glowing embers.]
>   (Id., "Le Balcon")

To that line I even prefer these from "Les Bijoux":

> Et la lampe s'étant résignée à mourir,
> Comme le foyer seul illuminait la chambre,
> Chaque fois qu'il poussait un flamboyant soupir,
> Il inondait de sang cette peau couleur d'ambre.

[And the lamp having resigned itself to die,
As the fireplace alone illuminated the room,
Whenever it heaved a flamboyant sigh,
It flooded with blood that amber-colored skin.]
(Id., "Les Bijoux")

But in some of the poems which were condemned, the same repetition becomes useless and wearying. When the first line said already

Pour savoir si la mer est indulgente et bonne,

[In order to know if the sea is merciful and kind]
(Id., "Lesbos")

why again repeat in the fifth,

Pour savoir si la mer est indulgente et bonne?

It remains nevertheless true that those stately condemned poems, added to the others, produce a wholly different effect. They are restored to their position among the greatest in the book, like those crystal, haughty waves which majestically rise after the evenings of storm and which broaden the boundless vision of the sea with their alternating crests. One's emotion is still heightened when one learns that those poems were there, not just like any of the others, but that, to Baudelaire, they were the chief pieces in the book; so much so that he first intended to entitle the whole volume, not *Les Fleurs du mal*, but *Les Lesbiennes*. The title finally chosen, now inseparable from literary history, was not found by Baudelaire, but offered to him by his friend Babou. It is more apt. It extends to other themes than Lesbians but it does not exclude them, for they are essential to Baudelaire's aesthetic and moral conception of the flowers of evil.

How did Baudelaire come to take such a special interest in Lesbians that he wished to adopt that title for his splendid volume of verse? When Vigny, angry at woman, explained her by the mysteries of the breast nursing the infant,

Il rêvera toujours à la chaleur du sein,

[Forever he will dream of the warm bosom,]
(Vigny, "La Colère de Samson")

by the physiological peculiarity of woman,

La femme, enfant malade et douze fois impur,

[Woman, that sickly child and twelve times impure,]
(Id., Ibid.)

by her psychology also

Toujours ce compagnon dont le coeur n'est pas sûr,

[Always that companion whose heart is never sure.]
(Id., Ibid.)

it is understandable that, in his disappointed and jealous love, he should
have written:

La Femme aura Gomorrhe et l'Homme aura Sodome.

At least, he opposes them to each other as unreconcilable enemies:

Et se jetant de loin un regard irrité
Les deux sexes mourront chacun de leur côté.

[And casting from afar a mutual and wrathful glance,
The two sexes will die, apart from each other.]
(Id., Ibid.)

Not so in Baudelaire:

Car Lesbos entre tous m'a choisi sur la terre
Pour chanter le secret de ses vierges en fleurs
Et je fus dès l'enfance admis au noir mystère.

[For Lesbos of all men on this earth elected me
To sing the secret of its virgins in bloom
And from childhood on I was admitted to its dark mystery.]
(Baudelaire, "Lesbos")

That "liaison" between Sodom and Gomorrah which, in the parts of
my novel recently published, I have entrusted to a coarse individual,
Charles Morel (it is on such brutes that such a role usually devolves),
it seems that Baudelaire, in a strange privilege, assigned to himself. Why
did he thus assume it, how did the poet fill it? It would be fascinating

to know. What is understandable in my Charles Morel remains shrouded in the deepest mystery for the author of *Les Fleurs du mal*.

* * *

After those great poets (I have not had the time to talk on the role of ancient cities in Baudelaire and of the scarlet color which they put here and there in his work), it is no longer possible to quote real geniuses, until one comes to the Parnassians and the Symbolists, who will not be discussed here. Musset, in spite of all, is a poet of the second rank and his admirers are aware of it, for they are now allowing a part of his work to rest for several years, free as they remain to return to it when they tire of cultivating the other part. Tired with the declamatory character of the "Nuits," which are nevertheless the goal toward which he strove, they alternate with those ambitious compositions shorter and lighter poems:

> Plus ennuyeuse que Milan
> Où du moins, deux ou trois fois l'an, Cerrilo danse.

> [More tedious than Milan
> Where at least, twice or thrice a year, dances Cerrilo.]
> (Musset, "A mon frère revenant d'Italie")

But, a little further down in the same piece, one is disheartened by lines on Venice, where he left his heart. The temptation is then to try poems of merely documentary interest which describe for us the balls of the fashionable season in Musset's day. Such hodge-podge is not enough to rank Musset among the poets, despite the ludicrous enthusiasm with which Taine celebrated the music and the color of such lines. Amateurs of Musset then return to the "Nuits," to "L'Espoir en Dieu," and "Rolla," which by then have gained a new freshness. Delightful tales in verse like "Nanouna" alone retain their liveliness and blossom all the year round.

Lower still along the ladder must be relegated noble Sully-Prudhomme, whose profile and gaze were both divine and equine but who was not a very robust Pegasus. He has ravishing beginnings of elegies:

> Aux étoiles j'ai dit un soir
> Vous ne me semblez pas heureuses.

> [To the stars one night I said:
> You do not seem happy to me]
> (Sully-Prudhomme, "Les Solitudes")

Unfortunately the piece does not stop there: the two lines which follow
are ghastly and I do not recall them well:

> Vos lueurs dans l'infini noir
> Ont des tendresses douloureuses.
>
> [Your lights in the black infinite
> Have a sorrowful tenderness.]
> (Id. Ibid.)

Then at the end two lines full of charm. Elsewhere he confesses with
some grace:

> Je n'aime pas les maisons neuves.
> Elles on l'air indifférent.
>
> [I do not care for new houses;
> They look indifferent to me.]
> (Id., Ibid.)

Alas! at once, he adds something like:

> Les vieilles ont l'air de veuves
> Qui se souviennent en pleurant.
>
> [Old ones seem like widows
> Who weepingly remember.]
> (Id., Ibid.)

At times the concluding lines of "envoi" to the reader are worthy of
Musset, less alert but more thoughtful and more sensitive, truly pleas-
ing. But all that is very far from equalling the romantics and the great
Marceline Desbordes-Valmore. One poet alone continues, before the
Symbolist era, the tradition, sadly impaired, of the great masters: Leconte
de Lisle. He reacted usefully against a language which was growing lax.
Yet he differs less than we might think from what had preceded him.
Here are two lines, proposed as a game:

> La neige tombe en paix sur tes épaules nues
>
> [Snow on your bare shoulders peacefully falls]

> L'Aube au flanc noir des monts marche d'un pied vermeil.
>
> [Dawn on the black side of mountains walks with purple feet.]

The first, which we might take to be by Leconte de Lisle, is by Alfred de Musset in *La Coupe et les lèvres*. The second occurs in what is perhaps the most seductive poem by Leconte de Lisle, "La Fontaine aux lianes." Leconte de Lisle purified the French language, cleared it of foolish metaphors which he pitilessly hunted. Yet he himself resorted, felicitously, to "the wing of the wind." Elsewhere, it is "the amorous laughter of the wind," "the crystal dew drops," "the fire gown of the earth," "the cup of the sun," "the ashes of the sun," "the flight of illusion."

I have seen him listening with sarcasm in his eyes to the finest pieces of Musset; but he himself often is only a more rigid and equally declamatory Musset. The similarity is at times so hallucinating that I confess having trouble in remembering if

> Tu ne sommeillais pas, calme comme Ophélie,

> [You were not asleep there, calm like Ophelia]
> ("La Fontaine aux lianes")

(which I know for sure to be by Leconte de Lisle) is not by Musset, so close to a line of the latter it is. Leconte de Lisle had his own curious phrases and circumlocutions. To him, animals always were the Chief, the King, the Prince of something or other, just as Noon is the "King of Summers." He would not write "the lion," but "Here is thy hour, O King of Sennaar, O Chief"!; not "the tiger," but the "striped Lord"; not the black panther, but "the Queen of Java, the black huntress"; for "the jaguar," the "hunter with noble hair," for "the albatross," the "King of Space," for the shark, the "sinister roamer of the watery steppes." Let us stop here, or else all the snakes would have to be brought in. Later, in truth, Leconte de Lisle gave up the use of such epithets and, like Flaubert with whom he has much in common, did not want to let anything come between the object and the words. In "Le Lévrier de Magnus," he describes the hound with the same literalness and fidelity which Flaubert might have shown in his *Légende de Saint Julien l'Hospitalier:*

> L'arc vertébral tendu, noeuds par noeuds étagé,
> Il a posé sa tête aiguë entre ses pattes.

> [The vertebral arch tense, knot over knot stretching,
> It laid its sharp head between its legs.]
> (Id., "Le Lévrier de Magnus")

And much of it is just as good. Nevertheless, I would not have rated Leconte de Lisle as the last poet of some talent before the Parnassians and the Symbolists, if there were not in him a delightful and novel source of poetry, a feeling of freshness, probably brought over from the tropical lands where he grew up. . . . If, without resorting to any extraneous information, we allow a few lines of Leconte de Lisle to return spontaneously to our memories, we are struck by the role constantly played in them by the sun, and by suns in the plural. I do not mean only the ashes of the sun, which recur many times, but the "joyful suns of naïve years," the "barren suns which are now but shadows," "so many suns which never again will dawn." All those suns drag after them reminiscences of ancient theogonies. The horizon is always "divine." Ancient life is inexhaustibly made

> Du tourbillon sans fin des espérances vaines.
>
> [Of the endless whirlpool of vain appearances.]
>   (Id., "La Maya")

And those suns are doomed to nothingness:

> L'esprit qui les songea les entraîne au néant.
>
> [The mind which dreamt them carries them to nothingness.]
>   (Id., "L'Illusion suprême")

That subjective idealism palls on us; but it may be forgotten. The light then remains, and a freshness which delightfully offsets it. Baudelaire also was haunted by the same tropical nature. Even "behind the immense wall of fog," he imagined his mulatto woman conjuring up

> Les cocotiers absents de la superbe Afrique.
>
> [The absent cocoa nut palms of proud Africa.]
>   (Baudelaire, "Le Cygne")

But one would think that he only saw that nature from aboard ship. Leconte de Lisle had actually lived there, had caught and relished every hour of it. When he alludes to springs, it is easy to feel that his use of verbs like germinate, spring, filter, is in no way pure rhetoric; even the substantive gravel is not put there at random. He actually underwent the spell of the "Fontaine aux lianes," a secluded site all to himself,

Qui, dès le premier jour, n'a connu que peu d'hôtes.
Le bruit n'y monte pas de la mer sur les côtes,
Ni la rumeur de l'homme; on y peut oublier.

[Which, from earliest time, was seldom visited.
Rumblings do not reach there from the sea to the shores,
Nor does men's rumor; oblivion is allowed.]
(Leconte de Lisle, "La Bernica")

Ce sont des choeurs soudains, des chansons infinies.

[They are sudden choirs, infinite songs]
(Id., Ibid.)

The azure sky is so gentle there that a bird may dry his wings in it:

L'oiseau tout couvert d'étincelles
Montait sécher son aile;

[The bird all covered with sparks
Flew upward to dry its wing.]
(Id., Ibid.)

in one of the poems, he does so "in a warmer breeze," in the other "in the warm starry sky."

A peine une échappée étincelante et bleue
Laissait-elle entrevoir, en un pan du ciel pur,
Vers Rodrique ou Ceylan le vol des paille-en-queue
Comme un flocon de neige égaré dans l'azur.

[Hardly a sparkling and blue opening
Would let one catch a glimpse, on a pure sky,
Of the flight of birds toward Rodrique or Ceylon
Like a snowflake lost in azure.]
(Leconte de Lisle, "La Ravine Saint-Gilles")

Lovely, is it not, my dear Rivière? Even if these lines do not come up to those of Baudelaire, should we not recall them to the modern reader, who reads such poor verse? The French people lately have learned to appreciate the churches and all the architectural treasure of their land. That would be no excuse to allow to fall into oblivion those other buildings, equally rich in forms and in thought, which rise above the pages of a book.

MARCEL PROUST

Baudelaire

by Georges Poulet

I

At the origin there is original sin. Before memory, before childhood, before all ecstasy and all disgust, for Baudelaire there are "two simultaneous postulations, the one toward God, the other toward Satan." This contradiction is repeated in every man in every hour; it is found in him from the first moment of his existence, and is most clearly indicated in the first period of his life; for "the child, in general, is, compared to the man, in general, very much closer to original sin."

Thus, from the first moment, there are two opposite tendencies in the child: one which, carrying him toward the infinite reality of God, makes him feel at one and the same the infinite imperfection of sensible and actual reality; the other which, carrying him toward Satan, urges him to adhere to the actual, to lose himself in things, to elicit from them animal pleasure: "When a child, I felt in my heart two contradictory feelings: the horror of life and the ecstasy of life."

If the ecstasy of life is the ecstatic acceptance of the present moment, the horror of life is, on the contrary, the movement by which, in rejecting the present, the human being from his very origin begets a sort of future time. The creature simultaneously throws himself upon the present and rejects it. The present is a prey on which he gorges himself and a misery which fills him with horror.

In the child, however, these two opposite tendencies, which later will tear the adult apart in the suffering of a time that is tragic, are as yet hardly distinguished, by reason of the strength of his faculties and the swiftness of his reactions. In the instant in which things reveal their insufficiency, the child (like the savage) finds within himself the necessary resources to make up for it:

"Baudelaire," *Études sur le temps humain* by Georges Poulet. Translated by Elliott Coleman. Copyright 1956 by The Johns Hopkins Press. Reprinted by permission.

The savage and the baby bear witness, by their naïve aspiration for the bright and glittering, for many-colored feathers and glistening cloths, for the superlative majesty of artificial forms, bear witness to their disgust for the real, and in this way prove unknowingly the immateriality of their minds.

Here is a distaste for the real, which, however, is immediately transformed into a possessive motion. Hardly, in his distaste, has the child had the time to aspire toward color than he becomes drunk with it, absorbs it into his imagination, and forms of it a more sparkling reality, a more iridescent moment:

> The child sees everything *in its newness;* he is always *drunk.* Nothing resembles more what is called inspiration than the joy with which the child absorbs form and color. . . . It is to this profound and joyous curiosity that must be attributed the fixed and animally ecstatic eye of children before the *new,* whatever it be. . . .

Thus the ecstatic drunkenness of the child is that of a void which is filled up, of a poverty made rich and full. He does not have the time to perceive the imperfection or the materiality of the perceptible life, because he redeems it, reinvents and spiritualizes it, in the same instant and by the same movement that he perceives it. Out of a repugnant or horrible world, instantaneously, unknown to himself, in play, he makes a magic world, a plaything. Instinctively, even in and of evil, he finds and remakes a paradisaical state:

> Pourtant, sous la tutelle invisible d'un Ange,
> L'Enfant déshérité s'enivre de soleil
> Et dans tout ce qu'il boit et dans tout ce qu'il mange,
> Retrouve l'ambroisie et le nectar vermeil.
>
> [Yet, under the invisible tutelage of an Angel,
> The disinherited Child is made drunk with the sun,
> And in all that he drinks and in all that he eats
> Recovers the ambrosia and the rose-red nectar.]
> ("Bénédiction")

From that moment there is discovered the ambiguity hidden in our incessant nostalgia for childhood. It appears to us in memory as an authentically paradisaical state, a state in which, *naturally,* action was the sister of dream. We dream of it as Adam dreamed of the lost Eden: as a state of perfection which has been ours, and which we would have enjoyed *in time,* on the earth; a continuous state of ecstatic happiness, in which our aspirations have been satisfied and our nature completed, in which duration was constant, in which the same moment was continued, always new, always like unto itself, in the same wonder. The magic memory of childhood masks us and makes us forget original sin. We forget that there never was a time when we were neither fallen nor disinherited. We dream of regaining a state and a time in which, like the child, we would be *always drunk,* without thinking that with the child this drunkenness was only a momentary precarious victory, which it was unceasingly necessary to obtain anew, over the dread of things, over the failures and perversions of the creature, by the magic of the imagination.

II

There are moments of existence when time and extent are more profound and the feeling of existence immensely enlarged.

There are days when man awakens with a young and vigorous spirit. His eyelids hardly released from the sleep that sealed them, the external world offers itself to him set off in strong relief, with admirable clarity of contours and richness of colors. The moral world displays its vast perspectives, filled with new splendors. . . . Exceptional state of the mind and the senses, that I can without exaggeration call paradisaical, if I compare it to the thick gloom of common and daily existence. . . .

In these happy hours which are illumined by "the latent poetry of childhood," the mind regains its freshness, and the adult becomes *childman,* ". . . possessing in each moment the spirit of childhood, that is to say, a spirit for which no aspect of life is *blunted.*"

Thanks to the intensity of this perception that has become childlike once more, nature resumes its radiant aspect of former times. It again becomes spiritualized, even supernatural. All its secondary qualities, tonality, sonority, limpidity, vibrancy, take on a sharper and deeper import. The hyperacuity of the senses "gives all tints a resonance." Each sensation in the field of consciousness appears stronger, more alive, more distinct, as if a greater margin bordered it and detached it from other sensations. Each sensation illimitably follows its trajectory and seems by concentric waves to invade a stone one has thrown into it. On the other hand, all sensations seem multiplied: they become an infinite number, deployed and projected in musical space. The enormously enlarged horizon discloses an immensity throughout which there vibrates, fragrant and resonant, an iridescent spray, a substance inexhaustibly formed of vapor of water.

To this indefinite amplification of space there corresponds an indefinite deepening of time. It seems as if sensations could never cease to move the affected nerves, sensations interminably prolonging their particular note through all duration. Simultaneous or successive, they meet, they touch, they respond, they form of their harmonies and analogies temporal echoes which reverberate them in transposing them:

> Comme de longs échos qui de loin se confondent
> Dans une ténébreuse et profonde nuit,
> Vastes comme la nuit et comme la clarté,
> Les parfums, les couleurs et les sons se répondent

> [Like long echoes that mingle from afar
> In a dark and profound unity,
> Vast as the night and the brightness,
> The perfumes, the colors, and the sounds respond to each other.]

In this "state of poetic health" time appears under the form of a multiplication of ideas and images; but a multiplication in the interior of a framework, within its limits: a profusion of temporal riches in a cornucopia whose sides are indefinitely extendible. Certain intervals, in which we resume consciousness, allow us to measure them:

> This imagination lasts an eternity. An interval of lucidity with a great effort permits you to watch the clock. The eternity has lasted one minute. Another current of ideas carries you away; it will sweep you around one minute in its living whirlpool, and that minute will be another eternity. The proportions of time and of being are disturbed by the innumerable multitude and intensity of sensations and ideas. One lives several lives in the space of an hour.

But, to examine the matter more closely, if the temporal proportions are disturbed, it is, strangely enough, in two contrary fashions. Insofar as images multiply, they seem to multiply time with them, to accelerate its course, so much so that one thinks that he lives with a prodigious rapidity, that he lives several lifetimes in the space of an hour. But, on the other hand, at each moment one becomes conscious of the real time that elapses during that interval, it seems that time must have prolonged itself in order to contain so great a substance of duration, extended its limits and slackened its pace. Observed *in its depths,* what passes away seems to be disposed over an infinitely greater *space* of duration, seems to have lasted for almost an eternal minute, a *vast* minute. It is, at the extreme, the conception of an eternity that is confounded with immensity, of a temporal depth that is analogous or identical to the spatial depth: "Depth of space, allegory of the depth of time."

> Space is made deeper by opium; opium gives a magic tone to all colors, and makes all sounds vibrate with a more meaningful sonorousness. Sometimes magnificent vistas, filled with light and with colors, open out suddenly in these landscapes, and one watches appear *in the depth of their horizons* oriental cities and architectures, vaporized *by distance,* on which the sun throws showers of gold.

It is striking that in these paradisaical states (artificial or not, it makes no difference) objects at one and the same time appear very distinct and yet situated in the very depths of the horizon, in a far distance that idealizes them. It is the same with the images of the past which, awakened in their turn by the evocative magic of the images of the present, appear one after another, or all together, with the same clarity as they once did, the same charm, the same affective power, the same actuality; but situated, nevertheless, at the far depths of an immense temporal horizon, infinitely withdrawn to the end of an expanse of years that seem centuries old, and that are nevertheless effortlessly traversed by the powerful flight of memory.

To the magic of the present is thus added the magic of the past:

> Charme profond, magique, dont nous grise
> Dans le présent le passé restauré!

> [Deep, magical charm, with which we are made drunk
> In the present by the restored past.]

If in these moments of "poetic health" the one who lives them is a child-man, that is not only because he has mysteriously "regained the spirit of childhood"; it is not solely because he feels and imagines anew as a child does; it is also because, beyond the "deep years," he is reunited with the life of his own childhood, finds along its road all perceptible memories, all affective memories, and literally becomes once more the very child he had been:

> Many an old man, bent over a pot-house table, sees himself living again in a circle of people and places that have disappeared; he is drunk with his vanished youth.

It is not simply that the interval of years is abolished, nor even that the mind suppresses distances in order to reach such a point of its former existence. It seems rather that what happens here is an extraordinary intercommunication in the mind of all parts of lived time. As one's gaze freely moves over the whole spatial mass that is offered to it, so the spiritual gaze sees spread out all around it the vast regions of completed existence. The various epochs respond to each other, touch each other, adhere to each other, and prolong in each other their evocative echoes. Whereas in normal thought, the evocation of one epoch excludes the simultaneous evocation of another, and whereas it is impossible for it to contemplate its life except by a successive unfolding of images, in these paradisaical states in which the profundity of life appears, existence is seen, on the contrary, to be deployed over a duration that has become pure extent. In this new direction the joys or the sorrows of different periods do not exclude each other any more; within it, upon the same plane, are found adult and child, voyager and poet, memory and sensation. As in a landscape painting all the forms of nature, the farthest off and the nearest, the richest and the dullest, are found reclothed in an identical charm, which is that of the whole picture, so all the years of existence, different as they may be, distinct as may be their peculiar tints, are not thereby found to benefit any the less from the same "general color," from a harmony that is formed on the one hand by the infinite network of affinities from epoch to epoch and, on the other hand, by the emotive hue, by the "personal accent," which, ineluctably, whatever the special nuances of the moments of his life, the same human being indistinguishably gives to all moments.

Thus ecstatic time, by reason of its spatial nature, preserves no trace of what is characteristic of ordinary duration. It is a time-painting that differs from a pictorial painting by the sole virtue of its being projected upon a space that is extended *backward,* a space previously traversed. But this last comparison is really not exact, for if it is fair to say that existence appears as already *traversed,* it nevertheless also appears as being always *traversible;* an open space in which it is always permitted to roam, to feel, and to live; a space which seems the very continuation of the present *backward;* a retrospective expanse which is what the future would be for us if we were able, in the full force of the term, to *foresee* it, *fore-feel* it, before engaging in it.

Thus, there is no longer a question of an irreversible time. One does not feel cut off from his past any more than one feels cut off from space by the consciousness of the point where one is. There is no longer that vertical or transcendent dimension which the law of irreversibility introduces between each lived instant. In this state one is on equal footing with his whole life. There is no longer a contradiction between all the points of nature, between nature and ourselves. For the whole length of its course, and whatever the thoughts that succeed each other, time is always of the same tonality, at once general and individual: the time of youth; the time of paradise.

Lengthening of hours by the multiplication of sensations, by the reverberation of memories, by the discovery of the depth of existence; unification of moments, hours, and epochs by the profound experience of the harmony that exists between all the states of the *self*. At its farthest limit there is no longer either past or present, "nor hours, nor minutes, nor seconds." The *self* mingles sensations and memories in the same unity of feeling. The infinity of sensations, in manifold reflected brilliancy of detail, lengthens, spreads out, abates, and finally puts a stop to duration. The idea of time disappears:

> . . . the hours, slowed down, contain more thoughts . . . the clocks are striking happiness with a deeper and more meaningful solemnity . . .

> . . . in the depths of her adorable eyes I always see the hour distinctly, always the same, a vast, solemn hour, great *like space*, without divisions of minutes or of seconds—an immobile hour which is not marked by the clocks, and yet light as a sigh, swift as a glance.

III

No! There are no more minutes, there are no more seconds! Time has disappeared; it is Eternity that reigns, an eternity of delights!

But a terrible, heavy knock sounded at the door, and, as in hellish dreams, it seemed to me that I received the blow of a pickaxe in the stomach.

And then a Specter entered. . . . Time reappeared; Time reigns supreme now, and along with the hideous old man has come back his whole demoniacal train of Memories, Regrets, Spasms, Fears, Agonies, Nightmares, Rages, and Neuroses.

There is nothing more sudden than the fall of time. And nothing more tragic. For the time that then appears to the awakened ecstatic is a time turned upside down, a time out of joint, in which all the characteristics of paradisaical time are found once more, but the wrong way around, reversed and as if monstrously perverted by the fall into matter and into evil; a time of dream still, but of a dream that has become a nightmare. The temporal universe in which the dreamer finds himself is no less magic than that from which he has slipped, but of a demoniacal magic whose domain lodges below the normality of things, as the domain of the supernatural dwells above.

If, therefore, the paradisaical duration finds its exact analogy in spatial extent, the internal time finds its correspondence in the absence of space, in the void. Its symbol is the abyss. And as the time of ecstasy is achieved in eternity, so inverted time finds its end in death. Death and the abyss enclose all things and all thoughts:

> Morally and physically, I have always had the sensation of the abyss, not only of the abyss of sleep, but of the abyss of action, of dream, of memory, of desire, of regret, of remorse, of the beautiful, of number, etc.

In place of a plurality which was founded upon a unity and a harmony, there is nothing more now than a chaos of numbers. Isolated, separated, hideously contrasting forms repeat indefinitely the grotesque echo of the original duality. Each moment reaffirms in its turn the infinite difference between the two natures in man. Every instant attests the infinite difference between the actual and the eternal. Instead of a time immanent in the divine, we have now a time that is entirely covered over, as with a lid, by the inexorable transcendence of eternity:

> Styx bourbeux et plombé
> Où nul oeil du Ciel ne pénètre;
>
> [. . . Styx miry and laden
> Where no look from Heaven penetrates.]

But also at the same time each minute isolatedly becomes of mortal importance. No longer supported by anything, nor linked to anything, it finds itself possessing no other existence than its own. Reduced to itself, it has no meaning or value except the ultimate and definitive meaning and value which the judgment of the infinite transcendence forever confers upon it, and in the very moment. Thus, if the seconds are now "strongly and solemnly accentuated," it is because each becomes infinitely significant. Each instant, well or badly lived, continues to have been well or badly lived forever.

A new, anguished thought is thereby insinuated into tragic time. At the very instant when the instant *is,* it becomes detached, it falls, and in its fall a second existence begins, an existence in which instants do not cease—never cease—*to have been.* In this enormous lengthening of their spectral duration, they seem to extend eccentric circles into the gulf of the future, just as in paradisaical time each moment of beauty filled up with its growing undulations an extent of harmony:

> Who can think, without shuddering, of the infinite enlarging of circles in the spiritual waves set in motion by a chance stone?

Then appears the thought of the irreparable:

> . . . If in this belief there is something infinitely consoling, in the case where our mind is turned toward that part of ourselves which we can consider with complacence, is there not also something infinitely terrible, in the future case, inevitable, when our mind shall turn toward that part of ourselves which we can confront only with horror? In the spiritual no less than in the material world, nothing is lost. In the same way that any action cast into the vortex of universal action is in itself irrevocable and irreparable . . . in the same way any thought is ineffaceable:

> L'Irréparable ronge avec sa dent maudite
> Notre âme, piteux monument,

> [The Irreparable gnaws with his cursed fang
> On our mind, pitiable monument. . . .]

The irreparability of things is the indestructibility of the past. The Baudelairean remorse is nothing other than the consciousness of the irremediable character, given, once and for all, to a past that will never cease to be the past that has been lived. Whatever the future life may be, nothing it seems, will be able to wash away these stains. We are far away now from the tranquil possession, in the present, of a past perceived in the depths of memory like the natural prolongation, backward, of a magic present. Here is a past which, without ever ceasing to be present in the mind, also will never again cease to be separated from each moment in which it is present, by the irremediable and vertical incision of the law of irreversibility. In the time of evil and of remorse, of sin and of sorrow, the irreversibility appears under its most implacable form. There is an absolute discontinuity between our present self and all the rest of our life. The latter appears to us a contradictory thing; that which is ours and that which is not ours; the only thing that might be authentically ourself, the only thing that our self can neither relive nor efface.

We are now only the witnesses of ourselves. We recognize ourselves in our own memory, but it is with a most secret horror, with disgust.

Like Coleridge's Mariner, we carry a cadaver around our neck: it is our past. Our punishment is that of enduring ourselves. It is the punishment of the damned:

> Ah! Seigneur! donnez-moi la force et le courage
> De contempler mon coeur et mon corps sans dégout!

[O Lord, give me the strength and the courage
To contemplate my heart and my body without disgust.]

Meanwhile infernal time follows in us and about us a course which appears both the slowest and the most rapid. Taken between these extremities, at each moment when we perceive its flow, it seems to have passed away at a stroke, to have been hurled into nothingness. We feel it race on and carry us toward the tomb. We feel ourselves gnawed and eaten by it. We multiply our deaths; we live our own decomposition. But, on the other hand, irreversible time seems to become impoverished, to grow sterile, to rarefy. Its slowness becomes an intolerable oppression: a laborious succession of ideas more and more rare, more and more monotonous, which is finally leveled down and unified by the hateful hand of boredom.

Rien n'égale en longueur les boiteuses journées,
Quand sous les lourds flocons des neigeuses années,
L'ennui, fruit de la morne incuriosité,
Prend les proportions de l'immortalité.

[Nothing equals in length the limping days,
When under the heavy flakes of snowy years
Boredom, fruit of dull incuriousness,
Assumes the proportions of immortality.]

It is as if, in and out of the mind, everything universally tended to be immobilized, or petrified:

Désormais tu n'es plus, ô matière vivante!
Qu'un granit entouré d'une vague d'épouvante,
Assoupi dans le fond d'un Sahara brumeux!

[Henceforth you are no more, O living matter!
Than a granite encompassed by a vague affright,
Made drowsy in the depths of a misty Sahara.]

The Piranesian image of a staircase of infinite spirals which a damned person eternally descends into darkness, or that finally of a vessel caught in an ice field and frozen forever to the same spot, such are the emblems of the eternity in reverse into which infernal time issues; hideous travesty of the eternity in which flowed effortlessly and radiantly the happy hours of paradisaical time:

> Descendez, descendez, lamentables victimes,
> Descendez le chemin de l'enfer éternel; . . .
>
> [Descend, descend, lamentable victims,
> Descend the path to eternal hell. . . .]

IV

One must always be drunk. That says it all. There is no other point. In order not to feel the terrible burden of Time that bruises your shoulders and bends you to the ground, you must get drunk incessantly.

"Slaves martyred by time," men with glittering eyes, with hearts divided between the "horror of boredom and the *immortal desire to feel alive,*" contrive to escape from their human condition and to "possess themselves immediately, on this very earth, a Paradise that had been revealed to them":

> Those unfortunates who have neither fasted nor prayed, and who have refused redemption by work, demand of black magic the means of lifting themselves at one stroke to supernatural existence.

Wine, opium, hashish compose their dark paradise of artificial ecstasies:

> There one breathes a somber beatitude analogous to that which the lotus eaters must have experienced when, disembarking upon an enchanted island, lighted by the gleamings of an eternal afternoon, they felt born within them, to the drowsy sounds of melodious waterfalls, the desire never to see again their household gods, their wives, their children, and never again to climb the high sea billows.

Thus the immortal desire to feel oneself alive is transformed into the mortal desire of nevermore having to will or to do. In claiming to "subdue their will to the fugitive demon of happy minutes," men arrive only at subjecting their will to the obstinate demon of unhappy minutes. In vain they tell themselves: "What does the eternity of damnation matter to him who has found within one second the infinity of delight?" The abdication of the will which the instantaneous infinity of their joy involves finally delivers them up defenseless, "incapable of labor or energetic action," to all the tortures the demon of time inflicts upon them:

It is not to be forgotten that drunkenness is the negation of time, like every violent state of mind, and that consequently the results of the loss of time must unfold before the eyes of the drunkard, without destroying in him the habit of putting off his conversion till tomorrow, up to the point of the complete perversion of all feelings, and final catastrophe.

From then on, the drama of time becomes the drama of the will: of a will still powerful enough to desire, regret, and to feel fear, horror, or shame, but never strong enough to will; strong enough to transform the present moment into deficiency and suffering, but never strong enough to determine the present or decide the future.

Hence the desperate desire of escaping, if not from time, at least from the consciousness of time; the desire to have no more desires. To be able to stifle, deep within oneself, that last vestige of will by which one distinguishes himself from his own destiny, and by which he recognizes in himself the presence of misery. It is the temptation of sleep, the longing of the vanquished for all the brute resignations:

> Je jalouse le sort des plus vils animaux
> Qui peuvent se plonger dans un sommeil stupide,
> Tant l'écheveau du temps lentement se dévide!

> [I envy the lot of the vilest animals
> Who can plunge themselves into stupid sleep,
> So slowly the skein of time winds off.]

> Résigne-toi, mon coeur; dors ton sommeil de brute.

> [Resign thyself, my heart; sleep thy sleep of the brute.]

To know nothing, to teach nothing, to will nothing, to sleep, and still to sleep, that today is my only vow. An infamous and disgusting vow, but sincere.

The immortal desire to feel alive ends in the desire not to feel alive, in the *wish for nothingness,* for continuous night: a fall into the void, a total abandon to the time-abyss:

> Avalanche, veux-tu m'emporter dans ta chute?

> [Avalanche, wilt thou carry me down in thy fall?]

V

As long as I have not *the proof* that, in the real battle, that of time, I shall be beaten, I will not agree to say that I have made a failure of my life. . . .
   All is reparable. There is still time. Who knows even if perhaps certain new pleasures. . . .

In spite of himself the human creature continues to hope. For him there can never be absolute nothingness, nor total despair. There is never a postulation toward Satan without there being a simultaneous postulation toward God. To the feeling of the irreparable there is contradictorily joined the feeling that *all is reparable.* With the conception of a time that imposes a fate upon us, there is mingled the conception of a time that proposes to us a task:

   We are crushed each minute by the idea and the sensation of time. There are only two ways to escape this nightmare, to forget it: pleasure and labor. Pleasure consumes us. Labor strengthens us. Let us choose.

Let us choose. There is still time—time to perform one's task. And the task to perform is first of all this: to learn to will; to come to have, or to come once more to have, a will. But in order to will once more, it is necessary to be a double person: the one who wills; and the one who wills to be. Such is the stoic hero, such is the Cornelian hero. Baudelaire conceives a religion that would have for a God the type of man one would wish to be, and for worship the worship of himself, the constancy and concentration of the effort by which one is maintained at the height of what one wishes to be. The dandy must be "sublime without interruption." Thus there would be formed a purely volitional time, made of continuous effort.
   But in so deifying his own self, the dandy, or the Stoic, does not neglect any less than does the Epicurean, or the drunkard, the ineluctable reality of original sin. The ideal he gives himself is not a true transcendence. The human frailty he ignores is the authentic misery of sin and evil. The drunkard gives himself the illusion of an *artificial eternity;* the dandy gives himself the illusion of an *artificial duration.* The former in pretending to halt time, and the latter in pretending to impose upon time a forced continuity, take account, neither the one nor the other, of the true temporal conditions of existence. They forget that time is a contradiction.
   There remains, then, to make use of time, such as it is. There remains to utilize the small bit of will that one has, to try to conduct one's

daily business well. There remains to avail oneself of all his experiences, of all his miseries, but also of all his greatnesses, in order to give himself the courage to live and act from day to day. Like the music of Wagner, every true work of art, every action by which man has been able to obtain a provisory but notable victory over the forces of dissolution and dispersion, admits of a series of elements or stages, discernible to analysis, which constitute a *suggestive* method and a *mnemo-technic.* These elements are: *will; desire; concentration; nervous intensity; explosion.* These terms are not synonymous. They express a spiritual progress, a determined end. When assiduous exercise of the will in prayer, in conduct, in labor, brings to birth or revives a *desire* which is no longer instantaneously vaporized in dreams, but which is concentrated upon a transcendent object; when thus, instead of "throwing one's personality to the four winds," one gathers his actual resources about a "fixed idea" that is magically evocative, then there is rediscovered in the being and in the mind something of the genius of childhood, a *"nervous intensity"* which, in an *explosion*—analogous but not identical to the paradisaical ecstasy—permits the attainment if not of happiness at least of beauty: "Art is a mnemo-technic of the beautiful."

But beauty is not happiness. Following the approximative definition of Stendhal, it is only the promise. It is the acute experience of a reality *promised* but not yet *given.* It is at once what separates and what joins present and future: the present in which we are not happy; and the future in which we shall be. Beauty is the knowledge of what would be necessary and what we lack to give the moment its fullness. It is the consciousness of eternity which the moment is not:

> The beautiful is always, inevitably, of a double composition, although the impression it produces is one. . . . The beautiful is made of an eternal, invariable element . . . and of a relative, circumstantial element. . . . The duality of art is one fatal consequence of the duality of man.

From the double and contradictory character of human nature there emerges in the thought of Baudelaire the conception of a beauty which itself also has a double nature and a double visage: a permanent nature and a transitory nature; a face of grandeur and a face of misery. And, by the same token, there is discovered the possibility of living in a time which is neither the eternal time of the paradisaical states nor the miserable time of the infernal states; but a double time which, amid misery, contains the promise of happiness, which makes beauty rise up out of ugliness; a time which is simultaneously *lacking eternity* and *tending toward eternity.*

Human beauty, therefore, is not an abstract ideal. It is the reality of a concrete, matter-of-fact experience, of a *terrestrial* experience, by which thought makes to appear in things and in itself the double, transcendent relationship of the temporal to the nontemporal.

VI

But, first, what are things? "Incoherent pile of materials that the artist is called upon to put in order," "suggestive mass scattered about in space," things exist in nature only with a literally *insignificant* existence —like the words in a dictionary. They are, but they express nothing. They are scattered about in space, but they do not constitute a space. They succeed each other in duration, but they do not form a duration. Perceived by the senses, they are heaped up in the memory and form again there another pile of debris.

The imagination makes itself master of this meaningless pile of things. It detaches and reunites, discomposes and recomposes, "creates a new world, produces the sensation of newness." But this newness is not just another incoherence. This new world is a *significant* world. Colors and shapes, sound and odors have become signs. They have taken on a moral sense. They express the *human*.

In this new kind of evocative sorcery, Baudelaire no longer attempts to attain directly, by a sort of black magic, to a superhuman order which, beyond good and evil, would dispose its eternal enchantments. The problem he sets about is both incomparably simpler and incomparably more difficult: simpler because it is a question of expressing, by *natural* symbols, a *human* reality, and infinitely more difficult because this human reality is that of a being whose true significance consists in not being what he would be, and in straining to be what he is not.

From that moment the evocative magic becomes entirely different. It no longer expresses *states* of mind; it indicates and effects metamorphoses. It lays hold of the mind "in the number, the undulant, the motion, the fugitive and infinite." Far from attaining a moment where all the richness of times and spaces simultaneously develop their harmonies, it discovers or follows, in the depths of the years, a moment always different and always similar, which, conscious of its poverty, avid for the riches it lacks, constantly searches, outside and beyond what is, for what is not. There is no longer a question of embracing duration, but of pursuing in its totality the thrill that pervades and animates it, and never leaves off:

La mer est ton miroir; tu contemples ton âme
Dans le déroulement infini de sa lame.

[The sea is thy mirror; thou surveyest thy mind
In the infinite unrolling of its wave.]

In the infinite unrolling of existence, nothing is distinguished except the provisory. Just as the discovery of Copernicus changed the aspect of the cosmic universe, so the final thought of Baudelaire reversed the aspect of the interior world. The latter becomes a world without fixed relationships: a world essentially transitory; a world of contingencies in which the creature watches himself pass from the grotesque to the sublime, from ecstasy to debauchery, from fatigue to drunkenness, from corruption to salvation. All his faces and all his fates, all his actions and all his emotions, all his *selves,* contemporary or remote, present themselves to him in order to establish interrelationships that are always ceaselessly changing. Under the urging of memory and under that of the present, exchanges are made between present and past:

Par toi je change l'or en fer
Et le paradis en enfer;

[By thee is gold changed into iron
And heaven into hell;]

also by thee ecstasy is changed into disgust, despair into hope, contrition into expiation. Time becomes reversible, the past redeemable:

Affected by these pleasures that resembled memories, touched by the thought of a past unfulfilled, so many faults, so many quarrels, so many things reciprocally to be hidden, he started to weep; and in the darkness his hot tears fell upon the naked shoulder of his dear and always alluring mistress. She shuddered, she herself also felt touched and moved. . . . These two fallen beings, but still suffering from what remained to them of nobility, spontaneously clasped themselves in each other's arms, mingling in the rain of their tears and their kisses, the sorrows of their past with their very uncertain hopes of the future . . . pleasure saturated with grief and remorse.

Through the darkness of the night he had gazed behind him into the depths of the years, then he had thrown himself into the arms of his guilty lover, to find there the pardon that he accorded her.

In such a conception of the activities of the mind, it is no longer a question of *possessing* one's existence. Existence is not possessed. It is no longer a question of seeing in it an ensemble of relationships out of which "the fatality of temperament necessarily makes a harmony," since the fatality of temperament can—even back through the depths of the past—be transfigured and redeemed. Over the whole course of existence, any moment, at any moment, can be "saved."

In this faith, grief loses its sharpness, evil its irreparability, death its sting:

> My humiliations have been graces from God.

Thus Baudelairean thought comes to express simply the grievous consciousness of the human condition. At this point the depth of existence ceases to be an individual depth. It is no longer simply in the temporal spaces of its own life that the soul hears the echo of its plaints and it joys resound:

> It is a cry repeated by a thousand sentinels,

sentinels who, since the beginning of time, have exchanged the same cry with each other, a cry that is no longer that of a particular human being, but of a general being in whom human anguish resounds. And as a consequence the immense reverberatory field of duration appears in its veritable unity, joining to all the past ages through which the same sob has rolled, the prospective depth of the whole distance it leaps over in order to bring each age and each instant to the very borders of the eternal:

> Car c'est vraiment, Seigneur, le meilleur témoignage
> Que nous puissions donner de notre dignité
> Que cet ardent sanglot qui roule d'âge en âge
> Et vient mourir au bord de votre éternité!
>
> [For it is truly, O Lord, the best witness
> That we could give of our dignity,
> This burning cry that rolls from age to age
> And comes to die at the edge of your eternity!]

The Aesthetic Dignity

of the *Fleurs du mal*

by Erich Auerbach

Spleen

Quand le ciel bas et lourd pèse comme un cuvercle
Sur l'esprit gémissant en proie aux longs ennuis,
Et que de l'horizon embrassant tout le cercle
Il nous verse un jour noir plus triste que les nuits;

Quand la terre est changée en un cachot humide,
Où l'Espérance, comme une chauve-souris,
S'en va battant les murs de son aile timide
Et se cognant la tête à des plafonds pourris;

Quand la pluie étalant ses immenses traînées
D'une vaste prison imite les barreaux,
Et qu'un peuple muet d'infâmes araignées
Vient tendres ses filets au fond de nos cerveaux,

Des cloches tout à coup sautent avec furie
Et lancent vers le ciel un affreux hurlement,
Ainsi que des esprits errants et sans patrie
Qui se mettent à geindre opiniâtrement.

—Et de longs corbillards, sans tambour ni musique,
Défilent lentement dans mon âme; l'Espoir,
Vaincu, pleure, et l'Angoisse atroce, despotique,
Sur mon crâne incliné plante son drapeau noir.

[When the low, heavy sky weighs like a lid
On a spirit moaning beneath endless troubles
And, blocking off the whole horizon,
Decants a day more dismal than night;

When the earth is changed into a damp dungeon
Where Hope like a timid bat
Flaps her wings against the walls
And dashes her head against the moldy ceiling;

When the long lines of rain
Are like the bars of a vast prison
And a silent swarm of loathsome spiders
Spin their nets at the bottom of my brain,

Suddenly the bells leap out in a fury
And fling a hideous howling at the heavens,
Like homeless wandering spirits
Whimpering disconsolately.

And a long line of hearses without drums or music,
Files slowly through my soul; Hope vanquished weeps
And vile despotic Dread
Plants her black flag over my bowed skull.]

This poem is all of one movement. Actually, despite the period after the fourth stanza, it seems to consist of a single sentence; made up of three temporal dependent clauses, each taking up a whole stanza, each beginning with *quand,* and of a main clause with several subdivisions, which unfolds in the last two stanzas. The alexandrine meter makes it clear that this is a serious poem, to be spoken slowly and gravely; it contains allegorical figures written in capital letters, *Espérance, Espoir, Angoisse;* and we also find epithets and other rhetorical figures in the classical style ("de son aile timide"). The syntactical unity, the grave rhythm, and the rhetorical figures combine to lend the poem an atmosphere of somber sublimity, which is perfectly consonant with the deep despair it expresses.

The temporal clauses, describing a rainy day with low, heavy hanging clouds, are replete with metaphors: the sky like a heavy lid closing off the horizon, leaving us without prospect in the darkness; the earth like a damp dungeon; Hope like a fluttering bat caught in the moldering masonry; the threads of rain like the bars of a prison; and inside us a mute swarm of loathsome spiders, spinning their nets. All these figures symbolize dull, deepening despair. And there is an insistence about them which, if you submit to their spell, seems to exclude any possibility of a happier life. The *quand* loses its temporal meaning and rings out like a threat; we begin with the poet to doubt whether a sunny day will ever dawn again; for Hope, the poor bat, is also imprisoned and has lost touch with the world beyond the clouds—is there any such world? Even a reader unfamiliar with Baudelaire's other poems, who does not know how often he evokes the barred horizon, the damp and moldering dungeon of hell, who does not know how little use the sun is to him when it does happen to be shining, will grasp the irrevocable hopelessness of the situation from these three stanzas alone. Hopeless horror has its traditional place in literature; it is a special form of the sublime; we find it, for example, in some of the tragic poets and historians of antiquity, and of course we find it in Dante; it can lay claim to the highest dignity.

But in the first stanzas we already find things that seem hardly compatible with the dignity of the sublime. A modern reader barely notices them, he has long been accustomed to this style, established by Baudelaire, in which many poets, each in his own way, have subsequently made themselves at home. But Baudelaire's contemporaries, even those who had grown used to the daring of the romantics, must have been startled if not horrified. In the very first line the sky is compared to a lid, the lid of a pot or perhaps of a coffin—the former is more likely, for in another poem, "Le Couvercle," Baudelaire writes:

> Le Ciel! couvercle noir de la grande marmite
> Où bout l'imperceptible et vast Humanité.

> [The sky! black lid of the great kettle
> Where humanity simmers, vast and imperceptible.]

To be sure, Victor Hugo had proclaimed years before that the difference between noble and common words was done away with, but he had not gone so far, and much less had Alfred de Vigny, who of all the romantics was perhaps the most given to the tone of sublime horror. Of course damp moldering dungeons, bats, and spiders are perfectly in keeping with the romantic style, but only as properties in historical novels and plays, not in the sharp immediate present, not right beside or even inside the poet, and yet symbols for all that. The last word is *cerveaux,* a medical term. Clearly no realistic imitation is intended; on the contrary, the image of spiders in the brain is unrealistic and symbolic; but that makes it all the more degrading, for with spiders in his brain the suffering, despairing poet is denied the inward dignity conferred by such words as *âme* or *pensée.*

The three stanzas introduced by *quand* present a heavy silence. The fourth, which begins the main clause, brings in a sudden clamor: furious bells leap out and fling a hideous howling at the sky. Bells that leap furiously and howl at the sky! Anything more violent and outrageous is scarcely imaginable; such a combination offends against every traditional notion of the dignity of the sublime. True, *hurler* had been employed by the romantics in an orgiastic sense;[1] it seems to have been fashionable with certain literary circles in the Forties; but combinations of this sort occur nowhere else. Church bells that howl and leap with fury: seventy years later such an image would have been termed surrealistic. And, it must be remembered, we are not on the style-level of satire, where one might speak lightly of "clattering bells," but in an atmosphere of profound seriousness and bitter torment, and therefore on the style-level of the tragic and sublime. In the next lines the bells proceed to emit sounds that might be characterized as a persistent blubbering whimper; *geindre* is a childish blubbering, furious, meaningless, and ignored; no one hears the homeless spirits. And while this absurd hubbub is still raging, the last stanza begins. Once again there seems to be utter silence, the procession of hearses, "sans tambour ni musique," draws slowly through the poet's soul—this time it is the soul, "mon âme," whose last strength is exhausted by the sight (a procession of memories, a wasted life laden with guilt). Hope has given up looking for a way out; she is weeping; hideous Dread hoists her black flag over the bowed skull, and so this magnificent poem ends. As a picture in the grand style of total abjection and collapse, the last stanza, especially the last line, outdoes all the rest. For the rhythm and the images—the procession of hearses, the victor hoisting a flag over the enemy's captured citadel—all these are in the grand style; but the victor is Dread, of the poet nothing remains, no soul, no brow, not even a head; what has bowed down beneath the black flag is only a skull, "mon crâne incliné." He has lost all dignity, not before God, for there is no God, but before Dread.

In our analysis we have tried to bring out two ideas, both of which take the form of antitheses. First the antithesis between symbolism and realism. Obviously the poet's aim is not to give an accurate, realistic descrip-

---

[1] In E. Raynaud, *Charles Baudelaire* (Paris, 1922), p. 105, we find the following quotation from a play written in the 1840's:

> Quel plaisir de tordre
> Nos bras amoureux,
> Et puis de nous mordre
> En hurlant tous deux.

One is also reminded of Leconte de Lisle's poem about the wild dogs, *"Les Hurleurs."*

tion of rain and a damp moldering dungeon, of bats and spiders, the ringing of bells, and a bowed human skull. It makes no difference whether or not he ever actually heard bells ringing on a rainy day. The whole is a vision of despair, and the expository statements are purely symbolic. The data are of so little importance that the symbols can be changed without loss; Hope first appears as a bat, but the end, where she weeps in defeat, suggests the image of an infant or child, certainly not of a bat. Thus the poem cannot be called realistic if by realism we mean an attempt to reproduce outward reality. But since in the nineteenth century the word "realism" was associated chiefly with the crass representation of ugly, sordid, and horrifying aspects of life; since this was what constituted the novelty and significance of realism, the word was applicable to ugly, gruesome images, regardless of whether they were intended as concrete description or as symbolic metaphors. What mattered was the vividness of the evocation, and in this respect Baudelaire's poem is extremely realistic. Though the images evoked are wholly symbolic in intention, they forcefully concretize a hideous and terrible reality—even when reason tells us that such symbols can have no empirical reality. Obviously, there is no one by the name of Angoisse who can plant a black flag over a bowed skull: but the image of the "crâne incliné" is so overpowering that we see the gruesome portrait. The same is true of the spiders in the brain or the leaping, whimpering bells. These images strike with a realistic force that no one can escape; nor does the poet want anyone to escape them.

The other idea stressed in our analysis is the contradiction between the lofty tone and the indignity both of its subject as a whole and of many details. This contrast affected many contemporaries as an inconsistency of style; it was violently attacked at the time, though since then the "mixed style" has gained general acceptance. Modern critics, beginning in Baudelaire's time but more persistently in later years, have attempted to deny the hierarchy of literary objects, maintaining that there are no such things as sublime and base objects, but only good and bad verses, good and bad images. However, the formulation is misleading; it obscures the significant thing that happened in the nineteenth century movement. In classical aesthetics, subject matter and the manner of its treatment came to be divided into three classes: there was the great, tragic, and sublime; then the middle, pleasing, and inoffensive; finally the ridiculous, base, and grotesque. Within each of the three categories there were many gradations and special cases. A classification of this sort corresponds to human feeling, in Europe at least; it cannot be argued away. What the nineteenth century accomplished—and the twentieth has carried the process still further—was to change the basis of correlation: it became possible to take subjects seriously that had hitherto belonged to the low or middle category, and to treat them tragically. The subject matter of Flaubert or Cézanne, Zola or Van Gogh, is not "neutral"; one cannot say that their originality consisted solely in the novelty or perfection of their techniques; there can be no significant new technique without new content. The truth is rather that the subject matter became serious and great through the intention of those who gave it form. The same may be said of Baudelaire's *Fleurs du mal.* On February 28, 1866, he wrote to Ancelle: "Dans ce livre atroce, j'ai mis toute ma pensée, tout mon coeur, toute ma religion (travestie), toute ma haine . . ." [Into this abominable book I have put all my thought, all my religion (travestied), all my hatred]. He could not have written in this way if he had not seen all human tragedy, depth, and greatness in his subject matter and intended to express them in his poems. It is futile to ask to what extent he posed and exaggerated; posture and exaggeration were an inherent part of the man and his state of mind. All modern artists (since Petrarch at least), have tended to dramatize themselves. The artistic process requires a concentration on certain themes, a process of selection, which stresses certain aspects of the artist's inner life and puts others aside. It was not easy for Baudelaire to live with himself and make himself work. He inclined to exaggerate his state and to make a display of what he rightly felt to be original and unique. But his concentration on certain themes that were distinctly his own and the force of his expression leave no room for doubt as to his fundamental authenticity.

He is authentic, and his conceptions are large; his poetry is in the grand style. But even among those whose intentions were similar, he is an extreme case; he is distinguished even from Rimbaud by his inner stagnation, his lack of development. He was the first to treat matters as sublime which seemed by nature unsuited to such treatment. The "spleen" of our poem is hopeless despair; it cannot be reduced to concrete causes or remedied in any way. A vulgarian would ridicule it; a moralist or a physician would suggest ways of curing it. But with Baudelaire their efforts would have been vain. He wrote in the grand style about paralyzing anxiety, panic at the hopeless entanglement of our lives, total collapse—a highly honorable undertaking, but also a negation of life. German slang has an apt term for this spleen: *das graue Elend,* the gray misery. Is the gray misery tragic? One should not be in too much of a hurry to dismiss as Philistines the contemporary critics who rejected this form of poetry; what would Plato have thought of it? Baudelaire himself found a very similar term for his spleen, "ma triste misère." It occurs in his poem *"Le Mauvais Moine";* after a half ironic picture of the medieval monks, who painted pictures of death and the truths of religion to console them for the ascetic austerity of their lives, he concludes as follows:

> Mon âme est un tombeau que, mauvais cénobite,
> Depuis l'éternité je parcours et j'habite;
> Rien n'embellit les murs de ce cloître odieux.
>
> O moine fainéant! quand saurai-je donc faire
> Du spectacle vivant de ma triste misère
> Le travail de mes mains et l'amour de mes yeux?
>
> [My soul is a tomb which, miserable monk,
> I have paced for all eternity. There I live
> In a hateful cloister to which nothing lends beauty.
>
> O idle monk! When shall I learn
> To turn the living vision of my bitter misery
> Into the work of my hands, the beloved of my eyes?]

These verses present a new problem, though one implied in what has been said above. It is characteristic of the gray misery that it incapacitates one for all activity. Even those who cope with such depressions more successfully than Baudelaire, force themselves at best to carry on some routine activity; most of these are helped by their milieu or by an occupation that obliges them to do certain things at certain hours. In many cases this kind of activity has relieved or overcome the gray misery. But Baudelaire had no milieu or occupation requiring regular activity. Instead, he demanded of himself something far more difficult, something well-nigh impossible, and he succeeded: he managed to form his *triste misère* into poetry, to leap directly from his misery into the sublime, to fashion it into the work of his hands, the beloved of his eyes. His passion for expressing himself drove him into an unremitting struggle with his gray misery, a battle in which he was sometimes victorious; not often, and never completely enough to cast it off; for strange to say, the gray misery was not merely the enemy, but also the beginning and object of his activity. What could be more paradoxical? The misery that paralyzed and degraded him was the source of a poetry that seems endowed with the highest dignity; it was the source both of the sublime tone produced by the fact of working under such desperate conditions and of the breaches of style that sprang directly from the subject matter.

The poet's misery had still other aspects, the most painful being his sexuality. Sexuality was a hell for him, a hell of degrading desire (*Lusthölle;* I believe that Thomas Mann uses the expression in *Doctor Faustus*). Here again we shall stick to the texts and begin with a poem without any concretely erotic content:

> Je te donne ces vers afin que si mon nom
> Aborde heureusement aux époques lointaines,
> Et fait rêver un soir les cervelles humaines,
> Vaisseau favorisé par un grand aquilon,
>
> Ta mémoire, pareille aux fables incertaines,
> Fatigue le lecteur ainsi qu'un tympanon,
> Et par un fraternel et mystique chaînon
> Reste comme pendue à mes rimes hautaines;
>
> Etre maudit à qui, de l'abîme profond
> Jusqu'au plus haut du ciel, rien, hors moi, ne répond!
> —O toi qui, comme une ombre à la trace éphémère,
>
> Foules d'un pied léger et d'un regard serein
> Les stupides mortels qui t'ont jugée amère,
> Statue aux yeux de jais, grand ange au front d'airain!
>
> [I give you these verses, hoping that if my name,
> Like a vessel favored by a stout north wind,
> Should happily accost in epochs now remote
> And stir a dream one night in human minds,
>
> Your memory like a dubious fable
> Will clang in the reader's ears and torment him,
> Your memory suspended by an intimate
> And mystic chain from my lofty rhymes;
>
> Accursed one, whom from deepest depths to highest
> Heights, no one will answer for but me!
> You who like an ephemeral shadow
>
> Pass light-footed and serene
> Over the stupid mortals who have judged you vile,
> Statue with eyes of jet, towering angel with head of brass.]

Syntactically, this poem too consists of a single sweeping movement: the simple and solemn main clause ("Je te donne ces vers"); dependent on it a long and intricate purpose clause, the subject of which appears only at the start of the second quatrain ("Ta mémoire"); followed, in the concluding tercets, by the apostrophe in three parts ("Etre maudit à qui . . . ; O toi qui . . . ; Statue . . ."). No less lofty seems the content: a poem is solemnly dedicated to the loved one, in order that she may, at some time in the distant future, partake of his fame. The reader is reminded of similar passages in which earlier poets, Horace, Dante, Petrarch, Ronsard, or Shakespeare (some critics have even mentioned Corneille and Byron) have spoken in lofty style of their future fame, sometimes in connection with a beloved. The words "Je te donne ces vers," with the ensuing image of a ship putting into port after a long voyage, seem quite consonant with this sublime tradition. And the singling out of a particular moment (*un soir*) when the poet's fame will go into effect, recalls a famous sonnet by Ronsard. But then the reader, prepared for grandeur and dignity, is shocked by the word *cervelles* (in the first version the line read "Fit travailler un soir les cervelles humaines"); the value of the poet's enduring fame becomes strangely dubious. The reader dimly suspects what becomes a certainty in the next stanza: the fame of which the poet is going to speak will not enrich future generations and gladden their hearts; it will irritate and torment them ("ta mémoire . . . fatigue le lecteur ainsi qu'un tympanon"), drawing the future reader into a noxious entanglement. The distasteful memory of the beloved to whom the poem is solemnly dedicated will remain attached to the poet's proud verses "par un fraternel et mystique chaînon"—in other words, the memory is not proud or lofty, but base and unpleasant, and it will be drummed into the reader's mind with a perverse insistence. The whole poem is a piece of bitter malice, not only against the beloved (we employ the word only because no other is available), but also against the future reader; for now, retroactively, the *afin que* of the first line takes on an insidious meaning: the poet's purpose in his *rimes hautaines* is malignant: to tyrannize the future reader and avenge himself against the beloved. In the final apostrophe the latter theme is explicitly developed; for the apostrophe—in three parts—is a curse; the beloved is described first in relation to the poet, then in relation to the rest of mankind, and finally for herself. Here we shall not go into the separate themes—the poet at the mercy of an outcast; her indifference; the mysterious presence of this unmoving statue, this angel of evil. Yet in the end something akin to admiration and adoration enters into the curse, expressed in a last haughty gibe, this one at the "stupides mortels qui t'ont jugée amère." This poem, so rich in contradictions, sustains its lofty tone from the first to the last word. The curse ends with something in the nature of an apotheosis.

What all this means is known to us from other poems that deal directly with love or desire. Rhythm, form, and attitude place nearly all of them in the lofty style. But the traditional themes of sublime love poetry are almost wholly lacking; the accent is on naked sexuality, particularly in its terrible, abysmal aspects. If we are fully to understand the profound significance of Baudelaire we must recall the place of such things in the European literary tradition. Traditionally, physical love was treated in the light style.[2] In the older poetry the perverse or abject is scarcely mentioned in any category of style.[3] In Baudelaire it is dominant. Traditional echoes are not wholly absent, such as the theme of the worshipped beloved (Muse, Madonna), but they ring false; sometimes they sound ironic and always strangely disfigured. The intimate tenderness that had gained a place beside the sublime in the love poetry of the early romantics also appears here and there in Baudelaire ("Mon enfant, ma soeur . . ."); but it is not the same idyllic intimacy as in the romantics, which would have been quite incompatible with Baudelaire's temperament; in him it has a new and strange aftertaste.

Almost everywhere in Baudelaire the relation between lovers—or more accurately between those bound by sexual attraction—is represented as an obsession mingled with hatred and contempt, an addiction which loses none of its degrading, tormenting force for being experienced in full (yet defenseless) awareness. Love is a torment, at best a numbing of the senses; true, it is also the source of inspiration, the actual source of the mystical intuition of the supernatural; nevertheless it is torture and degradation. Sometimes the loved one is sick and no longer young, more often she is a kind of bestial idol, soulless, barren, and morally indifferent. Baudelaire's masterly rendition of synesthetic impressions, in which the sense of smell is dominant ("respirer le parfum de ton sang"; "des parfums frais comme des chairs d'enfants"; "forêt aromatique" of the

---

[2] "*Sum levis, et mecum levis est, mea cura, Cupido*," says Ovid, *Amores*, 3, 1, 41. But all that is finished since Baudelaire; light love in poetry has become *Kitsch* or pornography. As late as the eighteenth century, in Chaulieu or Voltaire, for example, it was very different. In this connection it is interesting to read Baudelaire's instructions to his lawyer when *Les Fleurs du mal* was prosecuted for immorality; they may be found in a number of critical editions and biographies. He stresses the serious character of his poetry over against the *polissonnerie* of some of the "light" poems of Béranger and Musset, at which the authorities had taken no umbrage. We need only read these poems to see how incredibly vulgar this erotic poetry in the "light style" had become.

[3] Even in prose such matters were seldom treated. A few mild allusions occur in Montaigne. Crépet, in his critical edition (Charles Baudelaire, *Les Fleurs du mal: Edition critique établie par* Jacques Crépet *et* Georges Blin [Paris, 1942], p. 431; cited in the following as FdM, Crépet-Blin), expresses the belief that Baudelaire had read these passages in Montaigne and refers to *Essais*, II, Chap. XV. This is perfectly possible, but it is certain that Baudelaire learned nothing from Montaigne.

hair) helps to create a unique impression, at once sensuous, cold, bestial, painful, demonic, and sublime. All this is sufficiently known.

There seem to be isolated exceptions. Among the poems known or presumed to have been addressed to Madame Sabatier,[4] there are some in which health and untarnished beauty are praised; at first sight they seem to belong to a freer and happier order of poetry. But if we consider these poems in context, we soon begin to question our first impression. First of all we find that exuberant carnal health is strangely equated with sanctity and power to redeem. We begin to interpret the beautiful but very strange line "Sa chair spirituelle a le parfum des Anges" (from "Que diras-tu ce soir . . .") with the help of certain other lines, such as

> Le passant chagrin que tu frôles
> Est ébloui par ta santé
> Qui jaillit comme une clarté
> De tes bras et de tes épaules,

> [The downcast passer-by
> Is dazzled by your health
> Which springs like a radiance
> From your arms and your shoulders.]
> ("A celle qui est trop gaie")

or

> David mourant aurait demandé la santé
> Aux émanations de ton corps enchanté

> [King David on his deathbed would have sought
> Health in the aura of your enchanted flesh.]
> ("Réversibilité")

There is something startling and incongruous about this spiritualization and worship of so blatantly carnal a magic ("L'Ange gardien," "La Muse et la Madone," or "Chère Déesse," "Être lucide et pur"). And as a matter of fact the picture is false. All this health and vitality is intolerable to the poet; as we have said before, the sunshine is of little use to

---

[4] "Semper eadem," "Tout entière," "Que diras-tu," "Le Flambeau vivant," "A celle qui est trop gaie," "Réversibilité," "Confession," "L'Aube spirituelle," "Harmonie du soir," "Le Flacon," "Hymne."

him; hatred and lust for destruction spring up side by side with admiration and worship:

> Folle dont je suis affolé,
> Je te hais autant que je t'aime!
>
> Quelquefois dans un beau jardin
> Où je traînais mon atonie,
> J'ai senti, comme une ironie,
> Le soleil déchirer mon sein;
>
> Et le printemps et la verdure
> Ont tant humilié mon coeur,
> Que j'ai puni sur une fleur
> L'insolence de la Nature.
>
> [Madcap who maddens me
> I hate you as much as I love you/
>
> Sometimes in a bright garden
> Whither I dragged by atony,
> I have felt the sun like an irony
> Tearing my heart.
>
> And the spring with its verdure
> So humbled my heart
> That I punished Nature's insolence
> By trampling a flower.]

These lines[5] are from "A celle qui est trop gaie," one of the poems condemned by the court as immoral; it ends with an outburst of destructive frenzy ("Ainsi je voudrais, une nuit . . . pour châtier ta chair joyeuse . . . t'infuser mon venin, ma soeur!").

The hatred and torment contained in these poems would have struck the taste of an earlier period as intolerable; no one would have looked at and treated the torments of love (and is one justified in speaking of love?) in this way; there is nothing comparable in the romantics, not at least in their poetry. Many poets since the Provençal troubadours have been prevented by their heavy hearts from enjoying the springtime. This may be called an almost traditional theme. One need only read Petrarch's 42nd Sonnet, "In morte di Madonna Laura" (*Zefiro torna*), to realize what a breach of style Baudelaire had committed.

---

[5] Baudelaire made many such statements. One of the most characteristic occurs in a letter to Fernand Desnoyers. It has often been cited, e.g., in FdM, Crépet-Blin, p. 463.

One cannot but conclude that all those poems in *Les Fleurs du mal* which deal with erotic subjects are either filled with the harsh and painful disharmony that we have been trying to describe—or else are visions in which the poet strives to conjure up torpor, forgetfulness, the absolute Somewhere-Else.[6] Almost everywhere we find degradation and humiliation. The desirer becomes a slave, conscious but without will; the object of desire is without humanity and dignity, unfeeling, made cruel by her power and by ennui, barren, destructive; quotations and analyses are superfluous—all this is well-known to the readers of *Les Fleurs du mal*. Still, we should like to cite a few particularly glaring and magnificent examples of breach of style.[7] In the "Hymne à la Beauté," we have the line:

> Tu répands des parfums comme un soir orageux
>
> [You scatter perfume like a stormy evening]

and a few lines further on the power of beauty is praised as follows:

> Le Destin charmé suit tes jupons comme un chien
>
> [Destiny spellbound follows your petticoats like a dog]

and this is how the lover looks to him:

> L'amoureux pantelant incliné sur sa belle
> A l'air d'un moribond caressant son tombeau.
>
> [The panting lover bending over his fair one
> Looks like a dying man caressing his grave.]

[6] The tender, beautiful *"Je n'ai pas oublié"* refers to a happy period in his early youth, spent with his mother before her second marriage. Apart from this, wherever we find a gentler, more tender sentiment in *Les Fleurs du mal*, it usually proves to be deceptive. It is genuine when, in speaking to the beloved, he argues flight, renunciation, repose, or a numbing of the senses; then we find phrases such as "Mon enfant, ma sœur," or "O ma si blanche, ô ma si froide Marguerite."

[7] Jean Royère (*Poèmes d'amour de Baudelaire* [Paris, 1927]) calls these breaches of style *catachrèses,* and gives an excellent description of them. Royère regards Baudelaire as a Catholic mystic; on the lines from "Hymne à la Beauté" of which we have quoted a part ("L'Amoureux pantelant . . .") he writes (p. 123): "I decline to comment more directly on such verses. I content myself with reciting them every day like a Pater and an Ave." There are many such exaggerations in his book and almost all his ideas strike me as arbitrary and dilettantish. But even so it is a beautiful book.

Among the portrayals of desire we have chosen two; the reader is invited to savor their rhythm and content:

> Je m'avance à l'attaque, et je grimpe aux assauts,
> Comme après un cadavre un chœur de vermisseaux
>
> [I spring to the attack, I mount to the assault
> Like a chorus of maggots besetting a corpse]
>   ("Je t'adore")

and

> Je frissonne de peur quand tu me dis: "Mon ange!"
> Et cependant je sens ma bouche aller vers toi.[8]
>
> [I tremble with fear when you say: "My angel!"
> And yet my lips move toward you.]
>   ("Femmes damnées")

Now the degradation of the flesh, and particularly the equations of woman-sin and desire-death-putrefaction belong to a Christian tradition that was particularly strong toward the end of the Middle Ages. It was inevitable that certain critics should have related Baudelaire to this tradition, especially since he was sharply opposed to the tendencies of the Enlightenment and since prayers or something very close to it already make their appearance in *Les Fleurs du mal*. It is certainly true that like the romantics before him, he was influenced by Christian-medieval images and ideas. It is also true that Baudelaire had the mind of a mystic; in the world of the senses he looked for the supernatural, and found a second sensory world that was supernatural, demonic, and hostile to nature. Finally it may be said—and indeed it has been said—that the view of sensory reality that we find in *Les Fleurs du mal* would have been inconceivable in the pagan world. But that is as far as one may go. We owe it to the Christian tradition to point out that although the central trend of *Les Fleurs du mal* would have been unthinkable without the Christian tradition, it is fundamentally different from the Christian tradition, and incompatible with it. Here we shall sum up the essential points of difference:

1. What the poet of *Les Fleurs du mal* is looking for is not grace

---

[8] This line is a good example of the romantic three-part alexandrine, with a caesura not after the sixth, but after the fourth and eighth syllables. It should be read and savored accordingly.

and eternal beatitude but either nothingness, *le Néant*,[9] or a kind of sensory fulfillment, the vision of a sterile, but sensuous artificiality ("volupté calme"; "ordre et beauté"; "luxe, calme et volupté"; cf. also the vision contained in "Rêve parisien"). His spiritualization of memory and his synesthetic symbolism are also sensory, and behind them stands not any hope of redemption through God's grace, but nothingness, the absolute Somewhere-Else.

2. In any Christian interpretation of life, redemption by the Incarnation and Passion of Christ is the cardinal point of universal history and the source of all hope. There is no place for Christ in *Les Fleurs du mal*. He appears but once, in "Le Reniement de Saint-Pierre," and here he is at odds with God. This notion occurs earlier in some of the romantics; but to the mind of a believer no greater confusion or error is conceivable. Even from a historical point of view it is a dilettantish misunderstanding of the Christian tradition. This second point is not basically different from the first, but complements it and gives a still clearer picture of Baudelaire's situation.

3. The corruption of the flesh means something very different in *Les Fleurs du mal* and in the Christianity of the late Middle Ages. In *Les Fleurs du mal* the desire that is damned is most often a desire for the physically corrupt or misshapen; the enjoyment of young, healthy flesh is never held up as a sin. In the warnings and castigations of the Christian moralists, on the other hand, the object of carnal temptation may have been represented as the creature of an hour, but for the present she was endowed with youth and full-blown earthly health. There was nothing decrepit about Eve with the apple; her apparent soundness is what made the temptation so insidious, and in Christian morality it is condemned. The poet of *Les Fleurs du mal* knows youth, vitality, health, only as objects of yearning and admiration—or else of malignant envy. Sometimes he wants to destroy them, but in the main he tends to spiritualize, admire, and worship them.[10]

---

[9] There is a passage in which even *le Néant* does not seem to be nothing enough for him. It occurs in the *Projets de préface pour une édition nouvelle,* toward the end in the paragraph beginning with the words "D'ailleurs, telle n'est pas . . ." (FdM, Crépet-Blin, p. 214).

[10] Cf. the lines to Mme Sabatier ("Ta chair spirituelle a le parfum des anges"); or the following from "Sonnet d'automne":

> . . . Mon cœur, que tout irrite,
> Excepté la candeur de l'antique animal

"J'aime le souvenir des ces époques nues" is another example of this, although the apotheosis of youth at the end ("A la sainte jeunesse . . .") is very startling in Baudelaire. Cf. the note in FdM, Crépet-Blin, p. 303.

4. In *Les Fleurs du mal,* Baudelaire is not striving for humility, but for pride. To be sure, he degrades himself and all earthly life, but in the midst of his degradation he does his best to sustain his pride. In this connection we might mention the lines of prayer in "Bénédiction" ("Soyez béni, mon Dieu, qui donnez la souffrance . . ."). They are very moving, but the idea that fills them is that of the poet's own apotheosis; singling himself out from the contemptible race of men, he appears before the face of God. Such verses could scarcely have been written before Rousseau's famous apostrophe to God at the beginning of the *Confessions.* Neither writer is innocent of self-aggrandizement.[11]

What I am saying here refers solely to *Les Fleurs du mal.* We have no wish to speak of the salvation of Baudelaire's soul, and it would be beyond our means to do so. It is easy to understand that important Catholic critics should have concerned themselves not only with Baudelaire but also with other desperate rebels of the nineteenth century, and attempted to interpret them as exemplary vehicles of the struggle for faith and witnesses to the triumph of Grace. Souls such as Baudelaire's are the *âmes choisies* of our time or at least of a time that is not too far in the past.[12] But that is not our concern; we are speaking not of the history of Baudelaire's soul but of *Les Fleurs du mal.* It is a work of despair and of the bitter pleasures of despair. Its world is a prison; sometimes the pain is deadened or appeased, and sometimes, too, there is the ecstatic pleasure of artistic self-exaltation; but escape from the prison there is none. Nor can there be. Jean-Paul Sartre, an acute and concrete thinker though his designs obtrude too much, has shown brilliantly[13] how Baudelaire the man consciously ran himself into a dead end and how he himself blocked off every exit or retreat. In order to determine the historical position of *Les Fleurs du mal,* it is important to observe that in the middle of the nineteenth century a man was able to fashion this character and this biography and that this kind of man was able to achieve full expression at just this time, so that he disclosed something that was latent in his age, which many men gradually came to perceive through him. The periods of human history prepare their prospective representatives; they seek them out, shape them, bring them to light, and through them make themselves known.

[11] Royère, loc. cit., p. 58, writes: "Baudelaire . . . ne serait peut-être pas éloigné d'une théologie qui mettrait l'homme, en quelque manière, au niveau de Dieu." But that would be the Devil's own theology. In this passage, to be sure, Royère is speaking more of the male than of humankind, but that scarcely makes a difference.

[12] *Âmes choisies* is from the *Mémoires* of Saint-Simon, but may have been used earlier in the seventeenth century. The principle of selection has changed since then.

[13] Charles Baudelaire, *Écrits intimes;* introduction by Jean-Paul Sartre (Paris, 1946).

There is no way out, nor can there be. The poet of *Les Fleurs du mal* hated the reality of the time in which he lived; he despised its trends, progress and prosperity, freedom and equality; he recoiled from its pleasures; he hated the living, surging forces of nature;[14] he hated love insofar as it is "natural." And his contempt for all these things was only increased by his awareness that he had never experienced or ventured seriously to approach a good many of them. He invoked the forces of faith and transcendence only insofar as they could be used as weapons against life, or as symbols of escape; or insofar as they could serve his jealous, exclusive worship of what he really loved and pursued with all the strength that was left him after so much hopeless resistance: absolute poetic creation, absolute artifice, and himself as the artificial creator. Here it is worth our while to take up a text, "La Mort des artistes," the poem with which he concluded the first edition of *Les Fleurs du mal*. In its final form (1861)[15] it runs as follows:

> Combien faut-il de fois secouer mes grelots
> Et baiser ton front bas, morne caricature?
> Pour piquer dans le but, de mystique nature,
> Combien, ô mon carquois, perdre de javelots?
>
> Nous userons notre âme en de subtils complots,
> Et nous démolirons mainte lourde armature,
> Avant de contempler la grande Créature
> Dont l'infernal désir nous remplit de sanglots!
>
> Il en est qui jamais n'ont connu leur Idole,
> Et ces sculpteurs damnés et marqués d'un affront,
> Qui vont se martelant la poitrine et le front,
>
> N'ont qu'un espoir, étrange et sombre Capitole!
> C'est que la Mort, planant comme un soleil nouveau,
> Fera s'épanouir les fleurs de leur cerveau!

[14] His hatred of nature often sounds Christian ("la femme est naturelle, c'est-à-dire abominable"; or "le commerce est naturel, donc il est infâme": both from *Mon Coeur mis à nu*). But it is so absurdly exaggerated ("j'aime mieux une boîte à musique qu'un rossignol," as he is quoted as saying in Schaunard's *Souvenirs*), that it all seems to boil down to revolt. On the Apocalypse as the source of his visions of landscapes without vegetation (e.g., "Rêve parisien," cf. Apoc. 21-2) see J. Pommier, *La Mystique de Baudelaire* (Paris, 1932), p. 39.

[15] The first version, which appeared in 1851 in *Le Messager de l'Assemblée,* is quite different, much weaker and milder; in the 1857 edition of *Les Fleurs du mal* the poem already has its definitive form, with the exception of the third line which runs: "Pour piquer dans le but, mystique quadrature. . . ."

[How many times more shall I have to shake my bells
And kiss your low forehead, dismal caricature?
Before I hit the mystic target
How many arrows shall I lose from my quiver?

We shall waste our souls in subtle schemes,
And shatter many a heavy armature
Before we behold the great Creature
Who has damned us to heartbreaking desire.

There are some who have never known their idol,
And these accursed sculptors marked by an affront,
Who chisel out their own chests and foreheads,

Have but one hope, O strange and somber Capitol!
It is that Death, soaring like a new sun
Will bring the flowers of their brain to blossoming.]

There can be little doubt that he is speaking of the artist's struggle
for something absolute; a striving, warped by bitter hopelessness, for
the idea or archetype in the Platonic or Neoplatonic sense. The *morne
caricature,* before which the artist humiliates himself like a clown, can
be nothing other than the debased earthly appearance; the poet expends
his powers trying to pass through it to the mystic archetype. Thus far
the poem, despite the extreme sharpness with which it expresses the
indignity of the earthly appearance, is still compatible with the traditional idea of an ascent to the vision of the archetype. But what is quite
incompatible with this long tradition is the way in which Baudelaire
speaks of the archetype itself. First it is called *la grande Créature,* which
has a sensual, pejorative ring, and which in readers familiar with *Les
Fleurs du mal* evokes demonic insensibility and sterile lust for power
(cf. "Hymne à la Beauté," "La Beauté"); and a little later, with evident
scorn, he calls it *leur Idole.* Still more shocking is what he says of the
striving for the archetype. In the whole of mystical and visionary literature this striving, however arduous and vain, was never represented as
anything other than great and noble; it was held to be the highest form
of endeavor and activity that a man could elect. But the author of our
verses calls it *infernal désir,* as though it were a vice. The methods it
employs are *subtils complots,* which wear out the soul. Those who never
get to see their *idole* are accursed and degraded ("damnés et marqués
d'un affront"). In the twentieth essay of his first book, Montaigne says:
"L'entreprise se sent de la qualité de la chose qu'elle regarde; car c'est
une bonne partie de l'effect, et consubstantielle." ("The undertaking

smacks of the quality of what it has in view; for the striving is a good part of the result, and consubstantial with it.") If this is true, and it is true, the degradation of the striving will degrade the goal. At the end of the poem, to be sure, there is a sudden rise; a hope seems to appear; its name is Death, "planant comme un soleil nouveau," and it will "bring the flowers of their brain to blossoming." This again might fit in with the tradition. Beyond the vision which is sometimes granted a living man in *excessus mentis,* stands the sight of God in his glory, and this can never be taken away from the soul that has been saved. But here, in Baudelaire's poem, death is not eternal beatitude; this is made clear by the words *étrange et sombre Capitole,* which also exclude any other form of pure fulfillment in transcendence; there is a raucous note, a veiled mockery in the whole tercet whose rhythm seems to mount so abruptly. But what then of the hope? How can nothingness be a new sun that will bring flowers to unfolding? I know no answer. There is none to be found in *Les Fleurs du mal.*[16] Instead we find, immediately after our poem, a description of death in "Le Rêve d'un curieux"; it ends with the following words:

> J'étais mort sans surprise, et la terrible aurore
> M'enveloppait. —Eh quoi! n'est-ce donc que cela?
> La toile était levée et j'attendais encore.

> [I had died unawares, and the terrible dawn
> Enveloped me.—What, is it only this?
> The curtain had risen, and still I was waiting.]

The archetype, *la grande Créature,* is for the poet an object of desperate desire and at the same time of contemptuous mockery. As transcendent reality it is nothing, or worse than nothing: a nothing which by its nothingness mocks and humiliates those who strive for it.

But here he is unjust to himself. It is his unswerving despair which gave him the dignity and weight that he has for us. The unswerving honesty that made it impossible for him to worship the Baalim for even one moment in a time without gods, is his greatness. His dandyism and his poses were merely a deformation imposed by the desperate struggle. Anyone who reads him feels after the very first lines that his aesthetic dandyism has nothing in common with the pre-Parnassian and Parnassian

---

[16] Crépet (FdM, Crépet-Blin, p. 518) calls "La Mort des artistes" "la plus mallarméenne peut-être des *Fleurs du mal.*" This is incontestable. But perhaps one may equally well say that there is no better indication of the profoundly different character of the two poets.

aesthetes, with Gautier or Leconte de Lisle. Baudelaire's poetry has a much wider range. And he cannot hide himself behind his work. Degraded, deformed, and sublime, he is right in the middle of it. It is a book consubstantial with its author, to cite Montaigne again. Paradigmatic for the whole age, it gave this age a new poetic style: a mixture of the base and contemptible with the sublime, a symbolic use of realistic horror, which was unprecedented in lyric poetry and had never been carried to such lengths in any genre. In him for the first time we find fully developed those surprising and seemingly incoherent combinations that Royère calls *catachrèses,* and which led Brunetière to accredit Baudelaire with the *génie de l'impropriété.* We have quoted a few of them in the course of this study. "Des cloches tout à coup sautent avec furie," "La Mort, planant comme un soleil nouveau," etc. The visionary power of such combinations exerted a crucial influence on later poetry; they seemed the most authentic expression both of the inner anarchy of the age and of a still hidden order that was just beginning to dawn. In an entirely new and consummate style, this poet, whose character and life were so strange, expressed the naked, concrete existence of an epoch. For his style was not based on his personal situation and his personal needs; it became apparent that his extreme personality embodied a far more universal situation and a far more universal need. Now that the crisis of our civilizations (which at Baudelaire's time was still latent, presaged by only a few)—now that the crisis is approaching a decision, we may perhaps expect a decline in Baudelaire's influence; in a totally changed world that is perhaps moving toward a new order, the coming generations may lose contact with his problems and his attitude.[17] But the historic importance of *Les Fleurs du mal* can never be shaken. The human structure that appears in these poems is just as significant for the transformation, or perhaps one should say the destruction, of the European tradition as the human structure of Ivan Karamazov. The form, not only of modern poetry but also of the other literary genres of the century that has elapsed since then, is scarcely thinkable without *Les Fleurs du mal*; the trace of Baudelaire's influence can be followed in Gide, Proust, Joyce, and Thomas Mann as well as Rimbaud, Mallarmé, Rilke, and Eliot. Baudelaire's style, the mixture we have attempted to describe, is as much alive as ever.

And yet I do not wish this paper to end with the praise of Baudelaire's literary achievement, but rather on the note with which it began, the horror of *Les Fleurs du mal.* It is a book of gruesome hopelessness, of futile and absurd attempts to escape by inebriation and narcosis. Ac-

---

[17] "Un état d'esprit auquel Baudelaire aura cessé de correspondre," says E. Raynaud, loc. cit., p. 307.

cordingly, a word should be said in defense of certain critics who have resolutely rejected the book. Not all of them, but a few, had a better understanding of it than many contemporary and subsequent admirers. A statement of horror is better understood by those who feel the horror in their bones, even if they react against it, than by those who express nothing but their rapture over the artistic achievement. Those who are seized with horror do not speak about *frisson nouveau;* they do not cry bravo and congratulate the poet on his originality. Even Flaubert's admiration, though excellently formulated, is too aesthetic.[18] Most later critics took it for granted that the book could only be considered from an aesthetic standpoint and scornfully rejected any other possibility from the outset. It seems to us that aesthetic criticism alone is unequal to the task, though Baudelaire would scarcely have shared our opinion: he was contaminated by the idolatry of art that is still with us. What a strange phenomenon: a prophet of doom who expects nothing of his readers but admiration for his artistic achievement. "Ponete mente almen com' io son bella" ("consider at least how beautiful I am")—with these words Dante concludes his *canzone* to the movers of the third heaven. But can such words be applied to poems whose meaning is so actual and urgent, whose beauty is as bitter as that of *Les Fleurs du mal?*

[18] Like Taine after him, he called Baudelaire's style *âpre,* and wrote: "Vous chantez la chair sans l'aimer." Aside from Ange Pechméja's letter, this is no doubt the most outstanding of contemporary judgments; J. J. Weiss should be mentioned as one of the contemporary adversaries. These and other critical remarks may be found in Eugène Crépet, *Charles Baudelaire: Étude biographique, revue et mise à jour par* Jacques Crépet (Paris, 1906), Flaubert, p. 359; Pechméja's letter, p. 414; Taine, p. 432. But the action against *Les Fleurs du mal* and the contemporary reaction to the book are treated at length in the other biographies. The most complete compilation of opinions is probably that of Vergniol in *La Revue de Paris,* August 1917.

Baudelairean Themes: Death, Evil, and Love

by Jean Prévost

The Themes of Baudelaire's Poetry

Baudelaire certainly does not have the extreme variety of subjects, of themes, and of tones found in Victor Hugo. But his poetical themes are broader and more numerous than those of Lamartine, for example. The *Fleurs du mal* offers horizons of an amplitude seldom equalled in any other single volume. There would have been scant, if any, gain in the book's being two or three times larger; if Baudelaire, for sheer mass, equalled Hugo, he would be hardly tolerable. Under the variety of topics, an extreme suppleness of form, a distinctive unity of tone and of feeling is perceptible, with the same tension and the same will. Baudelaire's contemporaries did not fail to notice it, when they mockingly compared him to Boileau, and Sainte-Beuve, unjust as he was in his estimate of the poet's greatness, nevertheless saw his deliberate attempt to transform and transpose. Different as Baudelaire may be from Pascal, aesthetic impressions akin to those produced by the *Pensées* are frequently experienced by those who reread the *Fleurs du mal*. Each of them in his own realm probes our feelings and our thoughts with a very acute knife, cutting narrow and deep furrows into the quick. Both are anatomists rather than contemplators of life; in a few words, they reach straight to the bone, and strip it of all flesh.

Listing the themes of Baudelaire's poetry would not be enough. First and foremost one must ask how the poet *wants* to transform that theme, and to which others he wishes to marry it. A survey of the simple themes, or of those which seem simple at first, could be made fast enough. Again like Pascal, and like all those who load their thought and their looks with passion, Baudelaire feels, sees, understands through antitheses. The most important picture of Baudelairean themes can only be had through contrasting touches.

Naturally it happens that the poet receives or undergoes dreams which he has not organized; even if he has perhaps provoked them through hashish or laudanum, he has not organized their visions. Let us consider the poem "Rêve parisien": nothing appears clearer or simpler, provided we do not look for sources too high or too far, in the clouds or in regions beyond the spirit, of what the poet actually found in a precise craftsmanship and in the resources of his art. That weird vision owes little or nothing to De Quincey, E. A. Poe, Novalis, or Gautier, whose vision was distorted (in the case of the first two through intoxication). Baudelaire is clearcut, even when he describes what is vague.

In "Rêve parisien," the poet sees nothing but his hotelroom. But the perspectives are distorted: the tables, the door, the shelves, the plinths, the plaster moldings on the ceiling, the mantelpiece become prestigious structures. To a vague and magnifying perception, all that shines becomes metal if it is very small, a sheet of water if it is larger. Thus the mirror on the wall can be in turn huge polished glass and a waterfall rushing down from the sky; a few bottles around a wash basin are enough to suggest a colonnade around a garden pond; the little vault of the fireplace, above a metal plate which vaguely shines, becomes an arch or a tunnel above an ocean. The lines on the ruled paper are turned into rivers which come down from the sky; the small fragment of sky which can be seen from the window is projected afar, into the infinite, and instead of standing upright, appears to stretch horizontally; it is a boundless sea, weirdly contained on its sides. And if nothing vegetal appears in that vision, it is because the poet does not have the slightest bunch of flowers in his room; he is honest and refuses to alter anything in that perception so simply and vastly distorted.

It must be distorted a second time, or rather it must be given a shape at last, and pass from a false perception into a work of art. Then only, along with the customary rhymes which associate the images ("crise" and "cristallise," "fééries" and "pierreries," "diamant" and "firmament"), images will appear which have been borrowed from Baudelaire's predecessors, in poetry, or perhaps in painting and engraving. For every sight which he contemplates or interprets, the poet is prepared by all the images he has seen, all the words he has heard.

"La Chambre double," one of the prose poems, with similar simplicity describes another aspect, a humbler one, of the reveries provoked by intoxication. This time, the phial of laudanum is mentioned; it interposes only a happy mist between reality and the poet's eye; it makes the shape of the furniture and the setting more harmonious; its sole task of hallucination, a very modest one, is to spread a veil of muslin between the windows and the bed. The loved woman is dreamt; she is scarcely believed to be present; even the dream seems to wonder about its own presence. The vision as a whole does not create objects, but merely transposes values and invests every commonplace object with an appearance of beauty.

The same "moral message" emerges from "Rêve parisien" and "La Chambre double"—that which is also proposed by Thomas De Quincey's confessions. The dream which has been voluntarily caused by the dreamer and to which he submits must be followed by a desolate awakening, a bleak and frozen return to earth. . . . But if Baudelaire knew, underwent passively, and recorded the dreams caused by artificial paradises, his dreams are vastly different. These, more vaporous and subtle than the others, are impervious to change and are not followed by that forlorn awakening; they emerge at the mind's highest peak of lucidity.

The Theme of Death

The idea of death, on which the *Fleurs du mal* ends, remains more real and more religious than that of God for the poet. Even in that idea, which might appear to be monolithic and without any diverse hues, similar to the mat black of painters, he finds contrasts. He consents to rest in "La Fin de la journée," but seems to have doubts about doing so in "Le Squelette laboureur"; with exaltation, he affirms survival in "La Mort des amants"; he denies it in "Le Mort joyeux," which sounds like a challenge to fear and to faith. The vague hope of a glorious blossoming transfigures the end of "Bénédiction" and of "La Mort des artistes"; but "Le Rêve d'un curieux" tells us that even our thirst for the beyond must be frustrated.

The man for whom nature was monotonous and narrow, and who saw the world through a few artists rather than in its original nudity, vaguely expected from death something which no longer would look like what was known, which would not be our shadow or our reflection on things, but a novel sensation. "Le Voyage" thus truly deserves to be the final poem of the book, the one in which the stages of the poet's life are, one after the other, most clearly marked: memoirs, in a word, but at the same time the memoirs of all of us. Once again, this time all encompassed in one poem, the world as he has seen it unrolls before our eyes; life, like the sea, wearies us with its monotonous and dazzling brightness. Let us close our eyes, first to rest them, then to implore wildly for newness, "du nouveau." Spiritual flame has extinguished the sumptuous spectacle of nature, and the sun is now only an inner one:

> Si le ciel et la mer sont noirs comme de l'encre,
> Nos coeurs que tu connais sont remplis de rayons!

> [If the sky and the sea are black like ink,
> Our hearts which you well knew are filled with bright rays!]

That enchanted and disappointed review of human things sacrifices everything to a last hope, the only one which life cannot take away. The world, so lovely in its images, has shrunk and wilted; love is a stain which obstinately lingers; the lightness of departures, full of fresh hopes when one set out at the dawn of one's life, appears madness to him whose dreams have regularly foundered on rocky reefs. Even the splendor of the Orient, not unlike the grey sadness of our cities, fails to conceal the powerless human misery. The only folly which comes up to our mad expectations is that of opium. One hope alone will restore to the poet the cheerful joy of his earlier departure; in the midst of the vain tumult of old temptations, it will blow like an off-shore breeze, the only chance of freshness; death is the only certitude left to man, and the poet attempts to make it the only hope.

The Triumph of Evil

Along with poems in which Baudelaire yearns for the good or for nothingness, there are some in which complacency in plunging into evil is triumphant. His conscientious examinations now appeal to God, now to the Devil. So exacting, so perfect in playing his part is the latter, that he ceases to be the enemy and becomes the object of a desolate cult.

In "L'Horreur sympathique," the misery of the unhappy libertine is relieved by his pride. There, as in "Le Rebelle," the soul agrees to persist in its evil incarnation. The damned one in "Le Rebelle" is content with saying: "I do not want." The libertine in "Horreur sympathique" refuses to moan; he wants neither the brightness nor the certainty promised to the elect by faith; on the contrary, he is "avide de l'obscur et de l'incertain." What matters it to him if he is expelled from Paradise? At last, he will confess his pride and his taste for Inferno. The two poems are close to each other: the taste for Inferno is but a fierce taste for freedom; in spite of all hopes, in spite of all the rewards promised to docile submission, I want to choose what appeals to me, "to prefer myself to my happiness."

"L'Irrémédiable" shows another voluptuous aspect of evil, another pride: no longer that of independence, but of lucidity. Yes, I have seen myself, I have gazed clear-sightedly at all the evil that is in me, and here I am, God of myself, fully aware of my good and of my evil. In its first part, the poem is a series of comparisons, borrowed from Vigny's "Eloa," Poe, and De Quincey. These comparisons which all bring the reader back to the poet recall the pieces entitled "Spleen," in which the soul, melting in melancholy images of the world, seems to surrender. But the Devil appears, and the poet's admiration for that character who "always does well all that he does" gives a clearer outline to despair. Thus the second half of the poem is introduced, in which the mournful joy of lucidity will give itself free play:

> Soulagement et gloire uniques,
> La conscience dans le Mal!
>
> [Unique relief and glory—
> Conscience in Evil.]

Examination of conscience does not necessarily constitute an exercise toward virtue for Baudelaire. A particular examination impels to energy and hard work; a general examination leads to despair, and to the acceptance of that despair. The Socratic "Know thyself," basis of all virtues, here becomes awareness of and consent to evil; the monastic meditation which leads to good resolutions is utilized against laziness, but it accepts and it exalts the vast realm of sins. We do not have to judge it from the point of view of a moralist, but from that of a lover of poetry. Bound as it was to the constant quest for new and adequate translation into words, it made the poet more acutely aware of his own particular being. It led him to borrow the language of religion for very secular descriptions, to merge into one the two desires to know himself and to judge himself. When he observes man, he starts with himself; lyricism and lucidity are thus married.

The Love Poems Addressed to Madame Sabatier

It appears that once at least Baudelaire experienced romantic passion of the kind which transfigures the loved one into an angelic creature. Most of the poems sent to "La Présidente," as she was called by her friends, or written for her, seem like the rites of a cult. The poet occasionally offered the same fervor to Berthe or to Marie, "the child, the sister," but then without pretending to lower himself before them. Does he find in this experience the great "romantic love," and are not those poems as beautiful as the great love elegies by Musset, Lamartine, or Hugo, closely allied to them in their inspiration?

For the romantics, passion is an exchange. The words and the feelings of the loved woman appear to occupy the first place there. She is almost like Dante's Beatrice or Petrarch's Laura, the inspirer, she to whom the poet owes his genius. The inspirer is aware of her role and of her mission, so that her beauty seems but a paltry thing compared to the loftiness of her mind or the impulses of her heart.

Not so with Baudelaire. "La Présidente," for him, is not a living goddess but a nearly mute idol. He calls her Angel, but praises chiefly the merits of a filly in her: splendid eye, beauty, blooming and contagious health. Curiously enough, the confessions in the *Journals* and the other love poems in *Les Fleurs du mal* evince an enduring taste, first instinctive and then reasoned, for the thin, much painted, rather sad-looking type of woman. Does he offer his adoration to this healthy and plump woman precisely because she is not "his type," because he can sympathize with that healthy and overflowing vigor without feeling any desire for it? Doubtless this woman, whom he had long known, a good partner at smoking and hashish parties, the mistress of several of his friends, held little mystery for him at the time when he decided to make her his idol. Biography allows us to see in that "love" only a poetical raw material, a pretext for sonnets; the written work confirms it. From his idol, he received only one confidence, out of which he made the stanzas of "Confession." He succeeded there in hiding the extreme banality of the avowal under the description of a Paris night and a simple and faultless rhythm. We owe it to his genius to imagine that, by himself, he would have treated the same theme more profoundly. Elsewhere, she is not supposed to speak ("Taisez-vous, ignorante! âme toujours ravie!"), but at times the demon in her speaks, at times the phantom of the idol; in other words, to the woman herself, the poet prefers the image of her which he makes or unmakes at will.

Poet that he was, he sought two things in Madame Sabatier whom he treated as a work of art rather than as a real being. As early as 1853, in one of the first poems which he sends to her, he shows it ingenuously. First, her refreshing and salutary atmosphere, the contagion of health and cheerfulness which might impart tone and vigor to him. He does

not wish to possess her; he wants rather, at times, to share in her robust-
ness and her easy-going gaiety; he wants to believe in the contagion of
physical good as the ancients did:

> David, mourant, aurait demandé la santé
> Aux émanations de ton corps enchanté. . . .
>
> [David on his death bed would have implored health
> From the emanations of your enchanted body. . . .]

But chiefly he asks from her a continuous surprise, an ever-renewed
opportunity for contrasts with himself. Obsessed with himself and his
own problems, in her he finds his perfect opposite. It may be a chance to
forget himself; more often still, an opportunity for comparing and opposing himself to her. That series of methodically developed contrasts
is the theme of "Reversibilité." The beloved hardly appears; only her
vaguest virtues are celebrated; she is the motionless wall against which
the foam of her worshipper's contrary passions, the tide of his impure
suffering, beats. The last stanza devotes three lines to her. There the
real woman appears as if she were a sum of abstractions, a being of
reason, an Angel, whose prayers the poet implores in concluding.

In most of the sonnets which come later, Baudelaire does not even ask
the loved woman to participate in her own cult. She does not even need
to understand herself, to wonder what kind of beauty she represents for
the poet. Baudelaire celebrates her eyes; he has taken them as his guides;
thanks to them, for a moment he ceases to be demoniacal or Christian.
He allows himself to surrender to a love of simple and superficial gaiety,
to admiration for the most natural and blossoming beauty. In a word,
under a softer and more refined shape, with a suave quality which his
elder and master did not have, he seems to profess the aesthetic and
pagan religion of Théophile Gautier; he instills into it a mysticism
without content, made solely of remote intentions and of purified images.
Nothing designates the loved one in particular. These chants of adoration could be equally addressed to all women whose eyes are normal:
for example

> Ils marchent devant moi, ces yeux pleins de lumière
>
> [They walk in front of me, those eyes filled with light]

in "Le Flambeau vivant," or the similar lines in "L'Aube spirituelle."
According to the poet's own declaration, "Harmonie du soir" is a flower
from the same bouquet of laudatory hymns: one may wonder whether

it celebrates a living creature. A Spaniard, more accustomed than a Frenchman to a poetry of dolorous filial tenderness, might suppose that the poem is addressed to a mother rather than a mistress. The "Présidente" is more exactly depicted in "Allégorie," if it is she who is designated in that poem, as evidence leads us to believe. There Baudelaire magnifies his model, but does not idealize it.

Upon receiving her copy of *Les Fleurs du mal* and rereading the poems which the poet had said were devoted to her, Mme. Sabatier never wondered why, in that volume of verse, she was more vague and indistinct, less real than Jeanne Duval. She apparently did not ask: "But have these pretty lines anything in common with me? Can I see and recognize myself there?" She did not wonder, because she was one of those women who assume a modest air when the name of *beauty* is merely uttered in their presence. She did not understand that she served Baudelaire only as an embodiment of the ideal, and that, in such an ideal, the poet had put nothing of himself: he had only put the very opposite of himself.

Chronology of Important Dates

1821, April 9	Charles Baudelaire's birth in Paris.
1827	Death of his father, François Baudelaire-Dufays, at the age of sixty-eight: his wife was thirty-four years younger than he.
1828, November	His mother married again. His stepfather is Major (later General) Aupick.
1831	Baudelaire's family went to live in Lyon.
1836	The family returned to Paris. Charles Baudelaire attended the Lycée Louis le Grand.
1839-42	Life in the Latin Quarter: debts, mistresses. His stepfather sent him on an enforced voyage (1841) to the Cape of Good Hope and Mauritius Island.
1842-45	Baudelaire began writing poetry, met his "Black Venus," Jeanne Duval, lived among Bohemian painters and poets, ran into debt, perhaps attempted suicide. He published his first art criticism in the *Salons* of 1845 and 1846.
1846-47	Publication of two long short stories, *Le Jeune Enchanteur* and *La Fanfarlo.*
1851	Publication of *Du Vin et du haschisch.*
1852-57	Publication of several of the poems, to be included in *Les Fleurs du mal,* in various periodicals.
1857	*Les Fleurs du mal* (original edition). A lawsuit is started and six poems are condemned as immoral.
1859	*Salon de 1859.*
1860	*Les Paradis artificiels.*
1861	Second edition of *Les Fleurs du mal,* minus the six condemned poems but with thirty-five new ones and with new divisions.
1857 to 1864	Several articles of literary criticism (on Flaubert, Théophile Gautier, Victor Hugo), of art criticism (on "Le Peintre de la vie moderne," 1860; Delacroix, 1863) and an essay on Wagner and *Tannhäuser* (1861), to be collected after Baude-

laire's death in *L'Art romantique*. Also, intimate papers, to be published posthumously as *Fusées* and *Mon Coeur mis à nu,* were jotted down between 1851 and 1864.

1864-66   Lecture tour in Belgium. Disappointments and despair. First attacks of paralysis.

1866 March   Return of the invalid to Paris.

1867, August 31   Baudelaire's death.

1867,   Burial at the Montparnasse cemetery.
    September 2

1869   Publication of *Les Fleurs du mal* by Michel Lévy, with Théophile Gautier's preface, as Vol. I of his complete works. Publication of *Le Spleen de Paris* (*Petits Poèmes en prose*) as Vol. IV.

Notes on the Editor and Authors

HENRI PEYRE, born in Paris in 1901, is the author of several books and many essays of literary history and criticism in French and in English. He has been teaching at Yale University since 1939.

ERICH AUERBACH, one of the most eminent German scholars in the fields of Romance philology and literature, taught at the Universities of Marburg, Istanbul, Penn State, and Yale. He died in 1957. His books on Dante, on French classicism, on medieval Latin and French literature, and his *Mimesis,* translated into many languages, have won him wide recognition.

CHARLES DU BOS, born in Paris in 1882, studied in Oxford, became well known in the nineteen-twenties through his several volumes of *Approximations,* and his books on Byron, Gide, Benjamin Constant. After he returned in 1927 to the Roman Catholic faith, his critical essays became, until his death in 1939, marked by a profoundly spiritual attitude. He is considered one of the five or six greatest French critics of the twentieth century.

ÉTIENNE GILSON, born in Paris in 1884, is the most eminent historian and interpreter of medieval philosophy in France. He was a professor at the Collège de France, lectured at several Canadian and American universities, was elected a member of the French Academy. Besides his many volumes on Scholasticism, he has published essays on modern periods of French literature, from Rabelais and Descartes to Baudelaire, Bergson, Du Bos.

FRANÇOIS MAURIAC was born in 1885 at Bordeaux. He became famous as a novelist after World War I, was elected to the French Academy in 1933, and received the Nobel Prize in 1952. He has also written poems, dramas, many volumes of critical and political essays.

JOHN MIDDLETON MURRY (1889-1957) became well known as a very young critic through his studies of Dostoevsky, Keats, Shakespeare. One of the best informed Englishmen on continental letters, he was the husband of Katherine Mansfield and among the early friends of D. H. Lawrence. His autobiographical volumes, especially *Between Two Worlds,* are revealing.

P[IER] M[ARIA] PASINETTI, born in 1913 in Venice, is the author of volumes of tales in Italian and of a novel, *Venetian Red* (1960). He holds a Ph.D. from Yale, and now teaches at the University of California at Los Angeles.

GEORGES POULET, Belgian-born critic, has taught at Edinburgh, Johns Hopkins University, and the University of Zurich, Switzerland. His studies on *Human*

Time and on *Interior Distance* are considered the most profound recent interpretations of French writers. He received the Prix Sainte-Beuve in 1950 and the Prix de la Critique in 1952.

JEAN PRÉVOST (1901-1944) entered the École Normale Supérieure in 1919, became known as a novelist, a writer on the psychology of sport, a translator. His books on Stendhal and on Baudelaire are among the most penetrating studies on those writers. He was killed in 1944 while fighting in the underground in southeastern France.

MARCEL PROUST (1871-1922), author of *A la Recherche du temps perdu,* was also an acute interpreter and critic of literature. He was severe on earlier critics like Sainte-Beuve and a keen lover of poetry (Hugo, Baudelaire), music, and painting.

PAUL VALÉRY, born at Sèté in 1871, first became known as an essayist and as a poet in 1895. After a long period of silence and meditation, he published his greatest poetical work in 1917 and 1922 and many books of essays and of incisive aphorisms. He was elected to the French Academy in 1926. He is considered by many as one of the greatest poets and prose writers of twentieth century France.

Bibliography

The best current editions of Baudelaire are those published in the Collection de la Pléiade and by Garnier. The most abundantly annotated edition of *Les Fleurs du mal* is by Crépet et Blin (Paris, Corti).

The best works on the life of the poet are J. and E. Crépet, *Baudelaire* (Paris: Messein, 1907); A. Feuillerat, *Baudelaire et la Belle aux cheveux d'or* (Paris: Corti, 1941); id., *Baudelaire et sa mère* (Montreal: Ed. Variétés, 1944); F. Porché, *Baudelaire, Histoire d'une âme* (Paris: Flammarion, 1945); G. de Reynold, *Charles Baudelaire* (Paris: Crès, 1920); Enid Starkie, *Baudelaire* (New York: New Directions, 1958).

On Baudelaire's poetry, consult J. L. Austin, *L'Univers poétique de Baudelaire* (Paris: Mercure de France, 1956); W. T. Bandy, *Baudelaire Judged by his Contemporaries* (New York: Columbia University Press, 1933); G. Blin, *Baudelaire* (Paris: Gallimard, 1939) and *Le Sadisme de Baudelaire* (Paris: Corti, 1948); C. M. Bowra, *The Romantic Imagination* (Cambridge: Harvard University Press, 1949); R. Chérix, *Commentaire des Fleurs du mal* (Geneva: Cailler, 1949); J. Hubert, *L'Esthétique des Fleurs du mal* (Geneva: Cailler, 1953); J. Massin, *Baudelaire entre Dieu et Satan* (Paris: Julliard, 1946); H. Peyre, *Connaissance de Baudelaire* (Paris: Corti, 1951); J. Rivière, *Études* (Paris: N.R.F., 1911); M. Ruff, *L'Esprit du mal et l'esthétique baudelairienne* (Paris: A. Colin, 1955); M. Turnell, *Baudelaire* (New York: New Directions, 1953).

On Baudelaire's art, versification, and criticism, consult Suzanne Bernard, *Le Poème en prose de Baudelaire jusqu'à nos jours* (Paris: Nizet, 1959); A. Cassagne, *Versification de Baudelaire* (Paris: Hachette, 1906); A. Ferran, *L'Esthétique de Baudelaire* (Paris: Hachette, 1933); A. Feuillerat, "L'Architecture de *Fleurs du mal*" (New Haven: *Yale French Studies,* 1941); M. Gilman, *Baudelaire the Critic* (New York: Columbia University Press, 1943); Guex, *Aspects de l'art baudelairien* (Lausanne: Imprimerie Centrale, 1934); O. Levy, *Brno* (Czechoslovakia: 1947); G. Macchia, *Baudelaire critico* (Florence: Sansoni, 1939); J. Prévost, *Baudelaire* (Paris: Mercure de France, 1953); S. A. Rhodes, *The Cult of Beauty in Baudelaire* (New York: Columbia University Press, 1929); R. Vivier, *L'Originalité de Baudelaire* (Brussels: Académie Royale, 1926).

Other essays which might have been included in a less strictly selective collection of critical pieces on Baudelaire are: Walter Benjamin, "Über einige Motive bei Baudelaire" (1939); B. Croce, in *Poesia e non poesia* (Bari: Laterza, 1919); M. Eigeldinger, *Le Platonisme de Baudelaire* (Neuchâtel: La Baconnière, 1951); T. S. Eliot, *For Lancelot Andrewes,* (New York: Doubleday, 1928) and *Selected Essays* (New York: Harcourt, Brace & World, Inc., 1932); Aldous

Huxley, in *Do What You Will* (New York: Doubleday, 1929); J. P. Richard, *Poésie et profondeur* (Paris: Editions du Seuil, 1955); J.-P. Sartre, "Introduction" to *Ecrits intimes* (1945) translated as "Baudelaire" (New York: New Directions, 1950).